Disclaimer:

- <u>This is a work of fiction</u>. Unless otherwise indicated, all the names, characters, businesses, places, events and incidents in this book are either the product of the author's imagination or used in a fictitious manner. As it was visualized in my childhood, no characters invented, no events fabricated. What was seen, and I remember, I have narrated. Only dialogues and substance are fabricated. Any resemblance to actual persons, living or dead, or actual events is purely coincidental.

- Author does not intend to hurt Geo-Political feelings of Soviet Union and religious sentiments and if felt so, he asks for apology in advance. The purpose is pure, to bring Light in Human life.

- <u>This is partly, a work of nonfiction, also</u>. It's not intended to be a source of financial, religious or spiritual and legal guidelines. Theories and hypothecations are not tasted, yet. Do choose, the advice from this writing after consulting with a professional. The author makes no guarantee of spiritual, religious, social, political and financial results by using this book.

- Please note that I don't make any guarantees about the results of the information applied here. I share educational and informational resources that are intended to help you succeed in spiritual, religious, political, social, economical and judicial subjects. You nevertheless need to know that your ultimate success or failure will be the result of your own efforts, your particular situation, and innumerable other circumstances beyond my knowledge and control.

Dedication

"This book is dedicated to those millions (Before 1972) who died in Siberian Exile & Gulag Camps of Soviet Union that compelled Himalayan Master (Yogi) to descend!

As well, it is dedicated to those three millions of people who died when Russia abandoned Communism and people choose to break through invisible prisons that made human life miserable. They paved the pathway to Spiritual uplifting and designed the SUN LAND!" (After 1991)"

This story is dedicated to all characters who compelled me to write this book- namely, Yestlin, Wombick, Albee, Zorcov and others. They lived in my memories.

DR. YOGESH AKRUWALA

My Visualization Series:

THE MOTHER

Chapter:1

Himalayan Yogi Arrives at Siberia.

Author

Dr. Yogesh Akruwala (MS)

[Cover Page is created by Vipul Makani, Nadiad.]

Table of Contents:

Forward

The Mother is the Universal Consciousness; from her, Universes are created, regulated and maintained. We, the human beings are the propellers of Her Program (Universal Program), Her Wisdom and Intelligence (Universal Consciousness). We as Human beings were created to bridge the Animal Life and Divine Life. The life cycle is stagnant on Planet Earth because a Man does not recognize his noble role in Nature and Planet Earth. This Series- The Mother is forwarded to the Mankind that is living in illusive fog and emotional whirlpools.

People believe it or not, but the Mother operates upon us at various levels of our life- body, body consciousness, Mind Consciousness and Sub-Consciousness.

This book is forwarded to whole of Human Race to bring Eternal Peace.

Yogesh Akruwala (15.07.2022)

How My Visualization began

(First few minutes of Visualization, I will narrate here.)

"At one evening at 9 PM, 1972 in my bed, I visualized as if I was in a theatre. A slide on screen showed a line being typed, "This is not an entertainment movie." It disappeared in smoking effect. (I had never seen titles on film screen disappearing with smoke effect in those days.) Next slide: Typing sound came: 'This movie is not indicated for ... heart problems, with blood pressure, dual personality, violent behaviors, weak emotional personalities and so on.' Few viewers left the hall and ticket fees were returned to them. Second line was typed: Let us stand up to pay homage to those 3 millions of people who died in Epic Civil War when Russia abandoned Communism." (A flame was lit on screen as all spectators stood up in silence for 60 seconds.) Next slide: F.....O....C....U....S. (Letters of FOCUS began to spread horizontally on screem from right to left end. F went to extreme left and S went to right. That way, width of screen was ascertained. It was about 135 degree wide screen! Now, 'F' letter began to move in center of screen and it came in front near the eyes of spectators. Rest of letters glided behind. S letter went too far. That showed the depth of screen visuals. 'This is 3D movie.' This sentence was hanging before the eyes. (It was truly 3D movie. I had never seen before 1972.) It showed that the width of screen was equal to depth of screen! (When letters were aligned, spectator was able to understand that the depth of screen!) Now, a sentence was typed: 'Do not touch any wires around, do not disturb hanging micro-speakers.' (Whole of theater had hundreds of speakers, under the seats and overhead.) Next line came: Audio Dangers will be pre-indicated by red signal on right of screen, upper corner while visual dangers will be indicated by signal on left upper corner. (Spectator can close eyes and ears.) Now there was silence with the same flame burning at center of screen.

Thunderous sound of OHM began and was amplified by various frequencies, various waves[1] and each wave merged with previous wave making great sound. Series of Ohm with different amplitudes and Time followed and merged the previous sound pattern making the resultant sound of Ohm so loud, extremely loud that every spectator (Myself) was terrified. Next moment, a puff of fire emerged from bottom of screen in center; as if there was fire to screen! Next puff and Ohm sound doubled the same fire that went high, engulfed previous flame, got twisted, rose higher and with third puff in fire, it made a little swell with whirling twist and it reached to midway of screen. The Ohm sound was on extreme and the fire in screen was looking like a snake! It was looking like a giant snake with sparkling eyes made of giant stars. It projected forwards into theatre after twist with hiss and Ohm Sound. Soon, it blasted with magnanimous sound showering thousands of stars into the theatre! (Starburst phenomenon was displayed so close!) All stars entered in theatre with great sound, rocks followed and lastly cosmic ashes followed and showered upon audience. All passed through the spectators with hissing sounds...whole of theater was converted that moment into a spaceship! So much of Luminosity and terrible sound...all stars passed through and at last clouds of dust was sprinkled over the spectators.

Now there was peace, screen showed bluish stars at distance in universe. Peace lasted for a long time and slowly a blue line began to join various stars and title emerged: THE UNIVERSE PRESENTS THE MOTHER". The letters of the Mother began to bleed slowly! Soon, the theatre as a spaceship was moving farther in space. Andromeda Galaxy was passing by. A background human sound came, "Where is your Sun?" It's impossible to spot our Fatherly Sun out of millions of stars. A circle was drawn to spot our sun at farthest point. The sound came:

'Our existence is so tiny, isn't it? Not even a tip of pin! And, we live by so much of arrogance! Mankind has yet not evolved to its real stature, even after millions of years of existence! Will

---

[1]Constructive interference is a phenomenon in which two waves combine by adding their displacement together at every single point in space and time, to form a resultant wave greater than before,

we call it an evolution if we came out of caves to bricked houses? We use swords and bullets today instead of bony weapons by prehistoric human race! Is it evolution if we wear fabrics instead of leafy covers? Real growth is not in mortal way; not in earthen way... it's measured by Vertical flight, Spiritual way! It's measured by virtues by which humans are defined! We are driven by consternation and self-made disasters and terrors! We are fuming organisms! Fear and violence are signs of basic animal life! Divine life is in different dimension.'

While journey towards Earth in our Solar system, the camera (vision) began to pass across the surface of Uranus planet, it was just bluish iced planet, little of core and all gases were frozen. Rocks and mountains were made of subzero ice. Camera went across frozen clouds (!) and vision was passing through valley of snow. Then soon, I saw crossing over of Saturn rings....sparkling crystals sprayed in the theatre and a huge Saturn passed from the upper margin of screen. Then rocks passed through the theatre and at last, Earth was spotted. Camera was coming closer to Earth! The Voice restarted:

"The Mother Nature gives us an atmosphere conducive for life over Earth (Earth was coming closer.) Earth offers a platform for lives of various planets (Aliens also!) here and rejoice! This is 'the' planet where Divine Life landed with most secret and pious Knowledge about the God, The VEDA, (What was spoken by God!) and this is the planet where God Himself visited multiple times to say 'Hello' to us! When God came on Earth; where were you, dear? Now, you are asking His address!

The man is yet not evolved; same hatred, same violence! But, the People of Soviet Union stood up against self - imposed Prisons and welcomed the New Era of Divine Life." (Now, the Earth was in center of screen.) Let us go to witness how Soviet Union struggled for Golden Era. The Sunland! Over to Siberia!

The camera entered in atmosphere of Earth and spectator experienced a free fall! Audience was as if dropped from the space!

It attained terrific speed and all began to wobble with the eye of camera. Earth was coming closer and audience began to scream! Down they saw white Siberia, camera was about to crash to ice-filled ground, when an electric wire running across two poles came in, so the camera plummeted over the electrical wire, viewers felt a jerk, jumped back in air and then slowly descended on ice-clad Siberian Plateau. That was railway line where camera or viewer landed. Soon, viewer (Myself) listened the whistle of a goods Trans-Siberian Railway. It assured that yes, we have landed on Earth! There was snow everywhere.

Meanwhile, a Walrus raised his head on a thick ice slab at left side of railway track. Two Siberian Dogs spotted Walrus and ran closer. They stopped to let the train go. Dogs and walrus remained on either sides of rails and train entered in the theatre! (End-on viewing!) Dogs began to cry with ominous sound, looking in air; same way, Walrus also raised his head in air and puffed and cried badly. Their cries filled the heart of viewers with sorrow and pains...as Engine of train entered in the theater! Roaring sound of engine of Trans-Siberian Train filled the theatre. First came in were the buffers, cowcatcher and then main cylinders to chimney. That moment, train driver blew whistles to keep dogs away! Gushing sound of pistons in cylinder came from right side, then coupling rods for wheels came in frantically, wheels rode inside theatre, carrying the boiler! Viewers can see everything through and through! The fire box came immediately and fireman pushed coals forwards, as if he sprayed coals on face of viewer! Hissing sound of vapors jets from valves and compressor chambers of vapors were crossing through theatre, now viewer saw the cab where railway driver and his fireman were working. All began to pass through theatre and would go out from the back! The spectators began to view the activities of Engine driver, the live stocks for food in different cabins, soon viewers saw prisoners! All were tied in chains, sitting around the cabins, with shattered clothes, ice-speckles on hairs and mustache bruises over head and body. All prisoners were just like animals of previous cabins. The camera came to focus on a young man shivering in chilled air blowing through open windows. The focus came closer to disclose how much he was tortured. The Camera focused over his face and entered in his pupils and went straight into memory. (Till then, Titles of characters were displayed.) That is how our story begins.

Author's note:

This is an absolute visualization of a young boy at his age 14 to 15, in 1972. All incidences, characters and story are fictional but they tally with history of Soviet Union and certain characters have resemblances with certain Soviet politicians of past. The plots and locations as well events and wars strategies also, show resemblance.

No difference is made in between a cave life of human race and today's civilized race. Manstill suffers from worries and fear! Violence has not reduced; weapons of destructions and protections are not changed! Instead of bone and stones, man uses knives, swords and bullets! Is it a mark of our evolution? Have aliens invaded Earth? We don't need extra-territorial enemies, we have enough of enemies in our society!

The Author has no intention to insult or damage reputation of anyone, any party, intelligence department of Soviet Government or community or religion. The Author regrets about unintentional insult if any, done. Definitely, it describes true stories of exile, oppression, wars, rebels, revolts and political conspiracy. Secondly, Author has used hypothecations at many places to link two theories or two events illogically without any proof. This is to establish links in certain areas like Religious Confluence. I request the reader to consider hypothecation as the bridge between the Known and Unknown! Wisdom should prevail. Reader is requested to take the story fictional as it is childhood fantasy (!) but at certain point, you will feel that has come true. Secondly, I also, tried to investigate from Google and Wikipedia as well other sources to correlate the places and events with its past and history as well to make information more interesting.

This visualization came in 1972 and its first incidence came true in 1991-when Russia abandoned Communism! Then, Russia was fragmented. Russia sent its military troops to invade Ukraine. I have seen tanks moving in streets of Kiev as well other Cities of

Ukraine, Armenia and Azerbaijan. I did not know the name those areas in my childhood!

It was such a hair-raising, exciting and terrifying story narrating how Russia abandoned Communism and stepped forwards into Golden Era. It was a story of 8 days and each day describes about 10 years of history of Soviet Union. That way, 5th day of my visualization is running for Soviet Union and still 3 days are to go; i.e. 30 years are about to come!

I have many limitations. I have had 'seen', not 'heard' as well seen in childhood! So narratives were difficult, the depth of thoughts, emotions were difficult to understand. I did not know the names of locations. For example, let's study a short visual (Video clip seen in 1972-3 and it came true in 1991 to 2022.):

'Mr. President of USSR headed and escorted by few Military Heads to a conference hall situated at 5th floor underground in Kremlin. An officer switched and a porcelain map emerged on huge table of about 20 ft*12 ft. size. It displayed a map of USSR- all territories, mountains and cities clearly developed from porcelain. It depicted miniature of Soviet Union. Officers of various departments and Military forces surrounded and stood with grim faces when Mr. President entered the hall. A military officer picked up an 8 feet long stick and pointed at South-West states of Soviet Union (I didn't know the names but they were talking about Ukraine, Azerbaijan, Armenia and Chechen districts.) and stroke at various areas and said, "Mr. President, these states, we are losing!" Mr. President looked at all Military heads who were silent; eyes filled with pains and sighing. He too, sighed; pressed his lips while staring at those states and said, "Erasure!" He whispered, "Send whole army but we can't lose an inch of Ukraine!" An Air Marshal whispered, "We have started air strikes but our troops resist to fire at own citizens. Ukraine has been our mother, who fed citizens for centuries. Military may rebel." Mr. President stared at Marshal and sternly ordered, "Flush off! Expunge. Start expunction before our army gets tired." He walked out of hall. Most of military officers looked at each other in dismay and began orders of execution. That day, Ukraine's destiny has fallen from skies to ashes."

I saw how Russia was fragmented in 'Commonwealth of Independent States', bloodshed in Caucasian territories on religious divide; saw Chernobyl Nuclear Explosion and how KGB was stopped to operate further. Sole purpose of writing this book is not to just narrate the past but to pave the pathway to Realm of Love, Brotherhood and Peace for the Mankind. The main purpose of this huge write up is to describe how mankind will rise and step up in Divine Life. Violence will vanquish from Human minds not by Judiciary, police forces or Penal Codes but by a shear desire of Love and Peace that will rise in every human heart! When human race will rise to higher level of consciousness, then all vices for which we complain today will disappear like a fog! Golden Days are coming to Mankind but our Race must elevate spiritual and emotional quotient or levels to welcome the New Era. Those who refuse to rise will perish!

This story will be in several parts:
1. The Mother: Chapter: I: Himalayan Yogi In Siberia
2. The Mother: Chapter: 2: Inception of Sunland (Awakening of Angels)
3. The Mother: Chapter: 3: Over to Moscow & Friends for Life
4. The Mother: Chapter: 4: The Sun Land
5. The Mother: Chapter: 5: Role of Mother Nature
6. The Mother: Chapter:6: New World Order: Confluence of Religions
7. The Mother: Chapter: 7: Sea Wave returns into Sea.

Information about Soviet Union:

Historical Background:

Tsar Nicholas II lost his powers during February Revolution and dissolved the USSR. Bolsheviks refused to accept the alternative governance and revolted in 1917. Vladimir Lenin led Bolshevik party and took control of Russia and formed Russian Soviet Socialist Republics. Civil War broke out between Communist Reds and whites! In 1922, Communist Reds won and established Soviet Union, making Russia Communist. Lenin died in 1924 and Joseph Stalin seized the power. He ruled Communist party till 1953. It was the period of Stalinization. Then Nikita Khrushchev came in power and worked in era of cold war. Leonid Brezhnev came in powers in 1964 and tried to make economic reforms but it created national decline by mid-1970 and Yuri Andropov came in powers in 1982. Later, Konstantin Chernenko led Soviet Union for a short time. Now Mikhail Gorbachev came up in May 1985 and suggested Glasnost (Freedom for Soviet people and release of thousands of political prisoners.) This led to dissolution of Soviet Union on 26h Dec. 1991.

Soviet Union was ruled by Communist Party of Soviet Union (CPSU), that considered itself as a shepherd and people as herds! They thought as if people are kids and all responsibilities lie upon ruling party! They considered themselves superior or people inferior to their talent and wisdom! They attracted total powers like an ocean that receives waters of all rivers on name of socialism, equality and just for all. They asked fishes to swim straight, that's what Communism means! Everywhere, 'Rules' ruled!

How such a system would like people more intelligent, more dynamic to them? That led to political Exile of wise, intelligent and professionals to Siberia. A silent deep freeze of Earth, the Siberia was bathed with human blood, filled with human cries and became graveyard of many innocents! This game was carried not for few months but for years together! It was referred as Gulag Camps which were spread wildly over Siberia (Eastern Russia) and Northern Russia. Political prisoners were sent to Taiga and Tundra forests to exploit the woods, mining and human constructions like railways and cities. Forests were shaved off and animals were poached for fur. All the trees were cut to the sizes of plants or shrubs in communism. Intelligent and people with high Emotional Quotient (Professors, advocates, doctors and engineers etc.) were thrown in Siberia to do labor till death! Thousands of such exiled never returned home. The cry of innocent people echoed in Heavens! The Mother Nature shivered ... when whole of life (Animals, Humans etc.) was subjugated to torture, annihilation and genocide...Mother nature turned and twisted the table. Welcome to the Visualization, The Mother.

Geographical Information:

From East to West, Soviet Union can have five geographical zones- Tundra (in Siberia), Taiga (Forest zone), Steppe or plains, arid zone and mountain zones. There are three plains- East European, West Siberian and Turan Lowland. Tundra is treeless marshy snow plains at North, near Finland, west to Bering Strait and runs south along Pacific Coast where Kamchatka Peninsula containing sleeping volcanoes lies. This is the land known for wild reindeers, white nights and white snow-filled terrains; known for long harsh winters and summer brings mosses, lichens and dwarf willows and shrubs out of Permafrost. Great Siberian rivers drain into Arctic Ocean, pass through lakes, ponds and swamps hampered by partial and intermittent thawing. Thawing shapes the landscapes by glaciations. Taiga Forest is as large as size of United States, is forest of spruce, fir, pine and larches. This is coldest zone too. Taiga forest extends towards Baikal Lake in South. About 33% people of Soviet Union live here, this is their ancestral lands. Steppes are treeless grassy plains where 44% population lives. This zone has moderate temperatures and so ideal for human habitats and agriculture- later suffers by unpredictable precipitations or droughts. Arid Zone are semi-deserts and desert are in Central Asia particularly in Kazakh Republic. Cotton and Rice production are through irrigation. This is the zone of spare human habitats and so this zone is good for Space Exploratory Activities. Alpine Terrain or mountains exist between Black and Caspian Seas (Caucasus Mountains that separates Europe from Asia.). It extends to Southeast as Tien Shan and Pamir that separates Soviet Union from its neighbors in South. Highest peak is Mount Communism in Pamir lie near Afghanistan, Pakistan and China. Pamir and Tien Shan are offshoots of Great Himalaya! Eural Mountains divide Europe from Asian part of Soviet Union. Eastern Siberia has long Kamchatka Peninsula with volcanic peak jutted down into Sea of Okhotsk. These areas of Far East, Central Asia part and Caucasus have seismic activities.

Geographical locations that are covered in this vast story: 'The Mother' are (1) Sea of Okhotsk (2) Siberia plateau (3) Kamchatka Volcano (4) Tundra (5) Taiga (6) Eural Mountains (7) Moskva River (8) Moscow (9) Trans-Siberian Railway (10) Many cities that came my visualization.

States of Soviet Union (1922 to 1991):

There were 15 Republic Russia. (From North to South on Western Border) Estonia, Latvia, Lithuania, Belarus, Ukraine, Moldova, Georgia, Armenia, Azerbaijan, Turkmenistan, Kazakhstan, Uzbekistan, Kyrgyzstan, Tajikistan. When Russia abandoned Communism, most of states were separated and they made a conglomeration called as Common Wealth of Independent States (CIS). Few Allies are worth noting: Albania (1946-55), Bulgaria (1948-90), Czechoslovak (1948-90), Hungary (1949-89), Poland (1947-89), Romania (1947- 68), German Democratic Republic (1949-90); then they became independent.

Soviet Union Administrative Divisions, 1989
DEPOSITORY
RUSSIAN SOVIET FEDERATIVE SOCIALIST REPUBLIC
(R.S.F.S.R.)
KAZAKH S.S.R.
Yakutskaya ASSR
Krasnoyarskiy Kray
LATVIAN S.S.R.
ESTONIAN S.S.R.
LITHUANIAN S.S.R.
BELORUSSIAN S.S.R.
UKRAINIAN S.S.R.
MOLDAVIAN S.S.R.
GEORGIAN S.S.R.
ARMENIAN S.S.R.
AZERBAIJAN S.S.R.
TURKMEN S.S.R.
UZBEK S.S.R.
TADZHIK S.S.R.
KIRGIZ S.S.R.
ASSRs and AOs in the Caucasus
1. Adygeyskaya AO
2. Karachayevo-Cherkesskaya AO
3. Kabardino-Balkarskaya ASSR
4. Severo-Osetinskaya ASSR
5. Yugo-Osetinskaya AO
6. Abkhazskaya ASSR
7. Nakhichevanskaya ASSR (Azerbaijan SSR)
8. Nagorno-Karabakhskaya AO
9. Checheno-Ingushskaya ASSR

KAZAKH   Union republic (SSR)
*   Union republic (SSR) center
          Autonomous republic (ASSR), oblast, or kray boundary
          Autonomous oblast (AO) or autonomous okrug (AOk) boundary

0   400   800 Kilometers
0   400 Miles

Section:

1

A: How I met Yogi!

1: Yestlin at Leningrad University

[St. Petersburg was an English name so was changed to Petrograd (1914-1924) at start of WWI in 1914, as former name was sounded too German! Later, after death of Lenin, its name was changed as Leningrad (1924-91) in 1924, 26th Jan. (Grad is Cyrillic word, or Slavic term, meaning by town, city or castle. It was derived from Gord, Grad, Horod, or Gorod. City is situated on Neva River, at head of Gulf of Finland on Baltic Sea. It's 4th most populous city in Europe today. It's port on Baltic Sea.]

Yestlin, a young student, walked through corridor of his collage, feeling exhausted and confused as he had not slept last night. He held a few books abreast by right hand as if they were precious to him. He received those books from an unknown old man in a public garden last evening; he had to return after one week, exactly at same time, same place but, someone else would come to receive![2] Whole night he had read his book and now he carried in hands to read in free time. He looked at his colleagues with red eyes.

He made a good student of himself, attentive to professors, witty in his answers. He had a habit to scramble his thoughts in corners of his notes. He had performed great in his exam of Second year. Now he was confident, knowledgeable and bit wise to have his own voice and own conclusions.

Yestlin was a voracious reader; his endless pursuance towards Knowledge attracted his destiny. His Quest attracted unknown people who brought him literatures of West and Europe, news about the internal turmoil of CPSU, corruptions and Mafias. He had knowledge more than his age; therefore he had hatred for Communist Party and its policies! The young man was imbibing bad news and was programming his mind! He read articles of dignified professors of European Universities, read biography of

---

[2]That was a way of internal circulation of illegal books about government policies and strategies.

Lenin, Karl Marx and history of Soviet Union prior to 1922; understood the laws, the fate of civilians, about Mafia (OPG-Organized 'Prestupnaya' (Criminal) Group) He was dreaded with pictures of mobsters, crimes sites and their connection with Europe and America. The whole world was opening in front of his 'innocent young' mind and young Yestlin had more to hate than love the world![3] The more, Yestlin read, more he understood about the underworld and KGB nexus and more he was dreaded. He exchanged books and pamphlets in theatres, gardens, in buses and trains as well in public libraries. A lobby with anti-communist agenda used to feed materials to youth freely. They had retired old aged volunteers who devoted time to find such innocent students too. They used to ask to return books after a week time at same place. Often Yestlin used to get provocative pamphlets (Xerox) against university and local authorities. Being the commerce student, he was influenced by Capitalism and began to hate the same pond in which he was breathing like a fish!

He studied the principles of Marxism:

1. Principles were:
    - Abolition of property in land and application of all rents of land to public purposes
    - A heavy progressive or graduated income tax
    - Abolition of all rights of Inheritance
    - Confiscation of properties of all immigrants and rebels
    - Equal liabilities of all to labor and establishment of Industrial Armies and agriculture
    - Gradual abolition of distinction between town and country

---

[3]Whatever the mind sees, will happen. Wherever the mind looks at, a man will reach there. The mind emits vibes and they will draw attention of synchronous or asynchronous vibes from all around. **A man should be vigilantfor what he thinks**! He may ruin his destiny by 'own' thoughts. *A candle light should not complain for surrounding darkness. Should a flower of Lotus complain about the mud in which its roots thrive?* - Yogesh

2. Long-term goal of communism is a society that provides equality and economic security for all.
    a. Principles of Communism were like sugar-coated bitter pills:
    b. Pros: Everyone gets equal chance in education, employment and low level of inequality and unemployment. Everyone will be educated.
    c. Cons: There is no unauthorized opposition to Communism. Individual rights were restricted. Violence was the immediate solution for dissent. Individual earning and savings were kept low, resulting into poverty. Employments were high but freedom and meaningfulness in work place were low. Powers were under a few people in government (Centralization of Power). Government can hide information and can keep people ignorant!

He slowly began to read the history of Soviet Union written by French and British Scholars. He unknowingly, became a favorable youth of anti-Communist lobby that wanted to spread hate for government in college students union. Once, he gave a short speech in a hotel, to a group of unknown people, and got a prize! A time came when he crossed a thin line between the wisdom and foolishness.[4]

*

One day, a professor discussed about inter-university debate in his class and pointed his pen at Yestlin thoughtfully and said," I think, you 'are' taking participation in debate next week, Yestlin! Will you?" Yestlin had a tremor to see at that strongly held pen pointing at him. (He felt as if it was a knife instead of a pen!) He hesitantly asked, "Subject?" Professor smiled and answered, "You would definitely love- 'The Future course of Economy in Soviet Union'.[5] Yestlin was short-sighted as he wanted to open his

---

[4] *'How much knowledge does someone need to live at peace?'*

[5] *Intelligence is an abstract quality and has no eyes! Wisdom gives an eye.-*

'mouth' but he was like a tiny 'fisha' in a pond! He thought, it would be a proud moment for him to step up on a stage. He forgot an advice his mother, 'It is better to live in low profile in this world. Too much of anything becomes poison. A bird in bush is safer than in skies, it can be easily spotted by shooters.'

*

Yestlin was on stage wearing white shirt, red tie and blue pants. A young handsome student was in focus of all professors and Dean who were sitting on either side. A videographer was ready to record his speech. Here, Yestlin began:

"Greetings, my Fellow Comrades!"He looked at audience with dignified gaze and turned at his professors with great respect and fatherly Dean!

'Future Course of Economy of Soviet Union'! I am a small person to predict the course. Who knows future; who can predict? Yes, I can portrait my views and you will agree upon."

"A Country has two types of wealth. First is The Human Power. It includes physical power, mental and emotional power of society. The physical power depends upon the population growth, the health status and jobs we get or opportunity for youth to work. It lies in hands of army, farmers and laborers and government strengthens those sectors but our Soviet Union has slow birth rate. (Students giggled out.) Addiction for smoking, alcohol and drugs is alarming in our youth of country. (Students started gossiping) We know that well directed youth builds great nation. When youth uses its hearts and emotions in illusive world of addictions, elsewhere it will fail to cultivate own intelligence and true realistic world. Illusive world is like 'Diverticulum', a way side 'second' house! (Yestlin had himself missed so many things in his life.) Professors chuckled.

We, the students are too 'sentimental', too emotional and our transactions are from heart to heart; vibes to vibes! Any vibration can draw our attention; can change pathway of life. That way, anyone can play with our emotions, friends! We can make a great 'herd' by synchronization of Emotions and can be driven into rebel groups or driven by Fear or deflected by hatred and deviated by temptations! Youth is the wealth and government knows better how to channelize it. (Professors were absolutely, stunned and silent.)

Civilization grows by intelligent people who dare to think different, act different! If youth is going nowhere, encircles in whorls, it is catastrophic to nation. We don't want to be a lift man who goes up and down whole day...but is going nowhere!

We are innocent by nature and we do not disturb anyone but, we must not forget that someone can disturb us. Someone may play with our destiny, so be alert and emit right vibrations, choose our own pathway. Nation expects fresh thought, intelligence and wisdom from us. (Hall applauded by clapping.)

"Second Wealth is the National Treasures in form of forests, soil, rivers, mountains, air and live stocks. Soviet Union is the richest in that way. I think, we should not tag prices to each asset endowed by Nature. The one who discovered a coin of money in past must be a great magician. Whole world can be hidden behind this tiny coin! You just need a coin and you can get whatever you desire! Bullshit! This ideology is devastating for our future generations. They won't know the real value of each stone upon which they stand and walk! I think everything is precious beyond the price tag! (Dean was much pleased.) Draining oils and mining is unabated in Siberia and Kazakhstan for Cobalt, iron, Coal, Gem, Gold, Lead, Molybdenum and Tungsten. Let the richness be hidden, our future generation will need them! They are the reserve for future! Nickel is depleted now; others are asbestos, diamonds, fluorspar, mica and Uranium, and so on; all are going....in air! We are draining the wealth of Nature that results deforestation of Siberia and Taiga forests for papers industries and construction purpose. Killing and poaching animals for fur and meat are uncontrolled. Nature's resources are under the Government

Treasury in form of assets and they covert them in form of currency! And currency is fluid like, it always flow out. Bald surface of Siberia will be haunting to our next generations. Converting natural assets into Rubble is not growth at all. There is something more, far more important than a coin of money or Rubble. Natural Resources must be judiciously used, must be weighed against a coin of Rubble. It's better to be simple than to be sophisticated." (Professors were happy at that comment.)

"Third Wealth is the wealth of Virtues the mankind is heir to. We know every child is getting education, but still we have long way to go. Educating youth for table work, computer work, for factories and administrations is a selfish angle. (He paused.) Intelligence and moral virtues are real power to society. They will confer to have independent judgments in young gen. If we fail to instill the values of humility, honesty and love in students, then we lose our one more chance to raise our society. I personally believe that these are the fields to focus so as the country can grow, otherwise people sitting outside on fence are shrewdly watching us." He ended abruptly.

The audience applauded, students were amazed at the brilliance. Yestlin saw professors clapping with smile and he bowed a little at them. He forgot that 'Clapping is 'the cheapest thing' mankind has learnt to give!' He saw the seat of dean empty. As he stepped down the podium, he received a slip in his hand, it read, "Dean Office, immediately." Pleasure in this world is usually short-lasting and how much a man pays for?

*

The Dean was staring at the face of Yestlin that made him confused. Yestlin was eager to hear of his Dean who began, "Excellent speech!"

Yestlin: Thank you, sir.

Dean: What thanks? (He shouted across the table.) Was it an entertainment show... hmm? Was it your voice or voice of some traitors? (You were vomiting your thoughts out of your head...!

You will ruin your fortune! Stinging unhealthy thoughts are not welcome by Communist Party of Soviet Union. (Yestlin was shocked while looking at red face of Dean.)

Yestlin: Anything wrong, sir?" (Hesitant voice)

Dean: Such competitions are organized to find fools from collages. Organizers watch for what the youth thinks about Soviet Union. Do you respect 'our Party' or not? They always nip off offensive bud from the beginning. This is not your nomad (village), this is St. Petersburg, a complex oblast that defeated Nazi! We survived difficult times of Seige of Leningrad in WW II. Remember you have no friends here and don't trust any professors and me too! Then, how did you trust unknown people who circulate anti-national materials? (Dean sighed and began to whisper.) Dear Yestlin! I am a father for you (He wanted to remind Yestlin that he had no father!) otherwise who would guide you, my child?" (Yestlin was feeling uneasy now. Dean gave him a long pause to think.) "Your speech was more than I expected from student of your age. We do not teach you that, isn't it? (Yestlin nodded.) From where did you come to know, all that stuff?" Yestlin became blank, so dean peeped in his eyes," Who is your 'teacher' or 'mentor'?" Yestlin muffled and spoke," Books! Books are my friends, sir!"

The dean blasted suddenly, "Books can take you to hell, also!" He became soft and asked, "From where you got books... hmm?" (Yestlin had no answer.) "B-u-r-n those books tonight, free yourself from such toxic stuff. It will seal your fate. People spread everything to weaken Communism understand? Why they gave books to you free? Burn them if you want to survive!" (He lowered tone now.) "There are wiser people in Communist Party (Yestlin nodded.) and they do neither like dissent nor suggestions. (Dean was about 60 years of age, thin lean face with wrinkles on forehead and long sharp nose like beak of a bird...was as if penetrating Yestlin! Yestlin was shivering now.) "We want PEACE so as government can work well and precisely! Understand, we want 'peace' from you! No words, no ripples and no turbulence!

Government gives you everything-free education, free shelter, electricity and food at collage, isn't it? And, they expect just 'Peace in Governance', understand? How can they tolerate your criticism? They would say, 'We have plenty of students! You are dispensable in this giant system. They do not want your advices. (Dean leaned forwards on table, turned his head on left staring in eyes of Yestlin, to threaten! His eye balls were rolling.)

Yestlin tremulously spoke a little," But, it was just a debate, an essay, my hypothecation, my imaginary theory....that's all. Why can't you take it lightly? I did not utter wrong words, you listened me."

Dean interrupted, "Even your video is prepared. A Thought has many angles and everyone will understand differently. You don't know where you are wrong. Thoughts, in Communist Party are stringently measured, valued and recorded."

Dean continued, "Your thoughts will write your history!' He paused long. "Don't trust anyone now onwards, keep your mouth shut, just learn to smile and walk away! Every third person you meet will be a spy, inclusive of your professors and me!! We love our Party and so are we, faithful. We seek chances to prove our patriotism." Yestlin recalled 'that' professor who pointed pen in classroom strongly and smiled at him sarcastically. Yestlin was perspiring and shivering.

Dean took the command," See, dear, I know you are innocent. You spoke what you read. Now, you will be asked who gave you books, from where you got?" Yestlin did not recall any names of those suppliers of books. He confessed that he met many people in garden, theaters and buses but had no contact details. Yestlin cried a little and said," I made reading as my hobby, as I have no friends, did not smoke or party with others at hostel."

The dean gave solace and whispered," Don't worry! I will work out for you. See, my child, at the earliest you go to park and return them their books. If there in none then leave books behind on bench and walk away! Someone else will get chances to read such books. Your room should be clear and empty by the evening. No clutters, understand?" Yestlin nodded.

Yestlin wiped tears, nodded, thanked him and left for his room. He decided to return those books at the earliest. At 5 PM, he was waiting for that old man in park but, as if that old man did know and he did not turn that day. Yestlin could not leave costly books on bench in evening. He picked up a city bus of same route and he met all the strangers in that bus. He placed his bag under his seat and fellow on next seat reminded him! Whole evening....he traveled with a weight on back, on his small heart and 1.35 kilogram of brain! (How much we upload our body, mind and soul?) Truly, books loved him so much!! He returned to hostel and decided to dump books in backyard garbage of hostel but there was a group of students making party there, late night. So, Yestlin decided to submit all the literatures to dean office next day. He, as exhausted he was, walked in lobby of hostel and found air of hostel misty and hostile! Too deep was silence! He opened door of his room and found a note on the table from his roommate," My mom is sick, leaving urgently. Take care." His room partner had completely, emptied his table and shelf; he had taken away all dresses too! His space was absolutely clean! He cried softly from unknown fear and began to tear pages of his notes frantically, missed his dinner.

*

While tearing pages on table, he recalled an instance when he was walking with mom in his farm in that evening. He leaped few steps in joy while walking through sunflowers crop tapping each dull looking sunflower as their friend, Lord Sun was setting! He whispered to flowers, "Don't worry, just wait for the morning! Sun will rise again, tomorrow!" The mother watched childish behavior of her son and said, "Remember, what you are leaving behind tomorrow when you will go to college!" Yestlin became serious and whispered, "Leaving behind my mom, my farm, these sunflowers and home!" The Mother added, "Don't forget your reason when you reach to hostel! You are going for study, not for girls and smoking!" Son looked in her eyes and nodded.

Yestlin evaded serious remarks of mother and cheerfully answered, "Yes, my mom, 'sincerely' I will study but, with little fun! I will have lots of friends in hostel!"

Mother abruptly interrupted, "There are no friends!"(Yestlin stopped dancing and became serious.) "Yes, you are not going to college to make friends! They are acquaintances. You may know many but they are not your relatives. They don't reflect who you are. People come in life with purpose and go. You will have to forget. No emotional bonding you will feel."

Yestlin: Then, who are my friends? How will I recognize?

Mother: To get a friend is like getting a diamond in coal mine! Those who stay long way, with you; share your emotions- joy or sorrow and support you in need are friends. They may be blood relations or friends. Friends are eternal, only fortunate will get 'Friends for Life'! Most of people die alone! (She paused and her eyes got wet.) If you get maximum five friends in life, on whose shoulders you can rest your head and cry loud in time, then you are the most fortunate man on earth and the wealthiest person too. Do not make friend, they will arrive in life as per destiny."

Yestlin answered, "Then, mother, I am that fortunate, will definitely get the best friends for life."

Yestlin wiped off tears and continued to tear off his notes, pamphlets and some books. It was about 11 pm and only his room light was 'on' in hostel. Security guard down from garden observed this light and smoked a puff towards his window.

And, someone knocked his door, heavily! Then multiple strikes followed on his door! Those thumbing noises were disturbing. Someone asked, "Yestlin, please open the door."

Yestlin trembled," Who are you?"

The reply came," Dean has sent us to help." As Yestlin opened the door, first strong man of 6 feet height gave a bold punch to forehead and Yestlin fell unconscious. Three people covered him with black cloth, lifted on shoulder and ran quickly downstairs towards a wagon. Two persons explored his room, gathered all his belongings, the books, the torn pages in his bed sheet and joined his team at wagon. Wagon disappeared in darkness of that night and Yestlin entered in dark world! Next day, the hostel activities were routine, none noticed about Yestlin. None questioned. He had no friends, all acquaintance all around! A man is separate in a crowd, a few knows! Here, the dean wrote a message to the mother of Yestlin and sent his staff for telegram.

*

The next day, dean gave instructions to students in common hall where room partner was sitting in front raw, "You came here, to study, mind well. We have sufficient books in our library; have able professors to answer you. I would tell you not to harbor unquenchable thirst of knowledge in your mind. Don't rely people or sources from outside. There are bad people as well. Anti-nationals, traitors will feed you wrong things, wrong for you. We have departmental stores, a good canteen, a gym; so you need not go out. Remember, too much of knowledge may be poisonous. And, let me tell you that we are responsible; have to answer your parents." After a pause, he said, "Go and concentrate on study."

*

2: Destiny called him 'on'!

Yestlin could not see anything when he opened his eyes in dark closet room. He had severe headache .He recalled severe blow on forehead at hostel room.) He saw things around blurred till he was able to see beams of sun rays entering through slits in walls. Yes, his cabin was a garage made up with logs of woods in remote area in outskirt of Koloksha, Vladimir Oblast, Russia.[6] Two feet snow covered the cabin from all around and he was tied up to chair without any protection. (He had a single coating- his shirt!) Slowly, he saw three monstrous persons sitting in front with their feet raised on table their boots facing him. They were silently chewing meatballs with juice dripping from corner of mouth. One man reached to Yestlin who gathered courage and asked, "Where am I?"

He said, "Soon, you will be without any address!" All chuckled. Yestlin asked, "Who are you?"

The man whispered, "Moirai, the Goddess of Fate! [7] (They laughed and soon, became stable.) We are from Officers from

---

[6]**Vladimir Oblast, Russia** is East to Moscow. Koloksha It is a rural locality and the administrative center of Kolokshanskoye. The population was about 1000 people and there were just 10 streets in Koloksha.

[7]**Moirai:**Fortune writing Deities. In <u>ancient Greek religion</u> and <u>mythology</u>, the **Moirai,** (Μοῖραι"lots, destinies, apportioners"), was known as the **Fates** (<u>Latin</u>: *Fata*), were the <u>incarnations</u> of <u>destiny</u>. <u>Roman</u> equivalent is the <u>Parcae</u> (euphemistically the "sparing ones"), and there are other equivalents in cultures that descend from the <u>Proto-Indo-Europeanculture</u>. Their number became fixed at three: <u>Clotho</u> ("spinner"),<u>Lachesis</u> ("allotter") and <u>Atropos</u> ("the unturnable", a metaphor for death).The role of the Moirai was to ensure that every being, mortal and divine, lived out their destiny as it was assigned to them by the laws of the universe. For mortals, this destiny spanned their entire lives and was represented as a thread spun from a spindle. Generally, they were considered to be above even the gods in their role as enforcers of fate, although in some representations <u>Zeus</u>, the chief of the gods, is able to command them.[3]

In the <u>Homeric</u> poems Moira or Aisa are related to the limit and end of life, and Zeus appears as the guider of destiny. In the *Theogony* of <u>Hesiod</u>, the three Moirai are personified, daughters of <u>Nyx</u> and are acting over the gods. Later

Secret service department, KGB.[8]" Yestlin soon, became shocked and unconscious. Someone had given him a blow on back of his head. All three persons went out leaving unconscious young man uncovered, tied up to chairs with open doors to let him chilled. There was about 2 feet of snow around the cabin in that desolated area. Nomad, Koloksha was about 1.5 km. away from this garage. After a few hours of chilling, Yestlin came to consciousness with shivering, he was awake when flood of sunlight entered in garage. He found six people entering in room. He heard a wagon stopping at his room that was hired from nearby railway station. His lips tremulously, wanted to request for mercy, but his lips were torn and cheeks were bloodstains frozen. Two strong persons stood at open door. Two persons with rifles stood behind his chair, two sat in front of Yestlin across a table. Yestlin could look around in day light and discovered that it was a garage! Garage was turned into Secret Local Court!

---

they are daughters of Zeus and <u>Themis</u> who was the embodiment of divine order and law. The concept of a universal principle of natural order and balance has been compared to similar concepts in other cultures such as the <u>Vedic</u> <u>Rta</u>, the <u>Avestan</u> <u>Asha</u> (Arta) and the <u>Egyptian</u> <u>Maat</u>.Rozhanitsy, narecnitsy, and sudzhenitsy are invisible spirits or **deities** of **fate** in the pre-Christian religion of the **Slavs**.

[8]**KGB** was an organization coming under Committee for State Security (CSS) from 1954 to 1991, descended from similar agencies known as Cheka (till 1922), GPU (till 1923), OGPU (till 1934), NKVD (till 1943), NKGB (till 1946) and MGB (till 1954). It was the secret police force working as main security agency to safeguard Communist Party of Soviet Union, that way, indirectly, it was involved in internal security, intelligence and secret functions of police. It was directly attached to Council of Ministers. It was like a multi-headed snake! Similar agencies operated in each of republics of Soviet Union- i.e. in every country that was the part of Soviet Union as well countries that supported Communist Party of Soviet Union (CPSU). **Its mottos were loyalty to CPSU and to motherland!** KGB was a military service, making internal troops for state security. It functioned for intelligence (State and Foreign) and counter-intelligence, operative investigative activities. It guarded Central Committee of Communist Party and Soviet Government and combating nationalism, dissent and anti-soviet activities. Yestlin was trapped in this clause.

Chief person began with his introduction, "Yestlin, I am your judge, Comrade Igor; have traveled 320 kilometers this morning, just to see 'bloody' you! (He became furious.) Why didn't you focus on study? Rats, what are you doing in hostels? (He paused, takes deep breath to ease himself.) You students in collages should not conspire against us, see!" He puffed on his innocent face in disgust. Yest! I can be the last man of help for you, got me? From here, see outside, wild wild wild Siberia is calling you. Do you understand?"

He tapped his cigarette ash from its tip. (He leaned on table.) "Your case is too complicated. You gave an inspiring lecture in hotel, they circulated and next week, pamphlets with your name came to public in parks, buses and stations. You are fixed there. Here, at Leningrad, you are planning for an organized crime against party. You try to recall their names who gave you books. They speak of your treason. Unless you transfer your accusation to someone else, you will be held for punishment."

"But, what is wrong in reading books? You should control those publishers, printers and authors who published such a matter if so obnoxious. I was an end user; I am like a drug addict!" Yestlin got a little courage to speak.

"*How much of knowledge is needed to survive in our society, do you know,* Hum? (Yestlin became silent.) Your answer: We have to pick up leaves to reach out to trunk of a tree and then to its roots. You are a leaf, I know! More of knowing, more painful it will be. Know more and you hate us, more! Communist Party is doing excellent,; bloody, do you know? Free education, hostels, lunch, sports and jobs, you are getting! How the hell, Americans and Europeans are going to help you? Why do you tolerate if they say, Russia is a prison? This is our Home and none should mingle their intentions in our matters. They pollute minds of thousands of students and start rebel groups." Igor suddenly shouted and thumbed his fist on table. "And, you are here in front of me, arguing on their behalf. Not giving their names. Shame on your parents! I take pity for your mother if I have to answer her."

(Yestlin was crying...and he became alert when he heard of his mother.) Yestlin literally cried, "Seriously...I don't know any name," And, two persons standing behind got irritated with same answers and slapped his head from behind. Yestlin was flung from his chair in either direction. He got confused, then became silent and recovered a little and looked blanked at Igor. Yestlin nodded his head, opened his mouth to answer instead he cried out and he saw blood mixed saliva dripping (He Hs tongue-bite.) Meanwhile, helpers opened the package of books on table, his notes and torn out pages came out. Judge Igor sincerely flipped torn pages and smiled at Yestlin. Why you tried to destroy...?" He questioned politely, "Hiding something? (Pause) And, protecting whom? You should not do this, my son!" He threw pages in air violently and papers began to fly in the room with chilled air blowing in. Igor asked scornfully, "If you don't love the land, then why you are here? Go to Siberia, our deep freeze, there are plenty traitors. You go and preach your capitalism and free trade theories. Go there; you have no place to live here."

Yestlin began to sob, "I won't do this, I won't read anything ... please! I do not know them, sir! Pardon me." Igor smiled at him, "Can't be so much innocent! I will never touch anything." Again security personal began to fist him from behind...a tied up defense-less lad was totally humiliated and beaten repeatedly.

Yestlin recovered and said, "I decided to return all books to them last evening; I went there in park and in bus but...none came around yesterday. (Sobbingly) I will...you tell me what should I do with these books?" The strong men standing behind Yestlin, were irritated and hit hard butts of their guns on his skull and back of chest! Yestlin screamed and stopped crying, but shivered in terror. Igor rose across table, twisted right ear so much as his pinch torn the ear. Yestlin didn't shout, he was as if separate from his body! He felt as if his death is near. His heart became too fast running! A streak of perspiration ran from his head to cheek. Here, Igor wiped bloody fingers and shouted in his ear, "No 'sorry' I will listen. I am a Rattle snake[9], first I sound like a musician, then I bite!So many feeders to you and you don't have a single name?"

"I asked, but they refused!" Yestlin answered. Judge sat back and puffed a wheel of smoke so as crying face of Yestlin was seen exactly in center! Next police officer laughed and remarked, "Excellent!" The Judge brought out files from his leather bag and placed in front of Yestlin, "You can't cheat. We don't believe on your face, tears and 'sorry' words. We go by evidences. It's our policy not feed those who hate us; instead, we kill. We have plenty of students...they will get better opportunity. See, these are their affidavits from students of your collage, against you, look!" He held a paper in front of Yestlin; security guard standing behind punched butt of his rifle in his occiput again...the head flung upon the table and returned back. His nose was smashed. Yestlin became unconscious for third time. Last words he murmured, "I need my advocate! Mom, call someone. They are wolves!"

Igor and his team waited for Yestlin to recover. But, he remained drowsy for a long time, and so they concluded the process. They took his all ten fingers impression on papers, took photos and they prepared the file. The Judge signed the verdict, 'Unsuitable to be admitted in collage. It will be wrong to feed such a youth! Not suitable to live in our society as a free person. Toxic! This young man in society is risky of his thoughts and actions. Best place for him is Siberia." Yestlin was still drowsy and verdict was heard by security guards! An assistant opened the stamp pad and Judge put his mark of red inked seal! The fate of Yestlin was locked that way, when he was comatose. The back door of wagon standing outside was opened, (It made noise.) and two assistants dragged Yestlin into wagon, his left hand cuff was hooked with the iron bar in wagon and he was just hanging on his own hand. He was still dozing.

Meanwhile, a sledge came from distance and the Judge and his team heard of shouting an old lady. She reached the Judge and screamed," My son?" her voice was echoed from surrounding hills. Igor felt a deep pinch. Security guard showed the old lady her son, pointing his gun towards the closed door of wagon. The mother of

---

[9](Vipera kaznakovi is a species of venomous snake in Georgia and Russia).

Yestlin grabbed the handle of backdoor and shouted," Yesli, Yesli...wait...I have come. Now I am with you! Nothing can go wrong. (She turned at Igor.) I will get the best advocate for him. See, your mom is alive!" She grabbed the coat of Igor and cried, "You finished your judgment when my son was unconscious, none to help him. Is this humanity? (She shouted.) Stop that wagon. Stop now, give us a chance to defend...!" Igor, the judge puffed smoke turning his head on a side and then smiled showing his dirty teeth! The mother became sober by now; she requested to show mercy, show her all papers. She whispered, "My son can't do wrong. His grandfather died in siege of Leningrad in 1942, he was Senior Lieutenant in Police, his father died in military at Turkey border and his sister was a nurse, who died 4 years back at Polish border camp. Patriotism runs in our blood."

That gang of six, in team of Igor remained silent, smiling at each other and Igor said, "Forget your son, O Mother, your son was a traitor! This cherry was sour among others in your sweet dish!" The Police signaled and the wagon started. Mother ran and grabbed handle of back door of wagon. Wagon pulled here despite driver saw her crying pitiably from mirror. As wagon began its journey, old lady was dragged on ice filled road behind. With the wagon, the fate of communist party, also began rolling downhills! Wagon was going to railway station where Yestlin would be transported in a local train under police security and then he would be deported to Siberia through Trans-Siberian Railway from outskirt of Rostov. The stone-faced driver had no pity for the old lady being dragged behind the wagon...she would not loosen her grip.

Security guard whispered at garage, "She should not have come here." Igor, the Judge pulled the gun out from wallet of security guard standing next to him and fired at old lady getting dragged behind wagon saying, "I love Silence!" The bullet was well, targeted at her heart from back...it blasted her heart and she became silent. Igor saw her dead, being pulled on backdoor of wagon. Her son, Yestlin was semi-comatose in wagon, taken to railway station. Igor and his team took deep breath, smiled at each other and drove their car away towards Moscow.

[After a kill, only silence remains in nature. It's better to have noises of Life! How does a stupid man ask for Extreme Peace? Every life emits the song of love, in nature. Voice is the mark of celebration of life. Whatever one speaks, it's a sum total of Ohm, hardly a few knows this truth. – Yestlin]

*

[Whenever a mother cries the Mother Nature also, cries. Biological mothers are directly related with Mother Nature.- Wombick, a friend for life, of Yestlin]

Yestlin opened his eyes in utter confusion! He did not understand what he had lost in that transition! Time was taking him too far, leaving his whole world far behind. Probably, he would never return in same world again. The last cry of old mother echoed in small hills on way to railway station. Her cry reached to sacred place on Himalayas at about 16000 feet height within snow capped mountains.

The cry of innocence can create massive shock wave. History has witnessed it in form of Revolutions against tyrant kings, governments and authority. True king shows humility; he allows, appreciates and accepts all the types of surface waves or thoughts. He gives freedom of expression. He won't fight with mirror images, he tolerates minor variables. He knows that he can't achieve a clean garden! Dried leaves are a part of the beauty of garden. And, what should he do about thorns? Ruler doesn't spend time to pick thorn and destroy; he avoids them or makes a use of them! He knows that surface waves on sea achieve equilibrium! He focuses on giant sea waves that that can swallow even giant ships or can hinder his progress! - Yestlin

Emotions are like small tidal waves of an ocean while strong emotional outbursts can create giant waves in sea. Weak emotions are nullified and balance is maintained. Existence knows an art of maneuvering to achieve Equilibrium. Life came out of uniting two halves of Zero! That's why everything tends to be zero! Everything wants to meet its counterpart. Male loves females. Joy meets sorrow, life is attached with death and association has to meet with dissociation to achieve zero experience. A friend can become enemy! Success is met with heavy payment from other fields of life. Day has a night to follow. All is about equilibrium. But the strong emotional outburst generates deep impact to higher Consciousness.- Wombick.

When the back door of wagon was opened, Yestlin with hand-cuff stepped down on the same foot-rest where his mother laid down her life. The dead body of old lady was thrown away on track of wagon in snow desert. It will devoured as a feast by foxes. Rest of carcass would be gulped by the glaciers. Today, he had lost everything in life! A little treasure was looted; a small nest was blown away in storm! The bird was battered and about to meet his destiny. When the innocent Mother was shot on her back by Judge Igor, it penetrated the thoracic spinal cord giving her a sharp pain. The bullet then blasted her heart filled with love for her son. That created a strong impulse in space. The way, a massive sea quake has capacity to generate Tsunami, scream of innocent people shakes up Mother Nature!

Soon, Yestlin began his journey from Valdemir railway station (210 km from Moscow), picked up Trans-Siberian goods train along with other convicts to Exile.

*

3. Gulag Camp and Siberian Exile:

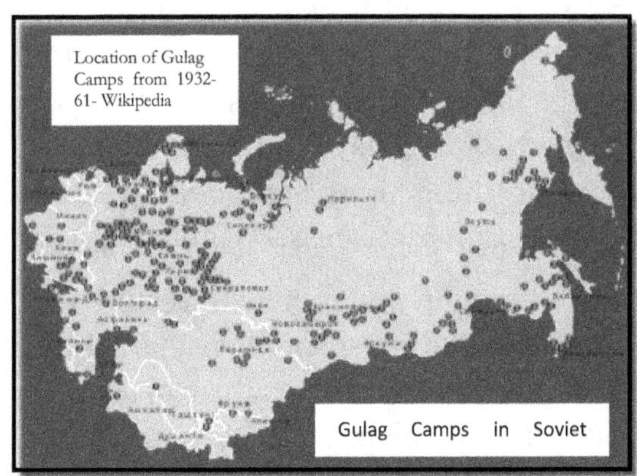

The Gulag (Russian: ГУЛАГ; acronym for Glavnoe upravlenie l agerei, Главное упра вление лагерей, 'Main Directorate of Camps')

Gulag was the Government agency in charge of Soviet Network of Forced labor Camps set up by order of Vladimir Lenin reaching its peak during Stalin's rule from 1930 to 1950s.

The Gulag was recognized as a major instrument of political repression in the Soviet Union, though official sources said it to be "corrective labor camps". The camps housed a wide range of convicts, from petty criminals to political prisoners, large numbers of whom, were convicted by simplified procedures, such as by NKVD troikas or by other instruments of extrajudicial punishment. The emergent consensus among scholars who utilize official archival data was that of the 18 million who were sent to the Gulag from 1930 to 1953, roughly 1.5 to 1.7 million perished there or as a result of their detention. But, there is no statement of official intent to kill them and prisoner releases vastly exceeded the number of deaths in the Gulag. This can be partly attributed to the common practice of releasing prisoners who were either suffering from incurable diseases or near death. Gulag has come to mean the Soviet repressive system itself, the set of procedures that prisoners once called the "meat-grinder". The arrests, the interrogations, the transport in unheated cattle cars, the forced labor, the destruction of families, the years spent in exile, the early and unnecessary deaths!

As an eyewitness, a prisoner described the Gulag as a system where people were worked to death. Many mining and industrial towns and cities in Northern and Eastern Russia and in Kazakhstan such as Karaganda, Norilsk, Vorkuta and Magadan (Here, Yestlin was sent.), were originally blocks of camps built by prisoners and subsequently run by ex-prisoners. There was an infamous system of labor exploitation whereas the inmates' food rations were linked to their rate of work production. That notorious 'you-eat-as-you-work' system killed weaker prisoners in weeks and caused countless casualties. After a proposal known as nourishment scale, that was rectified Administration faced ingenious problems. Forced labor was less efficient than free labor. In fact, prisoners in the Gulag were, on average, half as productive as free laborers, partially explained by malnutrition. Second problem was food shortage. Third was labor scarcity. During war in 1941, many laborers were shifted to front and labor shortage was intense. 'Do more with less food' came as a policy. Laborers were given rest of 5-6 hours and often had skipped meals! The use of Gulag camps was to build buildings, military settlements, roads, bridges, Trans-Siberian railway lines and even entire cities like Magadan- free of cost! They were employed in mining and deforestation. Less described the better!

Siberian Exile and Siberian Gulag:

Katorga (Russian: ка́торга, IPA: ['katərgə]; was a system of penal labor in the Russian Empire and the Soviet Union. Prisoners were sent to remote penal colonies in vast uninhabited areas of Siberia and Russian Far East where voluntary settlers and workers were never available in sufficient numbers. The prisoners had to perform forced labor under harsh conditions.

Forced exile to Siberia had been in use since the seventeenth century for a wide range of offenses and was a common punishment for political dissidents and revolutionaries. In 1754 the Russian government decided to send petty criminals and political opponents to Eastern Siberia. Sentenced to hard labor (katorga), the convicts had to travel mostly on foot and the journey could take up to three years and it is estimated about half died before they reached their destination. Later, instead of regarding it, a means of getting rid of disabled criminals or enemies of states, the Government began to look upon it as a means of populating and developing a new and promising part of its Asiatic territory. Trans-Siberian Railway was partly built by such prisoners. Others worked in the silver and lead mines of the Nertchinsk district, the saltworks of Usolie and the gold mines of Kara.

Those convicts who did not work hard enough were flogged to death. Other punishments included being chained up in an underground black hole and having a 48 lb beam of wood attached to a prisoner's chains for several years. Living standards were extremely frustrating, mean and pitiable. The Spoon was luxury, the walls of cells would get snow coating at night, often prisoners had to drink soups directly from pots.

After the change in Russian penal law in 1847, exile and katorga became common punishment for participants in national uprisings within the Russian Empire. This led to increasing numbers of Poles sent to Siberia for katorga.

Siberia has long had economic value for Russia. The production and export of these minerals makes up a major part of Russia's economy (approximately 3-4 percent of gross domestic product, or GDP), but Russia draws its real significance — economic and geopolitical — from its oil and natural gas resources.

Such prisons still exist in Siberia (2013) Although improved, prisons in Russia are still suffocating places. Mr Naymushin said: 'I have been taking photographs in the prison camps of Siberia for about 15 years, so my first impressions were of the past. Russia is thought to have about 850,000 convicts in its prison system, with many sentenced to forced labor. [Jun 19, 2013; taken from internet, Wikipedia and other articles]

(Such abuse of powers and humanity is painful to Saints from all over the world. A Human kills a human? Who will believe in future? But, the blood, and fleshes of humans gone to soil are fertilizers. Heavens are watching! Yestlin was sent for petty issue to Siberian Exile that was also the same story.)

4. Divine Kingdom at Himalay

Defining The Rishis:

Rishis[10] are the Holy Saints; the most pious, divine humanly embodied saints who do not indulge in human social behaviors. They stay high, live without food for a long period, wonder high in spiritual levels, say higher than Manipur Chakra in Kundalini science. Yogi is the one who is attached at highest anchor, called as Brahma or God and get infused into Brahma. Rishis are more than them...they derive Pure Knowing from Brahma or God. It's like a river returns after entering from Ocean to tell TRUTH.

Maharshis-(Maha-rishis) have ageless body and thoughtless minds, emotionless Chitta or Sub-Consciousness and stay in ethereal bodies; they travel in various Dimensions of Universe to other timelines and they visit to Himalayas at regular period. They see our world through their third eye. They are truly awakened souls. Otherwise, they stay in deep Meditation in certain occult caves or locus. Still higher, there are Five ('Panch', in Sanskrit) Great Masters (Parmesthi, in Sanskrit; 'the greatest, farthest Sages who do 'Good' to every life.) We call them 'Panch-Parmesthi'. It is a rare occasion to meet any one of them and rarest to meet them when they are all together. They are the highest Spiritual Regulatory Authorities who control clans of Gurus (Masters) on Earth, religions preachers in all types of religions. Functions of Parmesthi are very complex as it is universal. Few of them are as under:

- Uplift the spiritual level of mankind; as they know that the Gravity of Planet Earth and Mother Nature pull human life down to animal level. They know, 'A man is born like animal

---

[10]**Rishi**: They are Holy Saints spread all over, but remain in isolation. Most of them reside and do Yogic Practice along with their Masters in remote areas of Himalaya. They are bound to their Masters so as they can't preach to civilian unless the fellow become their disciple. That way, most of Teachings of Yogic Science and Devotional pathway have remained occult since ages. The One who is not bound to His Master will be free to preach to common man.

but he can be divine and Angel'. Mankind is the link between animal life and Divine life.

- Help many pious yogis or devotees when they find difficulty in their spiritual practice.

- They emit signals and the receivers of those vibes are transformed, become devotional. They become devotees, Yogi, Gurus and Preachers we see routinely, in society. Others become the finest mentors of groups of people.

- Nature runs in multiple cycles- Life and death cycle, Karma and Karma-fal (fruits of Karma) cycle. Electrons, protons are rotating cyclically; energy waves are rhythmical. Mother Nature maintains Equilibrium by sum total of joy and sorrow, association and dissociation. Ultimate experience is Zero. Dark forces are balanced by enlightened souls!

- Function of Paramesthi is to help human race by sending enlightened souls to poise Love against the Violence, Hatred and Envy.

- Paramesthi look many tricky matter of Mother Nature like Sublimation of Yogis and Devotees, well functioning of Dharma Chakra, look at whether every life gets a chance for re-birth. Everyone who dies will get a chance to return so as his dreams may come true or he may pursue his dreams or unfinished accounts, or he meets with his destiny.

*

'Question: Which Way? Gyan Ghati Says, 'Ours Way!'

A divine Goose, Rajhansa was flying across a valley in between two ranges of snow capped mountains (22000 ft. height) in deepest terrine of Himalayas near Kanchenjunga (3rd highest peak, 22800 ft or 8500 meters ht.). 'An Eye of Observer' that followed the divine goose, suddenly turned towards the mountain slope on left side and penetrated through ice and rocks into a deep dark bluish cave! Observer quickly, travelled through bluish tranquil tunnel in serpentine way lined with dark sharp and wet rocks jutting out at many places. Tunnel was too narrow for anyone to travel, was like a slit some where. It led to a deep cavity, a cistern, where four divine radiant souls (semi-transparent human figures) were floating in Dhyan (Meditation posture), few inches above the floor encircling a holy fire. Fire too, was floating without any woods; fires were through holy spirits of those Maharshris. The cave was as if, breathing and throbbing with Ohm. Ohm vibes were emitted from those Maharshis. The Holy spirits were just like halos or white silhouettes. Their auras were illuminating enough to shine in darkness. Divine fragrance was mesmerizing. It was a zone of pure consciousness and tranquility. The Oldest Grand Master was of 780 years of age, had long white hairs, white skin, curled up nails of about 6-8 inches and wa s almost frozen in look. Other Masters had long white hairs on beard and plaited hairs on head. They were of about 560, 410, 320 years of ages. Hardly, they were breathing once in 2 to 3 minutes! (They were live!) They were like floating humanoid figures, so transparent that rocks of opposite wall were seen through them. Serenity would compel anyone to bow down to them. The Peace that encircled them was special. (I will name them 1st M (or Grand Master, GM), 2nd, 3rd and 4th M (M for Master) according to their seniority.) When GM (1st M) came out of deep meditation, he opened his glittering eyes with a sigh! That made the peak of mountain shivered; little snow showered from its top. Soon, discussion began:

GM: (He whispered in discrete words.) "Who will tell them to 'look up', see from where they have come? You are not alone. Someone is watching from heights." A long pause followed. "Busy quarreling for pebbles at sea shore; they miss out roaring ocean' calling. When will they understand the purpose of their visit to Earth? They are not pigs or fishes!"

3rd Master: They are not quarreling, they have weapons of Havoc, want to kill each other. They are gripped with Fear and Violence. See the tragic state of the most intelligent species in this part of Space! Someone may feel like vomiting blood over their activities- exploiting, extortion, taking profits, exploiting children and women or people on name of God. (pause) Lord Krishna or Ram came for such a dwarf civilization! Ram eliminated one unjust civilization just to send message not to be like Ravana! Krishna could not save his own kingdom nor he could stop war of Mahabharat. Human race has witnessed so many Genocides; and learnt nothing. Then, Lord Buddha and Mahavir came to preach forgiveness for all so as they might Love each other. There, they failed. <u>A human being does not love, even himself</u>!!

2nd M.: Human Race is a strategically devised on Planet Earth. It therefore, came late to land here. Life on Earth (animals & birds etc) had no hope to sublime and return to root source (The Brahma or God) before the Doom's Day i.e. End of Kalp Day. Life is cyclical, rotational, and ever changing and sum total is zero! Life on this planet can reach to Brahma before the End of Kalp[11]. Human brain and heart derives vibrations (emotions or feelings) from any experience of this planet. From those vibes, he can sublime. That is why, all animals look at a man with holy expectation. The Mankind is the last 'Hope of Mother Nature'; the bridge to divine life through which even animals can cross the Nature. Same way, when Angels want to seek the Brahma of God, they dive down, take birth as Human being and then sublime. So much is dependent upon humankind and those fools are quarreling for pebbles! They run after rolling coins, spend whole life or prepare for wars to conquer the part of Planet. First, a man should serve his Soul, then others. The Soul is trapped here, on Earth since the inception of Universe! (Pause)

Once, this soul was dissociated from the God, like a Ray of Sun began journey leaving the Sun. when Soul entered in existence, it

---

[11] Kalp: Kalp is the Time, a period in which this Universe exists. It starts with the birth of Universe and ends with the collapse of Universe (Implosion). This widest span is the life of Universe. When it returns to its root source, the Brahma (God), Brahma Himself returns to Nothingness. Veda says the Maha-Visnu goes to sleep for another period of Kalp. That explains that (1) The very Existence in which Universe manifests, swings in pendulum from Being-ness to Nothingness. The very Existence is the Brahma or God. (2) To return to Brahma or God or Root Source before the Doom's day is the goal for most of living world, even for species of other planet, if any! And, the Mankind is the only hope for them. That is why, aliens are attracted on Earth.

was consumed by Fire Element, as binder of electrons and protons (Fire Element) to make an atom, an element (Air Element). The elements conjugated and they made the chemical Compounds (Water Element and Earth Element). Later, enzymes came into existence and so chemicals were able to be redesigned, re-created into another set of chemicals. **As if, the Enzymes had intelligence and the creativity or life**! Enzymes are synthesized in Ribosome attached to Endoplasmic Reticulum of a cell. Each cell has a Soul that way. Life, soon began, in true sense. Each life needed energies, so was asked to consume food (energy) and proliferate (multiply) and become 'the food' for next level life! Life starts of Yagya or the Self-Sacrifice and ends with Yagya. This is the Natural cyclical rhythm of Life. I take food and oh! I am the Food also!!

Each soul that has entered on Earth is moving cyclical from life to death to life. There is 'no go'! These animals and birds are pitiable that way, as they are returning in different forms of life since ages. Therefore, to bless them, gracefully, God or Brahma (Bhagvan) Shiv, 'our' Father, landed here at Kailash Mountain, Himalaya with Vedas and brought Human form of life on Earth. Shiv means Kalyan or Welfare or Good for all. Lord Shiva brought World Orders, inter-galactic order from Kailash Mountain! He defined the return pathway by Yog Sadhana Path and Devotional Pathway). Those animals that would evolve, would drop hatred and violence, feel love for other living creatures will ascend to Human form. They will enter in Human Embryo. Last animal post in return series, is the Cow. That way, the cows are the last post for animal kingdom and the Mankind is the last hope for life on Earth.

2nd M.: A man belongs to Higher Spiritual Order, not of the Earth. He is born to lift rest of life as possible and Bhagvan Shiv is calling him.

3th M.: Unfortunately, after birth, mind follows the sense organs. So, what is perceived is believed and valued. That way, young man values matters more than intangible treasures. Who can tell him that the life is beyond sensual perceptions! His truth is defined by words, logics and understanding. Really, it's the great species on earth but with narrow vision, so they fight for worldly goal like cats and dogs. Human life is wasted.

G.M.: By our request and prayers, Lord Vishnu descended in form of Shri Ram and Krishna on Earth, to abolish Sinful kings so as to liberate innocent people. It was because, those kings were pawns of Darkness or those who crave only material pleasures= lustful, materialistic and looters of fortunes of innocent people. They eradicated Rules of many kings but common man did not show a sign of improvement. They continued to live in rat race.

Later, Lord Buddha & Mahavir came with a message that a man can live with Love and Non-Violence! Then, we sent the Messengers and people voided Him. Then we induce devotees to come in society and spread message of Love for Krishna and Ram. People began singing Devotional Songs but did not evolve. Animals and birds found them, they loved devotees and yogis; but human society devised the books and imprisoned their sayings or preaching. Now, those so called Holy Books guide the majority of Human Race! Anyone can manipulate! Those Religious books are the instruments or weapons to rule the world. Soon, a quarrel started about superiority of religious book in their hands! Why don't they understand that Religions were devised for a life to sublime; that proves that a life is greater than any religion. Religion is its tool only. But, as of now, religion has its bearers, leaders, propellers and a source of imperialism, have an army. Religious leaders get wealth, reputation, king's lifestyle, have own judiciary and own punishments! They have attracted power by subjugation of their followers. Religious followers are 'silkworms', dying in their own shells!

None understands that Ram or Krishna, Buddha or Mahavir have come and all gone. You are still clueless, asking which way, my Krishna went! They don't know right dimension, to reach to own root source. They are trapped in words and words are trapped in holy books, like dried flowers kept in books! Dead yet, but they have fragrance! Man should be able to find messages or feelings from fragrance of words of Krishna, Ram or Buddha. Books are vulnerable for manipulation. Words will confuse them. With centuries, intentions derived from words will change according to interpreters. (pause) True religion will ask them to look up, follow the stars, return to your root source from where whole universe is operated; dwell there, in Peace. That vertical voyage is called Spiritual Path. That is the only way to bring Peace down on your Planet. *When a man will be a man rather than animal then, divine life will descend on Earth.* That is the challenge to Mankind.

2nd M.: Who will make them understand this! Each Human has a pot of Divine Love at his heart, for Brahma and he should not waste his love and Time for Earthen Matters. He should devote to his God or Krishna (Brahma).

4th M.: Today, the world is passing through tough times. Life cycle is disturbed, millions of human lives are the wastes. Most of animals and birds don't get access in their respective embryos. Every life needs a birth after death. One should get respective body to fulfill own destiny. If they are unborn, they don't get respective parents or embryo, then those souls stay unborn. Most of species do not get the chance of rebirth, because of human interference.

In Human race also, a pious soul may not get a chance of birth. Angels cannot descend as appropriate virtuous couple they don't find. All men and women are mostly, transformed into warriors. Marriages in human race have remained biological more, than love-filled conjugation with higher vibes. Men and women are 'polluted'; their vibes are lower and so souls from animal stream enter in human embryos. That way, <u>Human race has humans, half-humans and non-human sub-types.</u> *How saints and pious souls will choose appropriate place for return to Earth? Who will go down if Earth becomes a place of physical, mental and psychological warzone!* Every soul has right to return and they seek appropriate parents. **If Souls**

with Higher Spiritual Vibrations don't descend then Future of Mankind will be doom. Dharma-Chakra (Wheel of Religion) will stop soon and Nature will purge human race. Humans behaving like animals would make them a futile species!"

Rests of Masters remained silent with face down against their Grand Master began to speak to them after a hundred of years of silence.

3rd M.: Human brain can ascend beyond 10th dimension and can dip in Samadhi. Tapaswi[12], Yogis, Demons, Angels, Semi-Gods[13] need to return as human to self-reveal their Divinity on Earth. So, it's a major divine problem, human race has created out of its ignorance. <u>All are suffering from misfired human race from Angels to Inferior lives.</u> But, human life is too complex, my Grand Master! Have mercy!!

"Human life is not simple; a man can live in different dimensions, may travel in different worlds at one time! Few of his worlds run parallel or cross with each other creating conflicting personality. Biologically, he behaves like an animal and desires to soar high like Angels. Karma and Destiny of past lives call him at accurate times at various spots or places. From within his desires and unfulfilled dreams of past lives drive him forth and his destiny or enticements hold him backwards. Man is an organism with great conflicts from within. To add, Devotional practice of past lives and grace of his Masters as well parents remind him to ascend vertically, they say not to spoil pure love to this mortal world. Live responsibly on planet Earth but ascend to deliver your love to Krishna. Here, Earth soil has gravity; it pulls him to down while man wants to ascend vertically to Krishna. Human life is not like driving on straight line.

---

[12] Tapaswi: who does penance.

[13] Semi-God or Demi-God: (considered to be a Son of deity) A **semi god** can be mortal who worships, prays to and constantly praises a greater God but is also worshipped, prayed to and constantly praised by others. He is a-mythological being with more power than a mortal but less than a god.

Where a man is born, there are Leaders instead of Teachers or Gurus too. Leaders have been authorized in almost every field of life starting from 'religion' to 'Entertainment' to 'politics' and 'ruling', to 'economy' and 'social life.'. There are prisons or traps in which a small tiny child is smiling like a rose with thorns. There are prisons outside prisons and they are the reflections of inner conceptual prisons. Instead of killing Ravana and Kansa (Hindu Purana), <u>we need to focus upon individual person so as he can break his prison by himself and then he can attempt sublimation or ascension. All humans are the prisoners of Time and Space. Oh Grand Master! Bestow upon Grace</u>."

*

Divine Conspiracy

It is a moment of despair for Rishis. So many Yogis at Himalaya live hopelessly, continuing their Yogic Practice until the last breath. (If they leave their present body, when will they get chance of rebirth? Proper sublimed parents are not easy to spot.) Heavens have thousands of eyes watching on Human Race. All are eager asking when you are going to rise!

Grand Master now, concluded:

"We requested the Vishnu (Brahma) to help human race. They came as Krishna and Ram. Then, we saw enlightenment of Buddha. He walked over Planet by the self as well by his Radiance. Then we had sent messengers, Yogis, Rishis, Tapasi, Siddha and many divine people however human race has failed to awaken, arise and failed to understand what they all said. Today, thousands of Gurus or Preachers work on planet but, people have confused such masters." There was a pause! Question was poised, **"How can we enlighten the human brain? How they may combat the darkness from within?"**

Panch Parmesti (four of five Great Masters) sat in meditation, got an affirmation from Lord Shiva and decided not to request Bhagvan Vishnu to return. They would neither opt for next messenger nor next generation of Devotees to reach to human society. They chose Lord Sun to eliminate Darkness of Human minds from within. After all, it's all the play of Light and Shadows. The Light flows in Sine wave. So, they decided the time when the Dawn will reach to Human Race (not to the Earth). And, it would create great sudden impact to mankind. That was why, the Grand Master raised a question, "Someone should reach to Human Race to inform that-

- They are the Ray of Light, the Pure Soul. They are God's Children. (That way, they are all the family.)
- Earth is not your permanent Home! Finish your purpose of visit and pack up!
- Sky and that Light are yours, not the soil, its gold or diamonds!
- They have forgotten the pathway. Your purpose of life is holy, ethereal and not earthen! You came here to express and experience who you are. Now, if it's done, then open the wings of faith and love for God, and rise in skies. We are waiting since long! You lift yourself and lead others to follow you!'

Grand Master poised with a major issue: "Who will go to tell them; either be prepared for impending fury of Nature or awake, arise and take off from this basic model of animal life.

Nature will flush the civilization that is parasitic and yields nothing. If The Man is a burden to Nature then, they should remember the fate of Mars and other planets. We won't allow this to happen. (He took a deep breath.) Who will go there to awaken the humankind?

Second Master whispered, "One of us should take initiative." He looked at other Masters and then said. "Our wisest Yogi?! The Fifth of our Panch Parmesti!" (All of them honored as he was the youngest so more tuned with recent generation.) They closed their eyes and recalled their beloved Fifth Member, of 'Panch Parmesthi', the youngest Master of the age of 68 years! (We will call him as 'Yogi'.) Soon, a transparent human figure emerged from the rocky wall of that cave; its snow shattered and a young looking Yogi emerged through rocky wall, stepped forwards through rocks and reached to his Grand Master; bowed and he turned to each one of his Masters to offer salutation. He knelt at floor and sat in Vajrasana. He looked down and remained silent. He was about six feet height, oval sweet face, clean-shaved, no mustaches, had grey hairs and wearing white shirt and a trouser. He was an 'Ascended Master[14], who could speak various languages to communicate with people. All Masters bless their Fifth member.

---

[14]**Ascended Masters**: They are the spiritually enlightened beings who were ordinary humans in past incarnations. They have undergone a series of spiritual transformations originally called initiations. They can be called as "mahatma" or 'Great Soul' or Masters of the Ancient Wisdom who has ascended. A "Master of Light", "Healer" or "Spiritual Master" are Divine Human Being who has taken the Fifth Initiation and is thereby capable of dwelling in a 5th dimension. An "ascended master" is a human being who has taken the Sixth Initiation, also referred to as Ascension and is thereby believed to be capable of dwelling in a 6th dimension.

They don't die, but prefer to die by their choice at completion of their worldly tasks. They love the man, animals, birds and Mother Nature who become fearless in front of **Ascended Masters** or **Great Yogis** or **Mahatma**. One Example is **Sanat Kumars** in Hindu Religion. They are **Maitreiya** or Friend of every soul! They don't have discrimination. They stay away from every material issue as they are just vibrations, not even atoms! Therefore, they may disappear here and reappear there! They travel at many places in world as well in Universe, in blink of eye! They are the most beloved sons of Brahma, the God and they have direct communicating skill. Meeting the God is like going to next room of own house. They appear to be human but stay invisible and occult; the one who could see them is very special to them. They bestow Grace upon, by which they initiate Flame of Love for Krihna in heart of the one whom they meet. (cont.)

This Spiritual Hierarchy is a "Universal Chain" of Individualized God Free Beings, fulfilling Attributes and Aspects of God's Infinite Selfhood and Universal Consciousness Probram. In this Cosmic Hierarchical scheme, are Divine Beings of the Space, Solar Logoi or God of Sun or Fire, Beings of the Elements, Sons and Daughters of God, Archangels, Angels, Cosmic Beings, Ascended Masters then, the Twelve Solar Hierarchies (Rashis or Zodiac Signs, Nakshtra or Constellation) and Twin Flames of the Alpha-Omega Polarity and lastly, entire Galactic Systems. Ascended Masters are not the ruler but moderators of both parts of world.

Second M: You have heard our discussion. (Yogi nodded.) Will you reach out to society? (Yogi remained silent.) They are almost ready for wars, hold guns and missiles, fingers running on buttons...and people run amok with swords in hands in streets! They have been poisoned. **To save earth, help the Mother Nature and innocent people we have to send you to intervene. This will be their last chance of survival!** If they refuse, they will be purged by Nature. It's an urgent message for People of Earth.

Earth has become a giant slaughter-house. Who will tell the man that all are the co-existents of this time and all descended from Lord Sun. All are the Souls who were liberated from Brahma (God) who have taken shapes and various attributes to enter in this Planet. Lord Sun is their first Heavenly Abode. Life on this planet is trapped by invisible prisons. Elevate all the barriers and liberate birds, they will raise high in skies to heavens. *We are eager to see the release of divine souls from Earth. Tell them the God is nowhere in holy books; God is within you! They are the walking Temple, or Church...see! Worship your own God sitting within.* And, follow your inner voice." Yogi observed his Grand Master, who smiled lovingly and blessed him.

Yogi: Is it necessary to meddle in human matters? They are independent, have seeds of wisdom, love in heart and intelligence in brain. They will ultimately find which way they should go. Why we from Ethereal World should interfere in their world?

2ⁿᵈ M: They had enough time to show wisdom! If they fail to yield results, Mother Nature will purge and we can't sit here idly viewing annihilation. You are going to save the life as far as possible. (Pause) Today, many people are crying with injustice and pains. Wise people pray to God and ask, "Which way?" (He paused.) We at 'Gyan-Ghati', (Shangri-La) want to convey the message, "Ours Way!" You are going to represent us.

You are the most beloved and wisest young Monk. Meet with them on our behalf. You will meet resistance. You will face their powers, we know. They will reject changes in life, we know. However, **you need to convey our message of Love or perish!** They have higher levels of weapons why you have just the Powers of Ohm!" Yogi nodded.

Now, all became eager to hear Yogi. Yogi bowed them again, took their order, closed his eyes and remained silent for a long period then he stated:

"I will go. Their pathway of life is not horizontal, it's not enough to wonder on planet Earth, their pathway is outside in and from below upwards, towards the sky...a vertical pathway.

They are divine from birth! Being Human is the greatest blessing from Mother Nature. I propose to establish the Sun Land where awakened divine souls will live, and lit a flame in every heart. Love will breed for thousands of years. The human race will be friend to other species. He will share his Intelligence, Prudence and Love. I will establish such an environment for society. (All Masters were satisfied and blessed him.)

Yogi asked, "Now, tell me from where we start?" That was soothing to all Yogis and Masters sitting in various caves of Himalayas. One out of thousands of Yogi decides to return to human society. Most of Yogis are also, selfish!! Who cares for downtrodden life on earth? Most of Yogis seek Salvation.

Second Master focused on Globe of Earth and said, "Reach out there, to Siberia, Soviet Union. We listen so much of cries and prayers from there. Ask Lord Sun to bestow the Ghyan of Immortality to them. Soon, New Era will begin and you prepare the people to welcome the Sun Land. (pause) They have suffered there a lot; I think, it's the right direction. Begin from Siberia. Let the sun shine. We will rejoice when animals will be expelled from human flesh."

Yogi bowed and said, "I need to be illogical, unquestionable, without name, norms and calculations! Then, I can combat their mortal forces. I will prove that Heavens are indeed, imbedded in their genes. Heavens are not hanging high. As I understand, human race is a funny species." Yogi stared at his grand Masters who understood the gravity of tasks and they came out of their ethereal shapes, walked a little to cover Yogi from all round. They raised hands and made a coning covering Yogi, made a pyramid to bless Yogi for a long time. 4th Master started humming:

Ohm, Apyayantu Twaamagani Vakpranah Chakhsu: Kshotramatho Balamindriyani Ch Sarvani. Sarva Brahmopanishadam Maa Maham Brahm Nirakurya Ma Ma Brahm Nirakarot, Anirakranam-Stvainrakaranm MeStu. Tadatmani Nirate Y Upanishadts DharmaSte Mayi Santu, Te Mayi Santu. Ohm Shanti Hi, Shanti Hi Shanti.

Ohm! Your organs, speech, Life, Eyes, Ears and all Organs and my Powers be replenished (forever)! The Brahma (God) that is defined in Upanishads, I won't reject Him, and Brahma (God) will not reject me too, we have permanent Relation with Brahma. The Groups of Religions that are defined in Upanishads will come to reside in me, who is devoted to God! They shall be within me, with me, Ohm Peace be prevailed, Peace, Inner Peace!

Ohm, Bhadram Karnerbhih Shrunuyam Deva Bhadrah Pashyamakshbhiryajatrah. SthirenangainS tustuvanasStanubhiVyarshem Devhitam Yadayuh. Swasti n Indrah Vrudhashravaha Swasti n Pusha Vishwavedah Swasti n TaKshyo Aristanemih Swasti no Bruhaspatirdadhatu. Ohm Shantihi, Shantihi Shanti.

Ohm! O Godly Figures (Angels), while worshipping the God, our ears listen at consecrated words; eyes see holy and consecrated things. With healthy body and organs, while in Devotional Practice of God, we use our life in Divine Purpose. O Lord Indra (Vrudhashrava- whose glory is spread in all dimensions.) you protect and nurture our Cause and Destiny. O Lord Sun ('Pusha'- the Lord who nurtures the Planet Earth and 'Vishwaveda'- All Vedas- the One who has Spiritual Knowing from beginning of Universe.) bring Good for us. O Lord Garuda (Aristanemi-who controls snakes of Evil forces.) nurture our Good and progress. O Lord Jupiter (Bruhaspati- the Great Planet) please, bring us our Good Fortunes. Ohm Shanti (Peace), Shanti (Inner Peace), Shanti (Peace everywhere)!

Grand Master whispered out of love, "Mother Nature will stay will you, will pave your path. Go and return quickly. Hari Ohm." Next moment, all of those Masters disappeared from that cave! Sparkling stars rotated around and slowly disappeared in the rocks of cave. Divine fire was also, gone in dark stillness.

*

"We, all disciples always remember this conversation as it was a rare event to hear what Holy Ascended Masters talk about the Mankind. As well, it is important to notice that there are our 'Fathers' who are concerned about the humankind and Planet Earth. We are not alone. We are thrilled about Yogi who came in our life and lifted us to next level in Spirituality." –All Disciples of Sunland

5: Journey of Yogi to Siberia

A Fisher man sleeping in his small cabin Located at Earnaculam sea coast, Kochin, India, got an intuition by a whisper from bushes of coconut trees, to prepare his boat, for the Unknown. It was 11.30 PM.

He hurriedly got some bananas and Coconuts as well he packed clean white shirt and trouser (he had just bought for church rituals.) in plastic bag. He prepared his small boat and placed all requirements. He was staring at moon in curiosity who would come. His small boat was dangling with tidal waves. Mr. Murugan was a fisherman, living in a small hut near seashore. He observed a fog was created in a bush and then a sparkling halo. Soon, a divine figure stepped out and went towards his boat. Murugan shocked but ran towards him and approached politely. He saw 'Jesus' reborn, in that figure. He bowed down and Yogi placed his hand on his head, played with his curly hairs and smiled. Murgan showed fruits and a bag of white clothes there in boat. Yogi smiled at him, lowered his head for that obligation, said, "I have a long way to go. I should not be late. You owe this boat from me." He stepped in boat,Murugan released anchor and boat began to move off the shore spontaneously. Yogi was smiling at Murgan, he told him to go to church and ask if he wanted anything, Lord will happily grant your wish." Yogi turned his eyes towards horizon and his boat began to glide over the waters fast. Quiet Ocean surged suddenly and a giant wave lifted his boat and took far in horizon. Fisherman saw the boat moving as if, towards the full moon, that was in horizon. He saw the horizons till boat disappeared. He stood there as if frozen! He then, ran to talk to his wife and father....

A small vessel was dancing on surface of Quiet Ocean, like a baby playing in lap of her mother. 'Ocean is as great as my Himalay.' Yogi whispered. It was his first journey by sea. His boat was surfing effortlessly on surface of Great Indian Ocean. Crystal sky and sparkling moon and thousands of stars made it a heavenly scene. Tiny ripples on surface of Ocean reflected moon and built a spectacular scene. Yogi whispered, 'When the mind is absent, the tranquility is established from within outwards! When peace of Space and ocean meet with the peace of soul, one can attain Samadhi. All noises are from human mind. Nature is cool; planet, ocean and moon are cool!' Yogi bowed down to Ocean and offer prayer. 'Oh Sea God, take me to my destination.' Then, he slept in boat in meditation and boat moved effortlessly towards Java Sea.

Before dawn, ocean hilariously greeted him with high tidal waves. Initially, waves were gentle crawling to boat and made splashing sounds. Later, the waves aggressively crept towards him; sea had its own rhythm, own sounds and own playfulness! The way heart beats; ocean also beats! As if, the ocean was throbbing. Soon, tide came at dawn. Tidal waves were also harmonious exhaling mist; it appeared that sea was forging its own sea-song. When Yogi left beach of Kerala, the sea was absolutely sleeping and now it is awake and childishly playful and even notorious. In tide, the waves were murmuring and mesmerizing! Splashing of waves to boat was as if palpitation. Soon, the sea began to roar, its quavering harnessed its majesty. Giant water body on Planet Earth

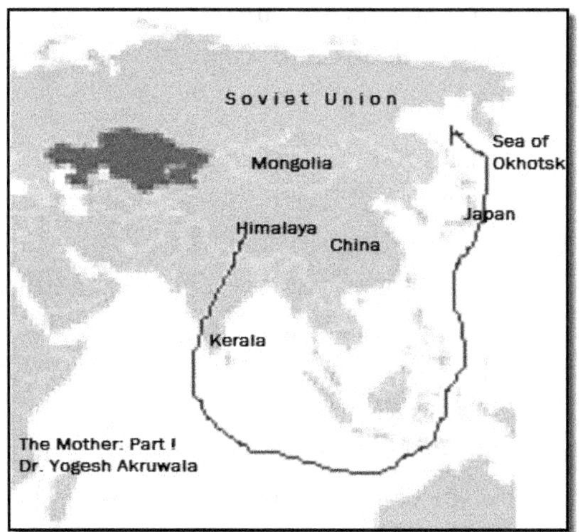

was so autonomous that none can understand who shakes and who makes ocean silent! Yogi thought that buoyancy is the basic character of ocean, it holds magnanimous ships. True sailors don't get afraid of sea. He experienced tanning bright daylights reflected from surface of ocean and soon, his peaceful voyage was transformed into a horrendous experience! Winds changed and dense dark clouds came over and brought rains and thunders! Mighty Ocean shuddered and giant Sea waves emerged. That sea storm flung his boat, there tiny toy like boat was lifted and moved the way striker spins over carom board! The sky became dark and lightening descended upon mighty waves. Heavy rains with thunders were terrifying and Yogi was carried away so swiftly that he crossed from Celebes Sea to Philippine Sea into Pacific Ocean. (This thunderstorm came to hide the boat of Yogi from eyes of fishermen of Philippines and other islands.)

When he entered in Pacific Ocean, giant Sea Whales surrounded and made loud slapping noises by their tails and fins. They began to encircle the boat and sent whistles and clicks to awaken Yogi. Yes, they had come to play with Yogi. First, they sprayed waters from all around to awaken Yogi from his meditation. They began to make noise, as if they sang songs by series of sounds for a period of seven to 20 minutes, all rhythmic and repetitive! Each whale had separate songs and they adhere to own tunes. They encircled the boat and continued to repeat the songs and whistling with spray of waters on Yogi. Their group began to rotate around the fast moving boat. Later, they came closer and Yogi outreached his hand to pat them individually. When a giant ship was seen coming close, the family of whales disappeared. Night brought silence again and Yogi crossed Japan Sea East to Japan islands.

As Yogi entered in Sea of Okhotsk, Siberia's deep tranquility came to wrap his boat from all around. Yogi saw glacial ice was coming upon sea ice. The boat was going to meet flat snow slabs soon. Sea of Okhotsk is very calm Ocean. The grease ice came first as the boat advanced. There were no ripples, no waves and no splashes to his boat. Boat was gliding northwards smoothly without any resistance. The Mother Nature became more still and the boat slowed down in vast ocean of congelation (Process of Freezing) of ice. White blanket of ice was making a floor; white 'wild' was the horizon, white fog descended and became still overhead. White clouds settling over the ocean slowly moved and suddenly disappeared as they were converted into crystal ice (A dangerous phenomenon, one can't see cloud sitting on ocean!) and white powder snow and crusts began to shower from all around. That made atmosphere sub-zero and but splendid. It created mesmerizing scenario. Hardly any contrast was left to perceive, looked like ghostly! But, for Yogi it was conducive to enter in meditation. Soon, the clouds settled on the boat hiding it from security guards boats. That way, slowly boat made a passage to reach to sea shore of Okhotsk, near Magadan, a port.

As the boat approached to coast of Okhotsk[15], the fog was lifted. The sun far in horizon reappeared with His golden glare! The birds began to sing and bears were looking at boat with inquisitiveness. They walked in snow along with moving boat. The man inside was

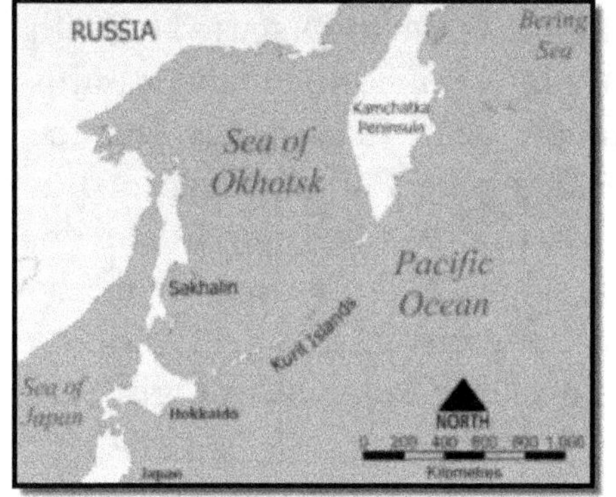

still sleeping (!) in meditation. As the fog was lifted, snow laden shore and its hills were visible in deep silence. Even boat was keeping pin-drop silence! It passed through ice and circumvented giant glaciers coming by side.

---

[15]**Sea of Okhotsk** is a marginal sea (~ 3000 meters deep sea near coasts) of Western Pacific Ocean, located between Kamchatka Peninsula on East and Kuril islands on Southeast, Japan's islands on South, Sakhalin islands on West and Eastern Siberian shore in north. *Okhotsk means urban settlement* and Sea was named after it. It has many military bases as well fisheries. So, Nature covered Yogi by fog and gave him a passage towards Seashore.

6: Yestlin runs for Life in Siberia

When Yestlin entered in a cabin of Trans-Siberian Goods Train with hands cuffs, he saw a series of young people, cuffed and brutally beaten sitting in line in the cabin. His cuff was tied to a chain with rest of prisoners. He saw gloomily at all co-voyagers of 'Train of Time'. All were frustrated, battered, chained with each other and sitting in a row in cabin around. Windows were open for 'fresh' air (!) and allowed the snow to sprinkle inside. All were sent for forced labor in Siberia. Yestlin stared at a few and found no face was criminal. Most of cabin-mates looked at him and sighed. He was youngest companion to them. As the train started off with rumbling sounds, all were thrust into unknown future towards Siberia. When that suburb station near Rostov was left the chugging sound of train engine increased. Chilled air gushed in through open windows. More Eastwards the train would go, coldness too would settle in those cabins. Old prisoners would die before they reach to destiny. Armed security guards were relishing hot drinks. Overall, there was dead silence in cabins. All prisoners were stooping to save own heat.

Yestlin turned his attention inwards, to imagine about fate of her mother; his eyes turned wet and tears were turned into pearls on eyelashes. Now, he knew why every victim had 'pearls' on his cheeks! After about a day of journey, a blanket of ice was covering floor of railway cabin and over all prisoners. Most of them were shivering, making chattering noise and clung to each other to each other to preserve heat. Soldiers were hitting them hard to stay apart. (They wanted them to acclimatize with upcoming Siberian cold.) No hot drinks were served since 36 hours.

And, Yestlin had an urge to go washroom. A guard unchained Yestlin from the line, took him to washroom with hands cuffs locked. He noticed the window of washroom without glass. Spray of snow came on his face and a 'bad' idea came in his mind! He frantically jumped out of the window! Young man dived through window of toilet but he screamed spontaneously as it was a bridge!

Luckily, the train was passing through a bridge over a frozen river. That scream alarmed the guards and they saw him going down from bridge over 70 meters. Security guards cried out, took position and there came behind showers of bullets to Yestlin. Yestlin saw a white blanket of ice down instead of river! He cried of wilderness. He kept his cuffed hands down to penetrate the

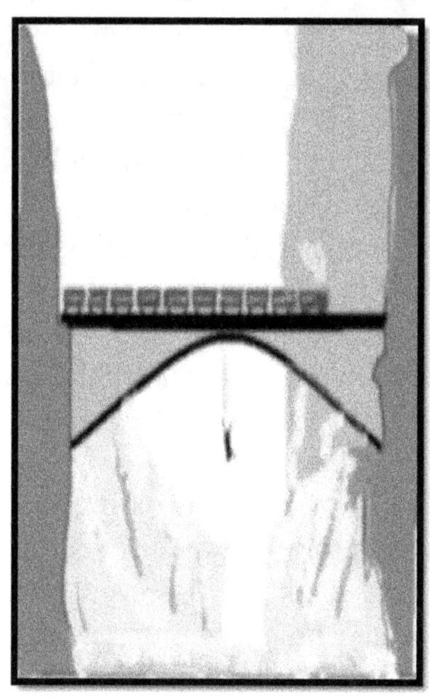

frozen river. Just before that, a bullet rubbed through his right calf! He screamed as he entered in river; a wheel of fresh blood splashed over covering ice sheets on river! As he entered deep in waters, the snow slabs came back in position, united but they had marked the entry level of escaped prisoner over the ice- A circle of blood splash!

The train stopped, guards opened fire over the surface of river. Yestlin was shocked in chilling waters[16] and so did not came to surface to breathe. Later, the train began to move and stopped at next station. The guard who allowed Yestlin to go to washroom was arrested for inquiry. A senior soldier shouted at security guards, "Let them pee or poo there in cabin, bloody, they are criminals of states!" After a few minutes, prisoners heard of barking squad of Siberian Hounds! They raised their heads from windows and trembled. An old civilian woman walking on platform looked at ferociously uncontrolled dogs pulling the band of security guards! Guards brought hounds to cabin where Yestlin was sitting. The dogs were taken to washroom to smell urine (A prisoner whispered, "Guards are themselves stinging!'); then

---

[16]**Chilled waters of frozen River:** The formation of icy spikes in waters goes towards surface but, when they conglomerate, become heavy and they settle down in floor. That way, the frozen rivers are too chilled at bottom.

squad rushed towards the bridge and down to bank of river. An old prisoner fainted at imagination of fate of escaped colleague. Soon, the dogs were seen, pulling the security guards on frozen river and reached there, where was a wheel of blood on ice slabs.

*

Hence, Yestlin fainted for a while! Wound of his right calf became frozen and num, bleeding stopped. He saw lots of bullets entering in river through ice slabs. Lucky enough, he took shelter behind a giant rock and then he made his way away from the bridge. He came to a bank of frozen river, got out with difficulty, hand cuffs were his limitations, he chattered looking at wide wild Siberian ice desert! He cried a little, whispered, "Not going to survive! Either they will find me...or Siberia will freeze me to death.", "Bloody Siberia! The worst freeze on Earth. And, see a small tiny 'me' is struggling for survival. What a fortune Siberia has in store for me, even if I survive?" He sobbed, but who was going to listen? He became wise (!) and walked randomly into vast plateau of Siberia. He had to run deep in Siberia, avoiding the forest of Tundra on his Westside; and tried to walk over snow so as his footprints would be hidden by fresh snowfall. However, few drops of his blood from calf wound inked on white snow as his trail marks! Yestlin had no idea where he was heading and who was following!

Here the Siberian Huskies dog squad was chasing him in snow desert. They came out of woods of Taiga and marched towards snow desert. They found drops of clotted blood and they jumped in air with ferocity! It was difficult to control them by guards, as they were trained by feeding with human flesh! When dogs spotted blood trail next time, they became uncontrolled! How long guards could run with their dogs? So, at one moment, they decided to release dogs from their chains. There they went, seven Siberian Huskies dogs (hounds) began their chase for human flesh! They would return to police station when the job would be finished!

Yestlin was pushing himself hard, exhausted and hypoglycemic! He sat on a rock and thought of digging a grave for himself in snow. He watched an eagle in sky and he whispered, "If I had wings!" Gradually, he became silent, sighing and crying had gone as none was there to listen at his cries! He again, began his journey to South-East in Siberia, thinking of sea there. He recalled his dean and uttered, "This fish has opened its mouth...and got 'trapped'!" He laughed loud that moment. Yestlin again, ran mad for his life.

Yestlin began to recall those old men who gave him books, the professor who asked to take part in debate, the dean and the night story when he was picked up from hostel. 'All had gone, leaving me damn alone here.' He was agitated and cried towards the sky, "What was wrong with me? Why you give curse? I was just reading." A breeze came to chill him! "There is no God! Innocents die here and devils live. Darkness is all around...while a candle has a life! Light of candle flame is limited while darkness is vast and infinite. There is no God!! He shouted and cried saying, "Mummy! Sorry! I didn't understand this world! All crowds and mobs are selfish. We have to die alone. I don't want to live here! I will not return to Earth again!!" he cried and wiped his tears and kept on running. "That bloody judge is, as if an alien! He had never been a young man, never had been a student!" He was trying to keep pace on glossy surface of snow glaciers. "For this, I was born here, Mom? This...this graveyard...? I have come walking to my own grave!" And he cried again. "Why the hell, I took birth here in Soviet Union? Government does not respect anyone and they have no wisdom, kindness for me!" He wiped his tears from cheeks and whispered, "I don't want to die this way! I tell you, mom...I don't want to cry this way in Siberia! I want to laugh like Sun!" And, he cried out openly, that was echoed from hills. Hills also cried that day. In answer, he heard the barking hounds from horizon.

Being alert like a rabbit, he began to run mad towards the high hills of Siberia. His cuffed hands and torn calf were his limitations. The tension mounted when he heard clearly of dogs. He became hysterical right and left on slope of uphill, indecisively and shouted, "Oh Jesus! I understand today, how you were crucified! This mankind has not evolved yet!" He breathed a little and whispered, "No! I don't want to die! My Jesus will not die twice!" As such, Yestlin had no time to question, no time stop and probably, had no time to breathe more! Meanwhile, he slipped down due to imbalance. He saw the band of hounds closer. Again he frantically attempted to reach to peak of snow capped hill and again he slipped miserably down; he cried loud and the dogs answered! Dogs hurriedly made a mad rush hoping on glittering snow surface and Yestlin also tried to reach over top of one hill. Now the dogs had seen him and he too saw his death closer!

He yelled for help and then a ghostly figure of his Mother (of Yestlin) appeared! She saw tragic end of her son. She too, shouted but a ghost can't do anything physically. She had no voice. She tried to assist her son but her hands were just ghostly! She ran towards dogs to stop them but was unable! What a ghost of mother can do except crying for her child? Again and again, Yestlin tumbled over the snow pits and glided a little down and meanwhile dogs reached him closer. Seven dogs and one man with hand-cuffs, pitiable was the scene!

Here the ghost of mother reached high and she spotted a silent boat coming towards the seashore. She heard of chirping of birds hovering over that boat; dolphins making circles around, emitting thin whistling sounds. Soon, they made grunting sounds to awaken the visitor on boat! They then, began to splash their tails in waters to make great noise. Walruses hopped from icy slabs around to reach to that boat! The boat was gliding spontaneously, through the icebergs, ice sheets and ice shelves. Far to West were forbidden Sakhalin islands[17], Uncountable

---

[17]**Forbidden Sakhalin islands**: few islands showed activities of swans and red-headed cranes. They made a great noise to awaken Yogi. Those islands were bird breeding grounds. Deep ice packs were dangling across the sea. Still Northern islands were the residential sites for fur seals and sea lions. Next were thousands of murres, a puffin-like species of swimming and diving shorebirds! They had nests there on islands; they too made a great noise to welcome the stranger.

hordes of thick-billed murres, puffins, fulmars and kittiwakes flied to reach on sea shore of Okhotsk, hovering around incoming boat. It was uncanny seeing skeins (groups of wild fowl, geese), flocks, lines and mobs of birds all careering to and from overhead, some setting on the boat without air-traffic control! Near the shore, sea waves began to tap the boat and the ghost of Mother of Yestlin reached there! She stood up on boat to see a divine figure sleeping (meditating) in boat, her cries stopped, she felt like bowing down to that sleeping angel! She could not disturb for her selfish purpose! As such, she was helpless in such a state! Meanwhile a whale came to help and it lifted the boat and shuffled. It shook the boat to wake up Yogi who at first saw the ghost of Mother, crying and requesting to help her son, there at hilltop near the shore. He sat and birds went in air singing. Yogi heard of yelling and barking of dogs. He immediately jumped from boat as he saw a young man fighting with dogs for survival, his first foot rested on thin sheet of snow (grease snow) and it just dangled softly! Next holy steps were over small ice balls jetting over sheet of frozen sea; he hurriedly walked towards sea shore of Okhotsk on surface of frozen sea of Okhotsk. Then, he speed up leaving icy specks dancing behind in waters!

The fog began to land over ocean and scene became picturesquely hazy! The golden sun wanted to rest as His representative has landed on Russian soil! It became cool and obscure in fog for a while. It was 4 am according to local Siberian Time. Now, days will be counted from 4 am to 4 am next day, that way, Yogi stayed in Russia for about 8 days and whole world was changed!

SECTION:

2

B. Yogi arrives at Siberia.

Day: 1:
[It was about 4 am when Yogi entered in Russia, so days of his stay are counted here, from 4 to 4 am next day. Every day, 24 hours coincides with about 10-15 years of history of Soviet Union.]

7: "Sorry, For Being Late!"- Yogi

It was 4 AM, Magadan shore was awake by clamor of birds and animals as they had spotted a guest coming in his boat. Sun was rising and so was the destiny of Siberia, too. An Indian Monk with white shirt and trousers came out of meditation and saw a ghost of mother requesting to help her son, at the top of hill. He saw first, Yestlin a young man screaming surrounded by Siberian hounds. Yogi got up from his boat, jumped on frozen seashore, ran towards Yestlin. He soon, began to run over thin frozen ice on surface of waters and landed on shore. Soft snow particles were dangling behind Yogi. Yogi's eyes were focused at hilltop. Yestlin appeared with about seven barking dogs all around. Someone biting his calves, one was on shoulder; another dog had ferociously picked up his nose and one torn his right ear. Yestlin was kicking and screaming.

As soon as, Yogi looked at them, the violent dogs became suddenly docile and silent; became still and as if frozen! And, the young man escaped from their bites, lost balance and dropped himself from top of hill and glided down over the slope of frozen hill. He had rotational course from hill to reach the holy feet of Indian Monk! Blood bathed body of Yestlin came under the feet of an Angel! Yogi bent down, placed right hand over the vault of head that eased his pains! He knelt, lifted the head of victim, accessed injuries (blood dripping from right ear and torn out nose) and sighed! Yestlin opened his dim hopeless eyes through frozen clots hanging over eyebrows and took first glance of Yogi who was tearful! Viewing the Mankind from 23000 ft. height of Himalaya is different than meeting the people crying. Talking of violence in a cave is easier than being witness. Yogi bent and whispered, "Sorry, For Being Late!"Tears in eyes of stranger gave comfort to Yestlin and he became unconscious. He reached to 'right' hand, and Yogi had received his first assignment in time, at Siberia! Nature does not waste time of divine people...her courier service is very precise and powerful!

Initially, dogs were as if frozen, on hill, someone was frozen with three legs in air! Yogi then, looked at them to summon by gaze. Dogs whimpered and glided on snow to descend and stood at distance from yogi, obediently. He took a time to find words, "He wasn't your enemy, isn't it? Humans are not your food either. Now, how will you repay?" Dogs whimpered and waved tails and sat down on snow. The shore was made of flat glacier meeting the shore. There, whispers of cold breeze and harsh breathing dogs were audible. Rest was like frozen grave.

Yogi sat down, took head of Yestlin in his lap, closed his eyes so tears dropped on cheek of Yestlin; he began to move his right hand from his head to toe and wounds slowly began to heal. He reached to heart level and eliminated his agony and darkness. Now, Yestlin had begun to snore! Yogi placed both hands over the head of Yestlin to study his past, got the proof of his innocence. Monk began to download the Russian and Slavic language from the memory of young man so as, he would communicate in regional language. Monk looked at the ghost of Mother. She showed her extreme happiness, ghost bent down in respect. Yogi smiled and blessed her. The Ghost glided in air, circled Yogi sitting with her son, came closer to Monk, bowed a little and then vanished slowly in air! Yogi closed the eyes, sat in meditation.

When Yestlin woke up, he was fresh and saw his head in lap of a divine monk. Yogi was looking at a peak of a giant mountain in East from seashore of Okhotsk emitting red signals. Yogi, without looking at Yestlin, asked, "What is that mountain for, Yestlin?" Yestlin gave strange look at distant mountain peaks, hiding in fog and fumes! He gave a confused look and became silent. It was Kamchatka Mountain[18] of Siberia. Yestlin was too young for such

---

[18]**Kamchatka Mountains**, Siberia: They are within volcanic peninsula of *1250 km length in Far* East Russia between the Sea of Okhotsk and the Bering Sea. Kamchatka is famous for the abundance and size of its brown bears. *Pacific Ocean makes eastern coastline while Sea of Okhotsk makes western. Its volcanoes are a UNESCO world heritage site. There is valley of Geysers too.* There are **more than 300** volcanoes on the Kamchatka peninsula, including 29 as active.

question. Yogi said, "There is something, 'not good' there! I get red

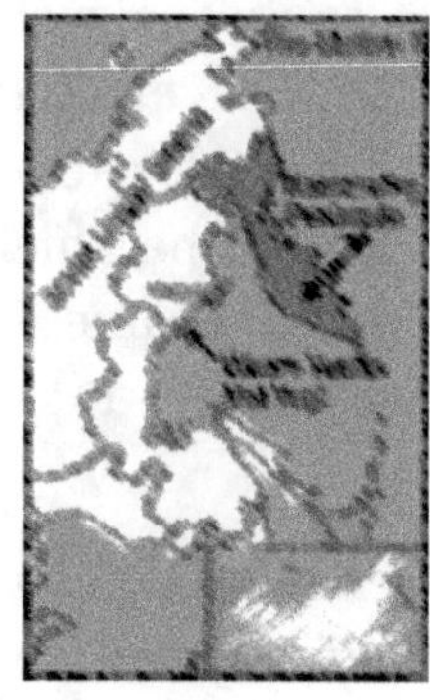

signals." and he smiled at Yestlin to reassure. Then he introduced himself, "Yestlin, Yogi, here, from Himalay!" Yestlin was fresh, painless and was surprised to find his wounds healed. That helped him recall his identity and he whispered feebly, "Yestlin!" buthe recalled that Yogi knew his name. He observed great aura and fragrance from Yogiwho was in white shirt and trousers. As he gazed at all the dogs surrounding them, Yestlin was frightened.

Soon, the dogs became alert on upcoming distant barks of another dog squad, coming from behind the hill and soon, a sledge appeared from end of glacier. Yestlin got shivered atview of shouting security guards on sledge raising their rifles in air. He looked at Yogi and whispered, "I am innocent!" Yogi nodded and said, "Yes, I know; no doubt!" The dogs around Yogi and Yestlin growled and got up! Sledge came closer at 40 feet distance; Yestlin crawled to hide behind Yogi. A sergeant of that squad got out of sledge, walked a little, yelling, "Mother's swear, I don't know you, but you have our prisoner. Give him to us." Other four guards came out of sledge and positioned with their aim at Yogi. The Yogi waved his right hand to slow down in their decision. Sergeant cried out to submit Yestlin and asked Yogi, 'Who are you?' in Sakhalin Ainu language. But, guards were in hurry and opened their fire. (They had not arrestedan escaped prisoner before. They understood, "A live prisoneris our liability atprison. Why to feed?"

Suddenly, rifles roared; firing began and all seven dogs went up in air sequentially to receive bullets. They rolled over in air so as to receive all bullets and fell dead on floor. Ice floor had splashes of blood all around. Meanwhile, Yogi furiously thumbed on glacier floor; glacier cracked and crack extended straight towards that sledge. It had fissured glacier deeply; widened to cover up sledge with all dogs and security guards from all around and that deep furrow passed past the sledge in fraction of second. Ice slab upon which sledge, dogs and guards stood, turned upside down taking them in ditch-filled chilled waters. The ice slab turned again. Various ice slabs came up, to their respective place to reconstruct the same surface as of before. Nothing was noticeable then, at site. Suddenly, one tip of sword of rifle pierced and then a muzzle came out of snow slab. It fired a single shot in air and then, became silent. The tip of sword of rifle jetting out from snow became a mark of their burial. Many a times, people do not recognize they have already reached to their burial place!

It all happened in one blink of eye! Dogs near Yogi had laid down their lives to protect Yestlin. Yogi approached to dying dogs; he moved his hand softly over their skulls to bless and they became quiet, permanently. Yestlin saw tears in eyes of Yogi. Probably, Yogi thanked dogs for bringing Yestlin to him, and laying down their lives to protect Yestlin. Soon, the glacier surface became soft and dead bodies of dogs began to enter in deep waters slowly.

*

Intimidated and frustrated as he was, Yestlin was stunned at the view of kill. He had seen something terrible and unbelievableincidence in a blink of an eye. His survival was so costly! A Himalayan Yogi had come for his rescue and seven dogs gave up their lives! He sawthe triumph of a man over mortal power. He knelt at feet of Yogi who lifted him from shoulders and said, "Yestlin, Innocence is to be adorned, protected. I have come from too far a distance to help people like you."

Yestlin concentrated to look at Yogi and found that he was an about 60 years old adult, a serene face with powerful aura, with so sweet and divine smile and eyes were so sparkling, too deep like a well, attracting him to dive in! He was indeed, mysterious! He had no mustache and no beards, was with thin white summer trousers and ordinary shoes at feet. Yogi had a special aroma.

Yestlin politely, with emotion of surrender, showed him his handcuffs and spoke, "Yestlin! (His eyes welled up.)I am a student who participated in a debate that resulted into exile. I escaped from train to Siberia and so, they are after me. They are going to kill me anytime. (He sobbed and Yogi embraced him. Then, he openly cried out that echoed in surrounding hills. Fog slowly, surrounded them. Birds became silent then after.

Yogi: Think as if, your dean has sent you to receive me! When you meet again, say thanks from my side. (Yestlin laughed so loud, that he cried at the end.)

Yestlin: You saved my life. I am all yours!

Yogi tapped his cheek with smile and said, "Spare your life for those who are waiting for you. Once your function is over, I will receive you, hmm!" Yestlin could not understand anything but smiled. Yogi whispered, "Okay, let's go to find a human habitat."

Yestlin hesitantly, asked, "Why?"

Yogi, "I am sure you won't stay here longer at seashore; you need Rabies vaccine, too!"

Yestlin screamed, "Are you crazy? I said, they will shoot me and you want to take me for vaccine." He knew medical centers are in government scrutiny.

Yogi smiled and said, "If not at medical center, someone at nearby city (Magadan)[19] will catch us soon. So, let's go. Siberia is calling us." Yestlin had no choice.

Clouds were gathering in horizon to welcome and showers of snowflakes began when Yestlin began his journey with Yogi![20]

---

[19]**Magadan**: is coastal establishment at Sea of Okhotsk; is famous for its **natural resources**. Gold mining and fisheries are the main source of income. Magadan is also well-known for its beautiful natural scenery.Most of the *oblast* is rugged and mountainous, except for small patches of lowland along the Sea of Okhotsk. There is some poor-quality swampy forest, or taiga, of larch, fir, and birch, but most of the surface is tundra. The climate is severely Arctic. There are a number of indigenous peoples—Even (Lamut), Yukaghir, Sakha (Yakut), and others, engaged chiefly in reindeer herding, fishing, and hunting. There is also a sizable Russian population. Gold is mined and there are deposits of silver, tin, and coal. Some timber is cut and salmon and other fish are caught in the Sea of Okhotsk. It's said that Magadan town was constructed by Gulag camp prisoners who laid down their lives who were buried there and there underneath.

[20]*In devotional practice, it's believed to be so much of luck, when a devotee has*

"When your Master arrives in your life; mind will seize, ego will melt and questioner will 'go'! He will open out a new pathway for you. New dimension will be opened." Yestlin (1973, March)

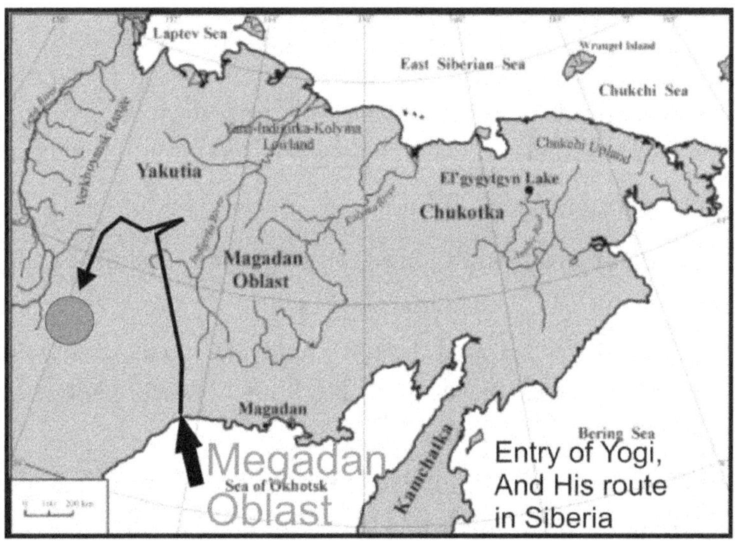

8: Welcome to Siberia:

Before leaving shore, Yogi showed Yestlin, the peak of a mountain in East jetting from dense clouds. He asked, "Do you know what is there on that mountain?" Yestlin took time to answer, "It is Kamchatka Peninsula, I read in my study books. There are active volcanoes there." Yogi said, "I see a red signal there, some sort of danger lies there!"

Yestlin looked behind the sea shore and saw a small boat 100 meters inside ocean. He saw dead bodies of dogs were sinking inside ice! He noticed that tip of barrel was standing as landmark of burial of border security guards. Snowfall had started and atmosphere became cloudy. He hurriedly moved to Yogi who was had gone far. On his voyage deep in Siberia, Yestlin had many questions. He asked, "You healed me; it's miraculous. Then, why did you not remove my hand cuffs?" Yogi smiled at him and said, "One man, one purpose…is the rule in Nature. Handcuffs are dealt by other agencies. We have to find them." That left Yestlin confused. During their voyage, when Yestlin got imbalance, Yogi held his chains of cuffs to pull him and he used to say, "See, the beauty of Chains in handcuffs!" However, he was reminding Yestlin that his hands were cuffed and he had to reach to someone. That way, Yestlin remained energetic and walked faster.

Two dark human figures in deep trench of Siberia were making their way towards high-hills. They were walking upon dangerous glaciers. Walking on a glacier was an opportunity for Yestlin, to see magnificent ice towers, deep caves, plummeting waterfalls and melt-water lakes. On left, giant snow walls were shining and floor of glacier was fissured at many places. The area was so deadly, appeared to

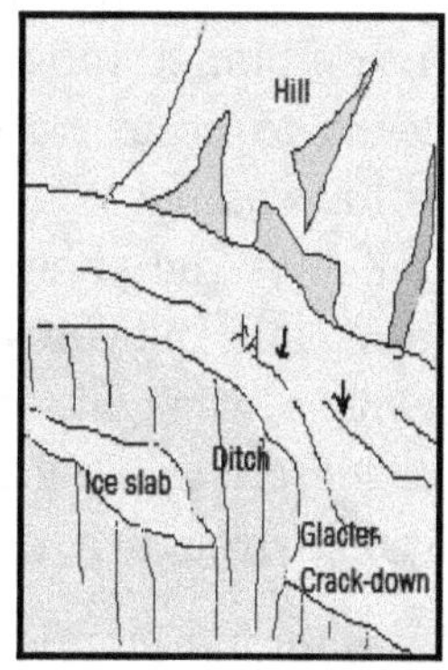

be haunted that Yestlin lost his faith upon Yogi! He pulled his hand and whispered in feared voice, "Don't you feel any risk, here?

(Yogi just, smiled in answer.) I say, why you insist for a vaccine? Why you risk your life? Why have you come here in Siberia? (No answer from Yogi) See, I don't need vaccine, okay? Better I should die rather than walking with you in Siberia. Freezing and dying areso easy here. Or, glacier may engulf me, or someone may shoot us bullets from any direction. Are we on stupid entourage in Siberia?" (This comment was serious enough for Yogi, but he smiled at him.)

Yogi pointed at frozen snow at side hills and exclaimed, "How beautiful is this Siberia? This Realm of Snow? You know significance of snow?" Yestlin was annoyed and did not answer. Yogi said, "This snow on mountains and on poles of Earth is the frozen reserve of water. Nature manages its equilibrium. More lives on planet, more snow is dissolved so more vaporization from Oceans to occur, to give more clouds and more frequent rains." Yestlin was not interested. So, Yogi questioned again, "You know what does the snow fall mean?" Yestlin nodded. Yogi answered, "Snow fall indicates presence of vapor in air. Good snow fall means a cycle of vaporization is well maintained. Snow fall is considered as Grace of Mother Nature. Lesser vapor means a possible draught." Yogi then, began to describe beauty of Siberia!

Hanging clouds, ice on either side, glassy shiny floor of ice and fog or mist in space obscured glowing sun. Space was luminous without source and objects became without shadows!

Yestlin found himself in heaven...the scene was mesmerizing. Yogi began to talk of tranquility. He asked Yestlin to keep silence in his head and feel the same silence that surrounded them. When Peace from outside percolates to inner core, a man becomes dissolved and comes in Being State. Yogi stood for a while teaching how to take peace from outside 'in' by focusing at tip of nostril! (Yestlin tried!) Observe how your inner self is tranquil without chatters of mind." Yestlin soon, began to dwindle and Yogi took him on his shoulder and continued walking on glaciers. Yestlin was again, semi-conscious.

After a time, again Yestlin was walking behind Yogi. He wondered where he was heading at! They felt the great fear as he was moving across the most treacherous terrain of Siberia local people were also, afraid of. He was frustrated of Yogi so,he cried out, "Why do you not understand me? We are not going to survive! Do you have suicidal tendency? Have you come to die here? Instead, allow me to die and you return!"(Yogi continued walking.) Yestlin said, "Okay! I give you certificate that you saved my life, okay? Now, I want to die here!" No hope...I am a failure!" Yestlin began to cry loud. Yogi stopped this time and moved back to him. Yestlin tried to figure out words while crying, "My mom died because of me! Whosoever will come in my life will die! O Yogi! Leave me alone and you return." He sobbed on right shoulder of Yogi saying his last words, "Let me die! Please! You save yourself! I am unfortunate." Yogi embraced him tightly and laughed softly.

Yogi chuckled saying, "Let me find a perfect burial place for you! (He laughed at Yestlin.) "Little away...walk few steps...forwards, little ahead, beyond your limits, please!" Yestlin followed him with a smile...he was so sentimental, wanted to run into Yogi to embrace because he wanted to break like soft ice and Yogi was pulling him ahead, who added, "Beyond our 'limits', destiny waits! Never stop walking, until you die! So take few steps...little more, Yestlin. Don't give up. (Yogi laughed at the end and hills echoed. His voice reechoed.) "Why are you in hurry to die?"

Yestlin smiled at Yogi, wiped of tears and answered, "Why should I be late?"

Yogi said, "Live not for yourself, Yestlin. Live more, for someone waiting for you since years, since ages! This life is a gift and you give to someone deserving."

Yestlin: Whom? Hmm? Whom?

Yogi: Friends for Life'! (Yogi was sincere but Yestlin became nervous and muttered, "I doubt about your wisdom now." Then, he loudly asked to Yogi, "Who is waiting for me in this hell? (pause) You are dangerously risky person to walk with! Either I am stupid or you are!" His sarcasm didn't work upon Yogi.

Yestlin stopped with thumping on glacier and shouted, "Stop, now! I am not coming." The Master became serious, concerned and showed him furrows of glaciers behind him. He whispered,

"We are not alone! These glaciers are 'alive'; they listen, they respond to your voice!"

Yestlin observed many fissures over that glacier. He saw a deep valley like trench on his left, created by frequent breakdowns of glacier. He tried to see the depth and chilling wind blew up from valley on his face. He screamed, "Oh! My God! " He saw his 'graveyard' there! He was walking on left side of fissured glacier that might crack down at anytime. His heart jumped out of fear, was terrified and cried loud, "Mummy! I am coming!" (pause) O Jesus! What kind of man you have sent to me! Instead of help, he has brought me in dangers!" Yogi began to hurry to cross that glacier. Yestlin yelled, "Wait, I am coming." and that 'Wait' word, echoed in glaciers, and glaciers answered him with cracking thunderous sound from unknown place! Cracking sound too, made a great noise that echoed and re-echoed from all around!

Glaciers crumbled, distant peaks of snow showered their snow! The air stopped and dead tranquility prevailed later. Yogi turned at Yestlin (they were few meters apart.) and asked to keep silence. Yogi saw a deep furrow on glistening surface of glacier chasing Yestlin from behind. Yestlin hurried to reach to Yogi and sharp cracking sound emerged from floor in next step! Edges of deep furrow vibrated showering snow. He took few more steps and furrow ran closer from behind. Its cracking sound was terrifying! It echoed in glaciers around. Yestlin began to run crying, "No, I don't want to die!" and he ran towards Yogi! Yogi laughed and said, "Why making late, dear!!" Both ran fast; furrow equally ran under their feet and soon, deep furrow ran past Yogi! Cracking sound shook the valley; both of them made last attempt to run for survival! And, the furrow was as if chasing, then it widened to take Yestlin first, inside! Yestlin screamed as he went down in glacier! Yogi ran into Yestlin, dived into fissure to pick up his handcuff so as both could fall together! Along with crackling sound, valley was filled with laughter of Yogi...as he had held Yestlin in his hands, while falling into grave!!

That Fissure eroded glacier and large chunk of ice slab crashed into valley on left! Their heart breaking echoes thundered the valley over few minutes.

Down they went with great fall of glacier for about 40-50 meters; Yestlin became 'deaf' for a while! He saw Yogi who jumped after him; held his cuffs and was laughing! Yestlin had never experienced such deafening, devastating sound of glacier! Both descended in between two great snow walls, right wall was firn[21], semi-transparent while left sided wall disintegrating towards valley! They entered in the valley, 50 meters down from surface, in between two vertical huge slabs of glacier! As left wall fell apart towards valley to release them from a trap. They landed on floor...and snow cubes or slabs followed over them. They were literally, buried under showers of snow. Terrible echoing noise continued in valley for long time. At the end, dead silence prevailed. Silence is eternal, permanent. The universe was born out of such silence and it bathes in, also! The Nature ultimately, tends to zero!

Yestlin thought that he was dead, reached to his grave! He was literally buried in pile of snow. A thick ice slab came to lie horizontally over those two persons, holding showers of ice slabs and rocks. That way, Yestlin and Yogi were saved from crush! Yestlin came out of pile and tried to find 'his' Yogi! He thought, 'I have reached so down, in so remote place on Earth!! Now, what worse can happen to me?" Meanwhile, he saw his Yogi coming out from pile of snow. He pulled Yestlin out by pulling the chains of handcuffs and saying, "Good, that you have this chain!" Yestlin while getting out of snow, retorted, "You are just terrible, can't stop joking here also! And, laughing for my cuff?"

Yogi chuckled with saying, "You are so sweet, Yest! Your mother was great." Yestlin began to stare at Yogi and who added, "You are really a noble person." Yestlin had heard something good about himself first time from someone, a stranger. He again embraced Yogi and tears showered on Yogi's shoulder. This was the first union of Yogi with Yestlin within the burial place!

Yestlin said, "Forgive me for my harsh words, I doubted you many a times." Yogi said, "A child can give what he can give! I didn't expect anything more from your level. So, I never mind bad words!"

---

[21]**Firn glacier**: An intermediate stage in the transformation of snow to glacier ice. Snow becomes firn when it has been compressed so that no pore space remains between flakes or crystals, a process that takes less than a year.

Yestlin was looking at crystal clear eyes of Yogi, tears came out while he said, "I stand upon my comment! You are a terrible man! Why did you dive behind me?" He waited for Yogi to answer, "You have risked your life, along with me, why did you dived after me?"

Yogi said, "Because, I love you!" (A True Master follows his disciple from one birth to another!) Yestlin felt sudden surge of pure love for that divine figure. He, who healed his dog bites, took him so far and did not leave even in glacier crush and dived after him was not an ordinary person.' Yogi was looking to him different, now. He with a so fatherly smile, came closer, placed his hand on his heart to bless him. He bowed down, knelt on snow wisely and stretched out his hands of cuffs towards Yogi with tearful eyes. He showed his cuffs and sat quiet. Yogi also, knelt down, took his hands very dearly to his heart, blessed him directly and whispered, "You are mine, Yestlin. Indeed you are!" That moment, four more eyes were wet! (Two more persons were viewing them behind snow walls!)

Yogi said, "Yestlin, you have come home! Meet your Friends for Life!" Now, Yestlin observed four eyes watching him from snow wall. It was scary as two persons emerged with spears and knives out of snow heaps. They were cruel looking, wearing furs and holding bony weapons. The one who was robust, short-statured, thick beard and wide mustache was facing at Yogi! He was stinging. Next person pointed dagger at Yestlin's throat. They were cruel and uncivilized[22]. They advised Yogi to remain silent. Yogi smiled at them.

---

[22] We usually, fail to judge a diamond by dirt it covers.

9: Friends for life

Yestlin raised his hands at those snowmen with lot of fear.

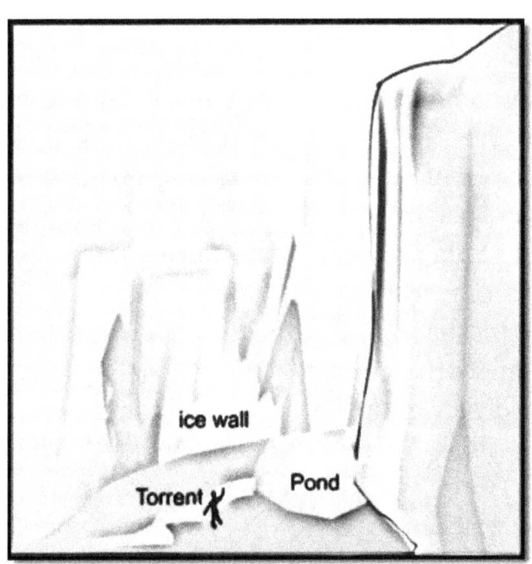

Snowmen saw his cuffed hands, looked at each other, came closer to inspect precisely the signs embedded on handcuffs. One of them whispered, "Leningrad police.". They observed for any marks of injuries and discovered none, except right red eye. They were surprised as Yestlin had no other marks of injuries. Leader asked Yestlin, "How did you get this cuff?" His speech was eloquent. Yestlin got courage and gave him details. He narrated how he met with Yogi and how they had travelled so far. The leader turned to Master and Yestlin said politely, "He saved my life

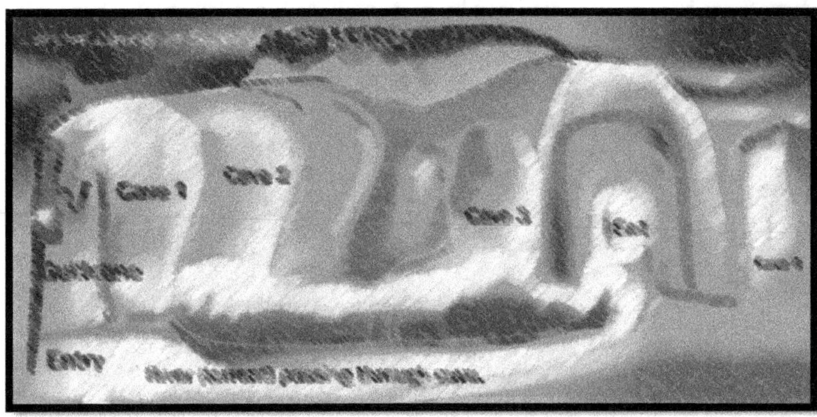

and he has brought me to you- as friends for life!"

Those two people were amazed to find a man with white shirt and trouser in Siberia with a smile and fragrance! His splendid aura and dignity were mesmerizing. They stood at a distance and did not dare to step forwards. They stepped back and bowed with respect. Immediately, they decided to take new guests towards the pool of blue chilled water, where torrent was disappearing underground. The first host took Yestlin, pinched his nostril, asked him to hold breath and jumped in waters. They disappeared inside! Next was the turn of Yogi and second host followed him. Yogi dived deep down in chilling crystal waters that had ice walls all around. He went for 20-25 feet down; then, they made a U turn while crossing a thick sharp metal plate[23]he emerged to surface and Yogi found an ice cave. Torrent was flowing through the cave and there were many many caves all around. Many cavemen and women were standing all around, in bizarre dresses to welcome them. A few came forth, helped Yestlin, pulled him out of torrent. It was extremely chilled atmosphere there. Yogi jumped out of torrent and did not require any assistance. Two hosts who escorted them came out last. A fellow caveman lowered the guillotine to close the entry into cave. Waters of torrent receded.

The temperature must be at near-zero level, Yestlin shivered and few cavemen brought warmed up fur clothing (Fur soaked in boiling waters) to cover Yestlin. Yogi refused to accept the warm fur. Soon, the cavemen noticed slight vapors arising from his wet scalp hairs and trousers and shirt! Slowly, Yogi's clothes became dry! Chief of Cavemen reached to him, touched his skin to access why clothes showed vapors; but he found skin of Yogi's hand normal.

Yestlin was taken to another cave, who surveyed about his 'future new home'! Cave had caves! He saw people were coming from their caves and crevices. It was a walled city of crescent ice! Cave had crystal-spiraled ice, with fractured sharp edges; prismatic display of ice seen in partitions walls in-between caves. It had various colors in reflection, looking like walls of diamonds.

---

[23] It was placed as guillotine to guard the gate of Cave, at entry level.

Waters were dripping from ice-blue ceiling, making the floor wet and chilled. Many cavemen were accustomed to walk bare-footed in caves! Floor was rocky, wet, covered with mosses and so slippery. He thought, 'Water that is dripping from roof everywhere and flows through caves drains the life of every cavemen!'

When Yogi turned on right, he heard of heaving sound of inward flowing air current, through sapphire blue walls from distance. He heard of little boy's groan from somewhere. Somewhere blue walls were lucid and warm! Deeper still, he smelled crackling fire with splintered branches and leaves being consumed. As a rule of cave, cavemen remained silent as cave was echoic. Voice was kept to minimal. They had custom to talk in nights. That way, cave was as if, haunted.

Cavemen began to come in central hall. A Caveman offered Yestlin a hot soup that was too nauseating. An old man sat near him, pulled the delicate hand of Yestlin and whispered, "See, my Child! I am your father, now. We make a family, isn't it? (His voice was very soft and he was emotional.) There is no life outside for next 50 miles. (His head nodded, as if he had tremors.) Do we make a family or not? (He wanted Yestlin to agree upon and Yestlin was staring at him with tearful eyes.) I came here exactly in same way you have come here, but few decades before! (He smiled, showed dirty teeth.) I am a doctor of 1937, so tell me if you have any pains or injuries!" He studied the inscriptions over the wrist cuffs to confirm from where Yestlin was 'dispatched'! Yestlin began to talk about his history. Other seniors quickly came around and attentively listened at. Next cave man began to cut chain of handcuffs. Meanwhile, people surrounded and Yestlin gave narration about Yogi, how he met and travelled so far. Soon, ladies group came, old ladies came closer to see Yestlin with lots of pain in their eyes as Yestlin was the youngest admission to their cave! He was just, 24 years old! She mourned over a thought, 'how this young man would live here, for whole of life?' Few of them, touched his soft skin of hands and pink chubby cheek and adorned. "Beautiful, you are!" an old lady whispered. As a mother, she took his head, smelt with love and kissed. Yestlin was annoyed and they made him cry. Old lady whispered, 'Cry! Darling! Crying is good for you." Soon, ladies began to sing 'a song of sorrow': That was a tradition to welcome any new admission. Newly arrived person must cry out and pray for death. Then after, he would feel this cave a comfortable and better home. They began in chorus:

> Why have you come 'here', O Dear! Why you came here!(2)
> Nothing is 'here' woo, why you came here!
>
> Stones of caves surround, whisper in your ears!
> 'Be like us', bury your love 'here'!
> Meat, furs, rancid smell; are the assets here!
> Dark world whispers in your ears…why you came here!
>
> Snow and wet caves are your home,
Your dreams will freeze soon, dear!
Futile Hopes will no longer throb in heart, here.
Gods don't look at us here.
>
> The One, you brought here, is different from us,
> He may fly back from here,
> But, you will live the life here! (Why?)

Ladies sang with various facial expressions, making lips like bears! At the end, they clapped at Yestlin as welcome gesture. Yestlin understood that he had to live here for whole life. He began to sob and then openly cried, like a small child….he cried! His yells echoed in caves and that shattered the soft heart of Yogi! He mercifully looked at all, sitting around him in main cavern; his eyes welled up. He closed his eyes and went deep in meditation. Everyone in cave was crying, embracing with each other. They were crying as they had passed through same welcome and had same rancid lifestyle. If no food was procured, then, they would eat the flesh of fellows who died. They had lived here for decades, here!

*

10. Yogi in Siberian Cave:

Yogi decided to help them to make them normal. He soon, made an illusion and different people began to emerge from the walls of caves. Crying stopped and surprise spread. In few minutes, hundreds of people emerged from the walls and they stood in front of cavemen. Soon, people spotted their own relatives- parents, family members and few close dear friends the cave men used to remember. They made a good crowd at one side of cave while living members of caves were thrown in surprise and exhilaration. The chief of cave saw his son calling him; his wife and mother were also, waving hands. He turned at Yogi and saw him in deep meditation. He raised his hands to stop all members to rush towards their family members standing there. He cried, "They are illusions, they are the ghosts!" The crowd controlled their emotions...and Yogi said, "They are truly, gone by now. They are dead by now. Please understand that the time is very cruel. Forget the past and come to stand on spur of percent moment. You are still, alive! Don't waste time in crying over your past. You must be responsible and reflective to your time! Get up and seek your egress in life." Soon, all illusive family members walked backwards towards the cave walls and disappeared.

There, the Chief of Cave Colony reached to Yogi, bowed a little spontaneously and introduced, "I am Wombick." Yogi smiled and whispered, "Wog!" Wombick felt as if a lightening fell on his head! His mother used to call him 'Wog' instead of Wombick, he was too shy and used to hide behind doors and curtains. Mother used to seek him whispering, "Wog!"

Wombick took time to recover and Yogi answered his query, "I look at you through and through, in your past." Wombick looked at the crowd, laughed and talked in Yukaghir[24] language.

---

[24]Yukaghir is spoken in two mutually unintelligible varieties in the lower Kolyma and Indigirka valleys. Other languages, including Chuvantsy, spoken further inland and further east, are now extinct. Yukaghir is held by some to be related to the Uralic languages.

Crowd became hilarious as they had someone who knew their past and future. Wombick turned abruptly towards the saint and all became silent. He wanted Yogi to talk about himself, his reason of visit. Yogi remained silent while Wombick had to speak, "You see everything, hear everything...Nothing to hide now! Now, it's your turn to tell us about you. How do you survive in shirt and trousers? You don't look like a traitor or a victim of CPSU[25] (Soviet Government). We have always received a victim here- crying for help; while you are smiling at us, joking at our pitiable condition. It looks as if you have come here for entourage! (Yogi laughed and nodded in negation.) He paused and continued, "I hope you are not a spy."

Yogi began: Yes! I am on entourage. I came from Himalaya, via sea route. I know a little about you people before I started from Himalay." He paused to continue, "Call me Yogi. Yogi means the One who remained conjugated with God. I am coming from height...(He showed by his hands how he descended like a rocket.) I have come because of you called me! Your pains, sufferings, cries, tears and blood baths have summoned me!! (Cave became silent.) I have nothing to take away from you, not even a sip of water from here. **I have come to give you** a smile on lips and a fear free breath. (Pause, he took a time to explain what is wrong with them.)

See, my dears! System is jammed, locked. Humankind is in Prisons and is governed by a few intellectuals. They rule to exploit and therefore, guide you where should you go. Communism is an instrument to them; they are sitting high, like an octopus. Every Nation is gripped by now. Governments work them and people pay to them indirectly. They have their armies; they have their spy system. They devour natural resources of every nation. Your mines and farming fields are their targets; your army and government are their assets. Terror is their business tactic. Unless you yield some result, they won't feed you. It's an invisible prison. Animals are free, but a man is not so!" Yogi paused and looked at ceiling of

---

[25] Communist Party of Soviet Union (CPSU)

the cave where crystal ice was shining like chandelier. He continued, "The goal of your birth is not to work for any system, any one else. They ask you to work to feed your family. That is wrong. *It's like you landed on a planet of non-humans. They ask their price to survive. Life continues to pay their prices.* They wish you may save a little to strengthen your dependency upon them." Most of cave community had not understood anything except the word 'they', 'price to survive' and 'dependency'. Someone raised question, "Who are 'they'?" (Yogi looked at him with deep silence. That made questioner nervous and he became silent.) There were so many intelligent people in crowd, they nodded as if they understood well. They raised their hands to stop any questioning. They looked at Yogi eagerly to suggest him to continue.

'They' means the 'system' that has captivated you. Life is free like an air. While here, are prisons and prisons inside prisons. Life is a flow beyond calculations, commerce, logics and mental planning. Prisons are invisible, as blocks at mental levels. And, we know that only Love gives wings to fly!" He stopped and observed a long silence. He had talked in English and Slavic language. None understood well, so Wombick asked, "Do you think you have said is what you wanted to share?" Yogi smiled in return.

He paused and looked at everyone categorically, then added, "Existence is halved. At one end, it's Matrix of multi-verse where mind operates, fear is obvious, thinking is required. At opposite end, Unity comes, where Love is experienced. There, no barriers, no prisons exist, every structure in between you and me collapses and open sky is created. Matrix breaks and vast Space is created. That is what I have a vision for you. (pause) I have come here, to access the truth, what we heard from Himalayan Heights is right or not. And it's true that human has become enemy of a human." Yestlin came and sat near Wombick. He had cuffs, still in hands; chains were cut. People saw his sparkling eyes like an 'Eye of Providence'[26]. They had seen someone as fresh as rose, smiling in front of them, talking of Love, non-dualism and Freedom. They

---

[26]God's Eye- that witnesses all, everyone, every time, everywhere!

had a visitor from skies...who had heard of their prayers. A 79 years old caveman, a professor of History, came forth with two assistants, to observe Yogi. He moved all around the guest. To focus on face of Yogi, he adjusted his worn out spectacle with a single glass; that too was cracked, so glued with animal fat. His vision was poor but what he observed made him believe in some prophecy. He whispered, "Jesus, he is!" All were eager to listen at his answer. A different smile came over his face, "Yes, I indentified him! My lord has come." He bowed down to the feet of Yogi. Yogi smiled innocently, withdrew his feet up and held the old man from shoulders and lifted to embrace him. Yogi whispered in his ears, "Let me be what I am, father!"

Yogi sat on a stone and asked everyone to sit wherever they are. Everyone was an attentive listener as most of them were scholars and graduates of various fields. Yogi soon, narrated about Himalaya Masters, their decision to send him to Siberia, his travel narration in sea, (Many were delighted to listen about description of ocean and whales and how he was awakened by birds and walrus!), how he met Yestlin and his mother at seashore of Okhotsk and how security guards died there. He described their journey on glaciers in beautiful way before reaching to them. Crowd laughed at Yestlin when they heard Yestlin was asking to die! Someone shouted from distance, "Yestlin, you came at right place to die...slow and but sure place!" All laughed and then they became tearful. All looked at Yogi as if, he had come as their hope!

Another man commented to Yogi, "You talked of invisible systems that have gripped all governments of world." An old man commented, "Don't get befooled! Don't take world's people simple, you talk and they will liberate us from Exile! **If words were mightier than swords, then wisdom would have ruled the human race**! Here, swords and bullets rule." Someone remarked.

Yogi answered, "Beyond the matter, words will stand, and beyond words vibes will work. All rays beyond Radio waves are mightier. After visible light, Ultraviolet, X-rays and Gamma Rays are vibrations. Truly, not the words, but vibes will work henceforth. All will happen in a blink of eye! (A lady laughed saying, "He is kidding!") Yogi continued, "In Autumn, who can believe spring will come. When spring comes, new leaves come first then flowers. You have started speaking in day time, chatting and arguing with each other, laughing and smiling upon me...are all indicators that fog will be lifted soon."

Meanwhile, habitats of nearby caves came and sat around Yogi. They wondered as people of this cave were cheerful, by now. Yestlin came closer to Yogi, showed his free hands, but with cuffs. Yogi noticed many people with similar handcuffs. That was their ornament, a wristlet and identification marks!

Wombick became confident, walked closer to Yogi, dropped his bony dagger and sat close to Yogi as his subordinate. (Then after, he always stood beside Yogi.) Wombick began to introduce everyone with names and narrated their designations. They were almost all learned persons. Then, he narrated how prisoners from Siberian Exile had escaped from various camps and come here in that cave. Then he described their lifestyle- going to hunt at night, eating raw meats, sometimes, they had ate flesh of own people who died of starvation! They had weapons made out of animal bones; use their fat as oil, wear their furs. Luckily, a few had glasses for old people! They would circulate among themselves.

The ice cave was discovered by Wombick when he came here hunting a Siberian Roebuck. Then after, escaped prisoners came and established a commune. The cave had different zones for habitation, kitchen, furs, weapons and grease. Wombick described his 'realm' and became nervous and whimpered a little but most of people were stone faced. The stones surrounded them, and they had become stony too! Life had come to shrink and stagnate into a small pungent cave. Later, all became silent. Yestlin sat on left and Wombick sat on right of Yogi. Wombick informed to Yogi, "You will find advocates, doctors, nurses, scientists, professors, teachers and political wise people here! Name a profession, and we have someone, here! Think, who are left in Soviet Union!" (Nobody could smile!)Two cave chiefs were observing the Yogi constantly from distance. Their eyes were fixed at the pious visitor. They had never seen such a man with poise in their life. All gathered in front of Yogi by now. Yestlin looked at Yogi and requested him to address the commune of cave.

11. Theory of Everything:

Yogi asked, "If you have question, you may ask." (Yogi wanted to judge the spiritual level as well he wanted to know what problem they have.)

A woman asked from back of cave, "Why did we suffer, though we were innocent, simple ordinary people? Was it our destiny? Our fault? Yogi closed his eyes for a moment and began to answer:

"It is not your destiny to suffer like this. Yes, it was your fault. It was due to your wrong choice. When you poise at destiny, you believe yourself innocent and enter in inaction. You curse your fate as well the God. But, when you take your responsibility of choice, you become alert, intelligent and wiser. Secondly, most of people suffer, as they are not looking beyond their family. Narrow angle view identifies that you are just an ant-going out for food and returning to its hole. Third, emotions create fogs that obscure your intelligence and wisdom. Now, stay away from creating Emotion out of any experience. It is the tactic of Dark-side to create emotion, a fog and blind your vision. Crowd or mob psychology starts from here. Politicians and leaders know how to create giant sea waves. A blind man is vulnerable for prey."

Now, flip the coin. Look, at the end of day, you will realize that *everything has fallen in right place; it was done by Mother Nature in perfection! Who are we to find fault in God's Plan?* Things are so accurate in Nature all over Universe, isn't it? Light speed is uniform all over in universe. It will reach in proper time therefore, what is reached to you, must be a God's Plan. See! Your sufferings have awakened Great Grand Masters at Himalaya; **all the focus of Spiritual Realm is hovering upon Russia! You don't know how important you are, by now. You are going to create wonder. The Siberia will become the Sun Land, the Land of Pious people, where Lord Sun bestows upon His Grace. And, I am the catalyst, forerunner of that torch."** Yogi looked at that old emaciated lady to say, "Wipe of your tear, Mother! Your tears have summoned me!" A shocking wave was spread.

Old man from somewhere asked, "What will you do?"

Yogi: Awaken you from within! Solution of all tragedies is in awakening from own sleep, own Ignorance. (pause) You are the Humans who has forgotten who you are. **Ignorance about the self and the NOW is called as Darkness Within**. When you will know that you are the Prince or Princess of Divine Kingdom, you will immediately wear crown of Divine Life. Then, your self-esteem and behavior will suddenly, change, choices will be different. <u>Therefore, I think, I should begin with telling you who you are.</u> (There was no resistance and no voice so, Yogi decided to go ahead.) We will have to go back to Origin of Universe and defining the God." (Everyone was surprised as Yogi linked their problem with Eternal cause.) All became attentive.

Yogi began:

"At the beginning, stop crying over the past; come to the Present by achieving balance and recreate the Future. Only, the controlled minds become wise, intelligent and progressive. **Promise, you may become angry but won't cry, henceforth. You are the Human, the only Divine Species of the Planet Earth with whom Angels and Aliens want to meet for their Cosmic**

Queries. Just, sit like a flame of a candle in a isolated area of cave...stay unshaken and be with me."

"Every cloud is wrapped around by a silent space. Each galaxy is also, wrapped by larger Space and deep Silence. Your problem of mammoth size is also, surrounded by a Space. **There's someone greater than this whole Universe!** Never consider your problems huge or terrible. When in pains, focus upon space that surrounds it. Miracles will develop as those clouds evolve in space out of Nothingness. <u>You need to shift your focus- from problem to Space it surrounds!</u> **The Space is The God.** The Space I refer is the **Universal Consciousness- the Mother** of all creation, its nurturer and controller. Instead of crying over problem, focus upon the Space and give your Callings as Worship." People had become absolutely, silent; they raised their hands with tearful eyes.

"<u>Now, let's focus on 'Who you are.</u>'" Yogi became upright and looked around with lots of love for that cave commune. A draught hit land was expecting the first shower of rains!

Let's go back in past and reach out at a spur of moment, when there was no Universe then, Time had not yet, started. Then, where was this Universe? The existence that was beyond the tick-talk of Time, the One who was there before the Universe was, was the Universal Consciousness, the ONE; we call Him as the Brahma or God or Bhagvan who was Invisible, Nameless and Attribute-less Entity. Our Rishis gave narrative of the God as "Supreme Element" or 'Dhatuh-Uttam' (The Greatest Element) in Sanskrit! From Him, whole Universe came into existence. Rishis logically named the Super-Element as the God or Brahma and His Attributes or Characteristics as the Mother or 'Mahatatva' in Sanskrit (From her, all Five Elements were derived- Fire, Air, Water, Earth and Space. Element and attributes are inseparable. That way, the God and Goddess are in Unison, but to facilitate narratives, they are described separate. Can you think of Oxygen without its characters? No! It's easy to describe the Brahma or God that way.

It is all hypothetical." All nodded. (Then, Yogi narrated according to this chart.)

All it began with OHM. It was the First Divine Vibration, OHM at the time of emergence of Universe. Ohm is the first Divine audible Sound of the Brahma, then came Light! Ohm is still audible to Yogis and Rishis. It has three pronged parabolic disgorge of energies from a center of Universe. Science narrates this as the First Gravitational Wave (FGW) or the Primordial Wave, we heard Him as OHM[27]. Brahma or God has no language as we have; His vibration, a Whisper or OHM has capacity to manifest in form of Universe! Soon, emission of Creative Energy began its course, in parabolic pattern from Epicenter of Universe. They were like Divine Snakes dispersing all over, opening various directions or dimensions for the first time. In each dimension, there is varieties of existence. This is the basis of Multi-Verse.

---

[27]**OHM** was the First Divine Vibration of Brahma (Someone narrates it as a whisper of God!) that manifested as a massive Electro-Magnetic shock wave.

The Brahma/ God	Attributes/Power
The FATHER (The SUPREME ELEMENT)	**THE MOTHER**, The Invisible Source of all Universal Powers and Programs, **Universal Consciousness, MAHATATVA**
HIRANYA-GARBHA (GOLDEN EMBRYO) from whom, all souls and spirits came out. The Divine Sun released Rays of Light and dispersed along with Attributes/Powers.	Mahatatva entered in Brahmand or invisible egg shaped structure where it was programmed by the Creator. When released, it made a sharp extreme vibration of few micro seconds with power of more than Gamma rays wavelength. It was OHM. Powers had parabolic journey.
Each spirit entered in a bond between two Quarks, electron-protons and comp-ounds as Graviton. Each spirit became SOUL to enter in an embryo and life began.	That opened various dimensions of Universe. They can be charted as Space, Time and various Energy levels. We are in lower second stratum of Existence. We call Bhu-lok.
See! Each one carries a Ray of God, the Soul. Without your presence, body dies. And, all spirits or Souls came from one Root Source, the Hiranya Garbha. We make a divine Family. Our body has so many chemicals...so many spirits we have within. You are a ship, carrying millions of Spirits and Soul...I ask you which way, are you going? You have no answer. You are stuck with survival issues.	Parabolic Energies condensed and Photon was created first. Light came first.(Fire), then sub-particulates (God Particles) came from condensation, butter emerges in butter-milk. Then atoms and compounds began and Universe was created. The Mother Part 1

FGW or Ohm has few characteristics:

1. It came in a fraction of second. All Energies of Universal Consciousness get dispersed in Micro-Second! Then after, the Epicenter of Brahma got empty. Everything was released with such a propensity. So, first there was Nothingness, Brahmand Or egg like invisible pool of Energy developed, then Divine Powers got released with Ohm Sound, then far away, photons were created and Light began. That way, Fire came after Ohm.

2. The energy of Ohm was greater than Gamma Rays, 10^{-23mHz}. Science has measured the Powers of Ohm, it was about 10^{-33mHz}.

3. This Vibration relying in all directions made a cosmic network upon which, who Universe precipitated. See, our galaxy is not showing a free fall. None has a free fall! All stars are received with love, by some invisible divine hands in form of Cosmic Gravitational Network, woven in Space! Space has negative

forces- Anti-Matters, Anti- Gravity, Anti-Magnetism and other that is why Universe conceived in Space can move smoothly. This is the property of Ohm.

4. Ohm or First Gravitational Wave can be divided in Units, Graviton! Energies from Spiraling Divine Snakes were sprayed, upon that network. They cooled; condensed and precipitated! The way, ice is created in freezing Ocean. Apart from Graviton, rests of sub-particulates are 'God Particles'. They are also, called as the unit of Ohm as well the Universe. They are the bridge of both worlds- visible Universe and Invisible Ohm! God Particles will make perceptible Universe while, Graviton is without mass and attributes but has Electro-Magnetic Potential (Graviton had Power of Attraction!). They create Universal Consciousness or the Nature as we call. They have their Program (Universal Program, that will run till the end of Kalp[28]Period.. They will create and sustain the Universe for the Life to manifest.

5. That way, OHM has Power of Attraction or the Divine Love! Aum or Ohm has power of unification and creating of the new conditions and New World. Ohm is the symbol of Love, derived from God.

6. Later, Gravitons helped other God Particles (Sub-Particulates or Quarks as Science says.) to unite, to get quantified and created the Universe. Sub-particulates made protons (two plus and one minus of God Particles) and Graviton rests in center of Proton! Neutron has two minus and one plus type of God Particle. Electron and Photons are God Particles in themselves. Then after, various Elements came in existence, from fusion of various numbers and types of God Particles. Photons and Electrons made FIRE Element. When Elements were created, they had gaseous form due to very high energy

---

[28]**Kalp (Aeon) Time**: In Hinduism, a kalpa is equal to **4.32 billion years**, a "day of Brahma" or one thousand mahayugas, measuring the duration of the world. Each kalpa is divided into 14 manvantara periods, each lasting 71 Yuga Cycles (306,720,000 years).

levels. (Air Element) Later liquid (Water Element) came in existence after compounds came to exist. Soon, complex compounds made solids (Earth Element) and Universe came as precipitations of snow, from fog!

7. When mass or quantum was created, it left behind anti-mass, anti-particulates and a Space around every atom! That is the Dark Matter and Dark Space. The Space is greater than the mass. Energy imbibed in Universe is just about 4% of total Universal pool. Rest is in form of Dark Matters of Space! (Listeners were enchanted and frozen.)

8. In Every proton, Neutron, atoms of Elements and compound, Gravitons exist as the binding agent that is without mass. That is Love of God for his creation, the Universe. He binds, He holds, He decides, when to disintegrate and He controls whole of Universe. He made Universe without raw material, out of nothing! And, He did not leave the Universe alone on its own destiny, He is sitting within! Same way, we are also, not 'cast away' on this planet. He is within you as the One who listens at me through ears, who perceives me through eyes and who sits within your body. As well, you are being watched and monitored (!) by Him.

This is how Powers of God's Attributes created Universe in nutshell. The existence that surrounds you is the Mother Nature. Now, we will study what the Brahma or God did in creating the Universe.

He, the Supreme Element or the God was transformed into a huge golden divine Sun. ('Hiranya-Garbha' or the Embryo having Golden Light emission.). The Divine Sun bear all the souls and spirits in his womb. You may understand or visualize that every Ray of Light of that Sun became the Spirit. His Light is different than the light of stars and Sun. Sun's Light has Photons, within it has photons and atoms. It has fierce fire! God's Sun has no Fire, no Heat, no atoms or God Particles! A Devotee at the time of Samadhi or Salvation will experience who he is, and it's called as Self-Realization.

When the Ohm resonated in Brahma, all Energies were released in spiral fashion. When Universe was under creation, the Rays of Light from Hiranya Garbha were released and they also, began their journey in Space along with those spiraling snake like energies flow. See! Element and its attributes can't stay apart! Those spirits (Ray of Light can be referred as Ray of Life) spread in space and reached to Sun. Sun is the first station of our souls. We were there before coming to Earth. There, we were the One, without differentiations.

As we know by now, how atoms and compounds were created; you will be interested in knowing how you as a soul, or 'Being-ness' arrived here on Earth.

Earth was a globe of Fire. When cooled, settled; Fire, Air and Waters were separated. Fire consumed Air, then, Atoms in Fire were cooked in Waters and compounds were created. That was, one way process but luckily, they were rotated in cycles like Oxygen, Carbon Dioxide, Nitrogen and Water cycles. Rest of Chemicals were as if frozen! Once Salt was created, Sodium and Chlorine were not separated so easily. As if, the system was locked, the Nature locked them here to give a constant atmosphere.

When the time came for Life to germinate, Enzymes were devised. They know how to and where to break chemicals and conjugate at certain points to form desired chemicals. Then, at next level, enzymes needed Energy to work...and so they devised cyclical enzyme systems like Krebs Cycle. Initially, the pre-life stage was inside the waters. Now, the Souls began their final journey to Earth as Ray of Life; they arrived as meteors but, they were invisible. As Soul is not made of matters, it is Ethereal, Cosmic you may say. Visualize as if, Souls came as Ray of Life on earth with their intentions to express the Self and experience the Life here. (These two are primary functions of every life.)Every chemical reaction, in cyclical life received His Ray of Life!

This Soul slowly developed DNA, genes and mutated to create series of Species. Now, a question came up. All souls in life will move cyclically as all species are arranged in food chain. Can they release themselves from endless cycle of taking food and being food? At Doom's day, everything will return to Brahma and that time-period is a Kalp. Should these souls wait till end? Certainly, not! This question is not for the Earth but for aliens of other planets. They also, seek Liberation.

After a long long time after creation of Earth, Brahma sent Regulator and Controller. God Shiva. He descended with Vedas on Earth, he devised Human Species as the bridge between animal life to Divine Life. All animals and birds expect something special from a man! They trust you. Mankind is the way to Liberation from life to death to life cycle.

Soul when enters in human embryo, it's blessed by Divine masters, Angels and Deities. They advised you not to get trapped in sensual information, in material world. Sense organs open outwards, and mind believes in those perceptions. So, you believe this world as the truth. While, the truth is in reverse. This Earth is your platform or launching pad. After finishing your primary functions (express yourself and experience who you are!) you should finish your unbalanced accounts. Then you will feel a peace that moment, you must decide to begin reverse journey to reach to your Root Source that is where the God or Brahma awaits for you.

See! You are the Ray of Life, or the Son of God and we make truly a family. Rest is non-sense, derived of vicarious mind! All pains, sufferings are just perceptions of mind! Open the eyes and you will perceive who you are! You as soul or Super-consciousness; you are here on this planet since millions of years! This life as human is so precious, now you understand the value. You have come here for multiple times as humans too! This Planet is your Prison! You will return to finish your accounts, fulfill your destiny and finish your dreams. Then you will get peace."

"Your pains and sufferings as a Man is due to Ignorance of Who You are. A Man behaves low, human life is sold cheap as commodity, so you have pain. Desires, acquisitions, lust, forces, envy, competition and violence are animal characteristics. That is why people complain; weep over the lost moments of life. Life goes in vain, in invisible prisons, or say, just in earning a piece of bread! Stupidity, isn't it?" Yogi ended his answer why people die unsatisfied and who they are.

Every person in cave was confounded for a long time. Something they had heard untold in this oration. Yestlin was in arms of Wombick...and weeping on his shoulder. None knew why they were so much emotional! They got some divine message from Himalaya; envisaged a call of Love from Holy Saints of Himalay[29] His aura was pulsating; his vibes, mesmerizing. There was an Eternal Peace outside and within the hearts of commune. They had lost something, gotten something! Someone saw Buddha in him, someone saw Jesus! Yogi opened his eyes, saw everyone differently and then closed the eyes taking everyone in meditation.

"A Human life is the moment of Pride among all lives on Earth, even Angels desire to be Humans and wonder on Earth, aliens also, intent to seek spiritual guidance from Human Race." Yestlin

"None of us had ever an experience of Meditation before, but we were lost in other space beyond the time! Meditation is not a doing...but it is a 'State of Being'! It is a staying united with higher self! Lower down come the sub-consciousness and conscious mind!"- Wombick

Leaving the Siberian Caves:

Later, Wombick took Yogi to show various parts of caves, his realm of 34 years! Living within a prison of hanging snow spikes made Yogi emotional. They sat on a rock, splashing feet in the torrent of waters. Few ladies brought their children to get blessings. Yogi smiled at Yestlin who was nervous at a thought, 'He might have to stay in that deep freezer for whole life! He was afraid that Yogi would leave him behind.' Wombick discussed about prisons all around. He drew locations on snow with his bony knife. He talked of types of torture in Gulag camps. People stood

---

[29] Himalay: A Sanskrit word, Him (snow) + Aalay (Abode of, Residence of) It's not Himalaya, but Himalay is correct word.

far in corner of caves watching Wombick talking politely. One witty person commented, "Yogi made a mouse out of our Siberian Tiger! I declare, Yogi has passed his first exam!" Everyone laughed loud and dispersed to hide!

Wombick asked, "You haven't told about your mission. Why have you come?"

Yogi: I have 3 purposes now: (1) To liberate you from caves. (2) to free prisoners from Gulag Camps, and (3) to prepare you for welcoming the New World Order. Night has to go, Wombick...prepare for Dawn. Tell them, to purify the self, be deserving for Grace of Nature or they will die. Upcoming period is the period of Spiritual Filtration."

Wombick asked after a long pause, "How will you do this?" Yogi smiled and said, "Me? I am not doing! I am just a catalyst conjugating two molecules and getting things done. There are many pending tasks of Mother Nature; I am supposed to settle. I am not going to get involved in your mess." He smiled confident and said, "Come on, Yestlin! We should go." Yestlin happily jumped up and suddenly, Wombick's voice changed, became strong, commanding, "No! You can't! (It was a rule of Commune that once anyone entered in cave, he or she would never leave the cave until death.) You should not (He corrected his words and tone.), and must not go out of this cave! It's not safe outside." Yestlin came forwards to Wombick, "I have seen Yogi in action. Who has come to help Mother Nature...who can do wrong to him? He is the One whom Siberia was craving for many centuries." Wombick hesitantly, said, "Then... I will come with you to guide till you cross Taiga Forest, there are colonies of bears there!"

Yogi softly controlled him, "Better, stay here until Yestlin returns. He will give you direction where I am. Then, you all will come out in open, leaving this cave forever, with full arms!" Wombick felt as if his heart missed a beat! Yogi added, "Bring other fellows, too!" Yestlin became serious; Yogi grabbed left shoulder of Yestlin saying, "Come on, you definitely need anti-Rabies vaccines!" Wombick began to chuckle at intimidated

Yestlin. He literally pulled Yestlin and became ready for sendoff. Commune gathered for farewell. Old ladies bowed down to fire and begged safety for Himalayan Monk.

They saw Yogi walking with one hand on Wombick and another upon shoulder of Yestlin and he blessed all of commune! An old senior fellow came across and warned, "Don't awaken sleeping giant. I advise you to re-think. Don't meddle with Communist Party. People are happy with government. And there are lots of risks for you." Yogi accepted his suggestions; he smiled at him, held him from both shoulders and spoke, "I am not going to work for you, people. It's you, who called me here; and I am a catalyst. And, about my risk? Ego dies, not me!"Now, Yestlin had just begun to love the cave as he did not want to go out with Yogi!

Flood gates were opened and water flow in torrent was increased. Cavemen placed two 6 feet long and 15 inch wide canoe made of Small curved log of woods in torrent of waters. Yogi and Yestlin stretched out in canoe, held the hooks very tight, took deep breath and canoe began to glide in water. Soon, they passed through narrow channel of rock in caves and torrent of waters entered in glacier immediately. Speed became tremendous; canoes revolved and landed in a pool of waters where many more torrents of waters were joining. They experienced a free fall and landed in a

water pool inside a cave all surrounded by ice. Here they left the canoe; cavemen pulled the canoe back. (Each canoe was having a rope tied at end.)

Yestlin and Yogi began outward journey on foot, along with the torrent. They emerged on the land somewhere about 1.5 miles away.

They sat on a rock, in sunshine to get dried out. Yogi was observing Yestlin with sweet smile. Yestlin was looking at Sunset, reluctant to see at his Master...was annoyed as Yogi was going to use him as bait! Everywhere was the kingdom of snow! Yogi pulled Yestlin and started walking, "This shall control our shivering." Far in horizon was the Tiaga Forest. Tall pine trees were standing still, as if they were in meditation. They were casting dark shadows in horizon upon white snow in foreground. Soon, clouds began to trollover Siberian plateau and entered in pine forests. There, they embraced each tree individually and then, became still! The tips of coniferous trees remained visible and clouds too rested in lap of forest, as the night was to fall! Yogi showed that to Yestlin and whispered, "Look, this world is the kingdom of Love! You know why we are separate? Why this Matrix was created? So, as wecan embrace each other! Dualism is there, then love is there in Existence! Look in this picturesque scene of sunset. Whom we will not love? Everything is beautiful and at peace because we are filled with love for all." Yestlin was bit confused so Yogi said, "When you feel love for many, for all in this scene, then you grow divine. And then why should I use you as a bait?" Yestlin felt shocked and he lowered his gaze.

The sun slowly became obscure in horizon. The heavenly picturesque scene was presented when light golden yellow clouds slowly trolled over plateau. Taiga forest on West was ready to receive them with dark shadows, white snow foreground, bluish water pools on a plateau and running rivers with their soft gurgling sounds.

There is nowhere in the world quite like Siberia. Its vast frozen landscapes are mysterious and intriguing. It's a land of contrasts and extremes, with majestic, snowcapped mountain ranges and icy-blue lakes to rolling green meadows and dense forests. Amongst the expansive tundra, rustic villages remain hidden from outside eyes, where the locals still live with uninterrupted values and traditions. Nature is unspoiled, and Siberia's breathtaking beauty is picturesque.

Yestlin whispered, "I feel, Master, I want to freeze here like those trees, those clouds! My life has come to standstill. I don't want to walk further. Let me be still like those frozen clouds! See, they also, have come here to rest!! Waters come to standstill, where constant grace of skies descend in form of snow flakes, sky is crystal clear like an eye of newborn baby, just I can see the galaxies of space through at night. Only heart beats and respiration reminds that I am alive!"

"This is the time to sit and ascend, as we are the humans. Humans should not be running after food, sex and pleasures in leisure times! Instead of sleep, he should enter in meditation. When life slows down, close the eyes and connect wit your higher center, your roots, the Almighty God, Krishna!" Yogi whispered lightly, so as not to disturb Siberian Air.

11. Taiga Forest

About Siberia and Taiga/Tundra Forests

Siberia extends from Ural Mountains (in South) to East between watershed between the Pacific and Arctic Ocean, from South hills of Kazakhstan and borders of Mongolia and china lie to Arctic Ocean in North. That way, Siberia falls entirely in Asia. Region of Siberia near Pacific Ocean is named as Far East in Europe and Russia. It covers 3/4th of land of Russia and has 23% of total population. Average temperature in January is -25 degree Celsius.

There are numerous mountains- common names are Altai, Baikal, Anadyr, Khamar, Kolyama, Koryak, Sayan, Ural and Kamchatka Peninsula in Far East. Major zones are Central Siberian Plateau and West Siberian Plain, Eastern Lowland, North Lowland, West Siberian Lowland. Siberia is known for Siberian Tiger, Kamchatka Brown bears and Polar bear.

Siberia is extremely rich in minerals- ores of all metals- (Nickel and Palladium from Norilsk, gold, lead, molybdenum, silver and zinc) as well gypsum, diamonds, diopside and coal. Oil and Natural Gas resources are abundant. At sea of Okhotsk, fisheries give 10% of world fish catch!

Taiga: The taiga is a forest of the cold, subarctic region. The subarctic is an area of the Northern Hemisphere that lies just south of the Arctic Circle. The taiga lies between the tundra to the north and temperate forests to the south. Alaska, Canada, Scandinavia, and Siberia have taigas. In Russia, the world's largest taiga stretches about 5,800 kilometers (3,600 miles), from the Pacific Ocean to the Ural Mountains. This taiga region was completely glaciated, or covered by glaciers, during the last ice. Large river systems like Ob, Yenisey, Lena are flowing northwards.

The soil beneath the taiga often contains permafrost—a layer of permanently frozen soil. In other areas, a layer of bedrock lies just beneath the soil. Both permafrost and rock prevent water from draining from the top layers of soil. This creates shallow bogs known as muskegs. Muskegs can look like solid ground, because they are covered with moss, short grasses, and sometimes, even trees. However, the ground is actually wet and spongy.

<u>Plants and Fungi:</u> Taigas are thick forests. Coniferous trees, such as spruce, pine, and fir, are common. Coniferous trees have needles instead of broad leaves, and their seeds grow inside protective, woody cones. While deciduous trees of temperate forests lose their leaves in winter, conifers never lose their needles. For this reason, conifers are also called "evergreens." Conifers have adapted to survive the long, cold winters and short summers of the taiga. Their needles contain very little sap, which helps prevent freezing. Their dark color and triangle-shaped sides help them catch and absorb as much of the sun's light as possible. In the taiga, tree growth is thickest beside muskegs and lakes formed by glaciers.

Taigas have few native plants besides conifers. The soil of the taiga has few nutrients. It can also freeze, making it difficult for many plants to take root. The larch is one of the only deciduous trees able to survive in the freezing northern taiga.

Instead of shrubs and flowers, mosses, lichens, and mushrooms cover the floor of a taiga. These organisms can grow directly on the ground, or have very shallow roots. They can survive in the cold, and with little water or sunlight.

Animals of the Taiga Many kinds of animals live in the taiga. All animals have to be well-adapted to the cold. Birds native to the taiga usually migrate south during the freezing winter months. Small animals, mostly rodents, live close to the floor. Many birds of prey, such as owls and eagles, hunt these animals from the trees of the taiga. Moose, the largest type of deer in the world, is able to live in the cold taiga. Like all deer, moose are herbivores. They favor the aquatic plants growing on the taiga's bogs and streams. Few large carnivorous animals live in the taiga. Bears and lynx are fairly common. The largest cat in the world, the 300-kilogram (660-pound) Siberian tiger, is a native taiga species. Siberian tigers live in a small part of eastern Siberia. They hunt moose and wild boars.

Threats to Taigas: Taiga ecosystems are threatened by direct human activity and climate change. Animals of the taiga, such as foxes or bears, have always been hunted. Their warm fur and tough skin, turned into leather, While, Tundra is the coldest biome on Earth where grass exists. It's characterized by permafrost! In summer, permafrost on grounds thaws and becomes soggy. While in winter, entire ground is frozen. Plants are small and stunted, have little room for roots to grow due to permafrost. Permafrost is any ground that remains completely frozen (-32degree F or 0 degree C) or cooler for at least two years straight. Then, partial thawing brings new waters with layer of sediments, gravels that

too freeze! Permafrost has frozen microbes that usually decompose bodies of woolly mammals and human bodies; decomposition would emit methane and Carbon Dioxide gases that may increase global warming. Permafrost holds twice as much of Carbon Dioxide and traps 80% of methane of planet! It prevents greenhouse effect. If all the permafrost thaws, 92 billion tons of carbon would be emitted! That way, industrial revolution adversely effects permafrost and harm more!

12: 'Come to Rest With Us, Here!'-Ghost

Slowly, soft frozen clouds hanging on Taiga Forest disappeared and forest became vivid. Pine Trees were more laden with snow. On right side, fresh clouds came down to rest on glaciers as if they were tired of journey. The life slowly, got frozen!

Yogi said in whispering tone, "Yest, Siberia is a perfect heaven! Peace and Stillness! Time has come to sleep! It's the breeze, flowing rivers and moving clouds, they say we are alive! And, we must rejoice our life. Those souls, who are non-living yesterday have entered into life today, one is Yestlin and another is me! Rest of existence is frozen!" Yestlin smiled as if he understood every word.

"Look above, stars twinkle and says you to come up! This Soil will engulf you at one day! Meanwhile, make this body as a platform for jumpstart! Rouse your Spirit from within! (Yestlin smiled.) This Siberia is so pious, so precious that... and the whole of it, is for 'you'! (Master wanted to say this pious world is for Yestlin or people of Soviet Union.) Yestlin! Thank God for this Siberia. Though life is hard, survival is an issue, but it's the launching platform for spiritually elevated person.

When you come to rest, feel nowhere to go, and come to Stillness; and you perceive same Tranquility around in Nature as it's here, then Yestlin, come here in future, sit down and enter in Yog and you will reach to me!" Yestlin nodded and smiled at Yogi...and then at sky and then back to Yogi! (He felt Yogi had become too complex!)

Yestlin was stuck to his vaccine program, he was too much worried from within so, he murmured, "We are going to sit here for Yoga, isn't it? Then, we are not going for vaccine, isn't it?" Yogi looked at him with surprise when Yestlin whispered in muffled sound, "I don't like..." He embraced Yogi and began to weep! "They will kill me!" A young man with so much of forces to live life fully won't like to die! His worry and cry were logical. Yogi consoled him saying, "Do you think I would allow anyone to harm you?" Yestlin cried saying, "Then, why do you take me to nomad (Village)?"

Yogi said, "You will be bold only when you face the reality, the storm, the pathway of Fire! That will transform you to be bold. How will you escape your sentence unless you face and finish it!" Yestlin wiped tears with trousers and Yogi smiled gracefully and said, "Where can you escape from the destiny? Yestlin? Face, receive or give out and balance your life. None can escape from Nature's Rules." Yestlin found a father in Yogi that moment.

They continued to walk in plateau across clouds. Yestlin suddenly found a cloud disappeared. When they reached there, they touched the frozen crystalline fog... it was that cloud suddenly frozen by a cold breeze.

The Master began to talk to Yestlin, "As I think, Siberia word has come from 'Sibiriya'; it means 'Land of 'Sibir'' (Sanskrit word-for classes of meditation and study of Spiritual Science.) Here, Rishis, Saints and Saga must have resided in Sibirs to do meditation and Spiritual study."

*

Meeting with Siberian Bears

Meanwhile, they saw cubs of bears rolling out of foggy landscape from pine forests. They were running joyfully, competing with each other, biting to slow down the next! Few bears popped out of their dens and more cubs began to chase towards human figures. Their parents came scowling to threaten humans figures not to harm their kids and asked their cubs to stop going closer to human figures. Usually the mother bear would swat to control uncontrolled cub! Here, she grunted to stop them! More brown bears groaned from forest and began to move towards humans. Soon, more families appeared in snow plateau and they stopped at a distance looking at fearless, two human figures waving hands to invite them closer! They were surprised! Yestlin hadn't encountered bear but he knew what real danger was, to face bear [30]!

He asked the Master to hide. Yogi was waving hand to call those bear cubs! Yestlin pulled his shirt and cried, "Please, run!" Yogi resisted. Yestlin saw a sleuth or sloth (group of bears) coming; he childishly left his Master, ran to hide behind a large rock at a distance. (He remembered why Wombick wanted to accompany them! And, Yogi recalled Wombick, if he had been here, bears would have attacked him as he was a serious enemy for bears!)

Cubs were as if, waiting for Yestlin to go! They happily jumped in running cold torrents and ran upon glacier towards Yogi! More grunting sounds came after them; mothers raised their tone and huffed strongly to return or to stop their cubs so their pace seized but, they glided into feet of Yogi! (It was so beautiful to see sliding cubs over glistening snow towards my Master.- Yestlin) Adult bears ran fast with snorting sounds. Soon, 20- 24 bears surrounded Yogi! Yogi bent and lifted two cubs, who stared at Yogi's eyes, then tried to rise over his shoulders and leak the face of Yogi! Their soft nails didn't hurt. Yogi's giggle sound while playing with cubs was heard by bears standing at about 50 meters distance. Soon more cubs entered in the play. They tore away his trousers at places. Then, came a team leader, a giant bear of about 5 ft. height and 12 feet length, unpropitious and dreadful bear walked from behind...and all cubs ran away! Yogi turned back and saw him sullen, well-intentioned royal bear standing about 15 feet away. He smiled at him; and opened his arms to call him with saying, "Thank you for coming to see me!" And, grizzly bear thought for a second, looked right to left, then hurried and rose to put two forelegs on shoulders of Yogi and face at parallel level of Yogi! Yogi stepped backwards due to heavy weight; observed him

---

[30]**About bears**: Bears are as such most intelligent land animals with complex and most convoluted brain in land mammals, 10 times larger somewhere! Bears can live in very diverse range of habitats, eat wide range of food. Black bear rear up on hind legs and knock victim with paws, eat one or two bites on arm or legs and then snap the head offthat is the most dangerous part of attack. People say not to play dead defensively to stop charging bear. Bears don't like lemon oil, lavender oil, orange oil and pine oil! Group of bears but he had not anything in defense.'

eye to eye, and mouth of Grizzly bear was watering...and he picked up right hand of Yogi in mouth and leaked with long tongue and then he forced Yogi to drop on ground, and over him, bear embraced! Yogi too, embraced him perfectly! Yestlin could listen at the laughing sounds of Yogi while he was absolutely covered by bear.

Yestlin was shivering and he closed the eyes behind his rock. But, soon, he heard his Master talking to Bear and bear also, started dialogues! The Bear was tearful at first. All bears came to surround them. Grizzle Bear wanted to convey his message by certain vocalization sounds. He stared at Yogi constantly, eye to eye and made 'teeth clacking' or 'jaw popping' sound suggestive of annoyance and agony. Other bears made huffing sounds from all around. It took about 15 minutes meanwhile Grizzly bear went on bellowing his angers by various sounds. Yogi again, embraced him by sitting on knees. Yestlin could listen Yogi saying, "Soon, Golden days will come soon; then you come with families when Sun will shower blessings from skies!" Again kids and other bears came trolling and Yogi blessed each one by placing his right hand on their foreheads. Soon, bears disappeared in forest. Few cubs wanted to climb on shoulders of Yogi and so, he promised, "When I will return, we will play in ponds...okay?" Then cubs returned behind their parents. The team leader, Grizzly bear gave direction towards some human habitat (Nomad).

Yestlin came running and fell at feet of his Master; for he was timid, silly and selfish behavior! He had no words; he had missed one of rarest opportunity of being with his Master. Yogi received him with smile, lifted and embraced! Then he said, "Don't leave me often! I will also leave you one day so suddenly!" Yestlin's welled up.

They entered in Taiga Forest at 10 PM; fortunately,sky was yet, bright enough. Yogi opened out and began to talk, "Bear Head had complaints, Yestlin, about hunting and poaching of bears and other animals in Siberia, probably more in East, in Kamchatka peninsula. His second complaint was about cutting of trees and deforestation. Third complaint was about blast activities for railways and mining. They have many problems, Yestlin, and one day, you will have to solve them!" Again Yestlin was clueless and asked, "Is there a solution?"

Yogi smiled to say, "If Fur is your need then either you be the bear or you design it artificially, intelligently, can't steal it from a bear! God has given them in favor. Human is not supposed to be here, as his body is not designed for extreme cold. Why don't they use intelligence and design for their survival, right now? Pleasure hunting bears is mean; when you hunt, you become an animal at equal energy levels. You seize to be a human." Yestlin tried to understand the stand of Yogi and walked silently.

After an hour of walk on snow through forest, they came to an area of abandoned wooden habitats, small empty huts, covered by snow. The area was as if, haunted and it was midnight now.

*

Meeting with Ghosts of Siberia:

Yogi asked Yestlin to stop for rest. Yestlin was exhausted and so he placed his head in lap of Yogi and immediately slept! Yogi chanted Ohm loud that terrified Yestlin! Yogi was sitting on a stone surrounded by group of pine trees.[31] Night deepened, Yogi was deep in meditation and there was an activity surrounding Pine trees. Cracking sounds came from snow-covered ground and, bizarre heads of hundreds of ghosts peeped from floor! Some were free, some were half-buried. Some were fog-like while some were of human sized transparent figures. Some were dangling over ground while some began to float in air current, from one place to another! Some were kicking and slapping another ghost while some were laughing mad at other's activities. Many ghosts were without arm or legs! Too scary was the scene! Many ghosts

---

[31] **Pine Tree** has fascicles from small buds that start on a dwarf shoot in the axis of scale leaf. Everywhere, one will find clusters of green needles- two to five needles make a cluster, routinely. Needles are the Pine leaves; they produce less oxygen. Needled Leaves having less waters won't get frozen in sub-zero temp and will survive in winters.

remained half-buried; stayed observant. They were happy to see two humans sitting in bushes. The One was divine, glorious and his aura inhibited them to go closer. Had it been someone else, he could have died by terrifying ghosts. And, then, more ghosts came from woods to surround Yogi and sleeping Yestlin! When Yestlin opened his eyes, he saw there, an army of ghosts.....that began to sway in flow of air, laughing mad!

Yestlin got up, looked at Yogi deep in meditation and still sat fearless! He shivered a little but he found his mother in ghost state, there. When the Master opened his eyes, ghosts saw stars in his eyes! His sharp luminosity was soothing and all ghosts became silent and still. The ghost of Yestlin' Mother came forward with a leader of Ghost colony! The Master raised his right hand to bless them and whispered, "Ohm, Shanti[32]!" And, all ghosts imitated! Ohm resounded from Pine forest. Yogi turned his gaze from left to right and blessed them. Ghosts felt soothing at heart, they became silent, at peace. Those, who were attached to their body buried in ground were released. Now they stoodlike a gang or band of soldiers. Yestlin saw them with ragged clothes and wounded body. A Leader came closer; he extended his neck for two or three feet forwards to Yogi and asked, "You look like a Saga! (in whispering tone.) Aren't you? (hollow tone)" Then, he flew and made a small circle around Yogi to observe around. Yestlin was frightened.

Yogi asked, "Here, why are you here? You are supposed to reach to your cities or towns so as you can get new birth."

> "Here, we, all are gentlemen, who came here to dwell for rest and peace. We are happy in graves; have eternal peace without your Yoga!..."Ghost Leader

Ghost leader shouted, "No! We won't go there! If we go there, we will soon return here in

---

[32]**Ohm Shanti!**Is a prayer to Ohm for Peace. Lift us to Eternal Peace. There are 4 layers of Sub-Consciousness: Energy or *Powers*, *Ananda* (Feeling Happy from within without external resources.), *Love* (finding everyone unified.) and *Peace*, what end-results when everyone is unified, no contrast remains and Matrix collapses. Then after, too far from there, Ohm comes as Root Source.

graveyards! They don't want us! (He paused and became blank. Ghosts never cry but make communication gap when they are subjectively emotional. They don't value differences, variety of opinions...they say, we need a garden of roses...then they will throw other flowers. If we take birth in Soviet Union, then they will send us back to here! Here, all are gentlemen, who come here to dwell for rest and peace. We are happy in graves; have eternal peace without your Yoga!" He laughed but again became silent for a long time.

"Why should I take rebirth as human; just to serve those rascals?" How much they have tortured us, with so much of planning! They feed us free bread and give free shelter and free education so as we can serve them like tamed animals.It's mouse-trap. No! I won't go to that society. (His voice muffled.) I am happy here. We don't need their food ration and we enjoy here, isn't it? (Last words he spoke loud so as every ghost answered, "Yes!") See, Monk!! We are happy! So, why worry? (He began to fly in pine trees; made a circle around saying... 'This is our Kingdom, we are immortals! (Ghosts on ground cheered and repeated his words.) No bullet can penetrate, no commander can whip, no one can give us an order, none can starve us, none will bury us in snow to freeze and die! We are buried here and alive!! We are better here!' (His painful laughter filled the space and all ghosts laughed mad.) He turned to Yogi and reached too close to whisper, "We are preparing army of Dead Men! Do something, so the Dead can take revenge!" (All ghosts cheered and made a great noise.) Ghost leader looked at Yestlin, so he reached and stayed in air, 5 feet from ground, and said, "You are Russian, and go fast and come back as dead! We will play games here!" Yestlin shivered and observed Yogi with tearful eyes.

"You asked me to do a favor so as you may take revenge. I see, you are happy here and not that concerned about your fellow citizen of Rus." Yogi smiled at the leader who bas annoyed, "I am here sleeping in my grave of my will, for my happiness, a ghost is always free!' He shouted.

Another ghost came and retorted to Yogi, "Go that way...there is nomad and medics are waiting for you! You were asking to Bears, just now!" (He showed direction.) Soon, you will return to us as ghosts."

The head of ghost became serious and asked, "Who are you, and why are you here with that Russian lad."

Yestlin intervened, "See, I am Yestlin, my mom is in your team!" All ghosts turned to mother ghost and got all stories. Leader said to Yestlin, "Return; run away to caves! I tell you how you will be killed slowly. First they will put you in cold stoned prison. Then, they will give you an impossible task in snow that will freeze your feet, nose and ears. You will get frostbites. Then, they will starve! So, you will melt and then will apply a rule food for work. As you weaken, you will be starved more. They will whip your back and butt for not finishing job in time. You will be working till 11 PM night in snowfall, without even a cup of soup! When I cried they torn apart my back; when I was agitated and shouted, they broke my bones; and, if someone would repel or fight back, or resist them then they would bury him in snow and subjected to die after feeding his face to their dogs! So, (turning to Yogi) I request, return to Himalaya. You are a delicate monk, your non-violence or yoga won't work in this world. This is our white Heavens! See, we were sleeping...why have you come to disturb?" He came very close to Yogi and noticed tears in his eyes. Ghost leader turned to his commune and exclaimed, "hi buddies, he has tears for us!" And, all froze! They had seen someone who cried for them! They all ran and made a circle to see the visitor with tears!

> "Sometimes, people like you do come on Earth, at a wrong time and at 'such' a wrong place! We as ghost also, enter in world early and repent. Are you going to preach those animals? They will remove shreds of your flesh! Unimaginably cruel they are! Go Yogi, go back to Himalaya! We, the dead, don't speak lies!"-**Ghost leader**

Ghost leader said, "Tears don't speak false. You are a genuine lover. We bow down to you." Then all ghosts bowed down with lot of love in their eyes. They had a hope. Leader said, "You have come to a wrong nation, at a wrong time. Sometimes, it happens! People like you also, makes mistake! Tell me, your intention and how can we help you. You have come to us so it's our responsibility to be responsible to our guest!" Many ghosts chuckled and Yogi also, laughed out.

"Okay, my Lord, what can you do for us? Preaching? Who listens? We are more animals. And, preaching to them at human society? They have momentum rush in life. Remember, the government is unimaginably cruel! Right man but at wrong time and wrong place. (He sighed.) If you want to preach, preach to us, we have time, none has spoken with love! So, start! (Few ghosts again laughed.) We, the dead, don't speak lies! Trust me, O monk! Siberia is not a heaven like your Himalaya! This is bloody Siberia! Here, we kill or they will kill us." Yogi smiled at his narrative. Again ghost leader circled Yogi around and made a swing to meet Yogi face to face, saying, "Tell me, what you want to tell, hmm!" To Yestlin, he was annoying, too arrogant.

Ghost leader had someone to listen to him so, he restarted, "System is such that they need intimidated docile flock in society that obediently would cultivate in farms, run factories and become clerks in office. And they would go home exhausted and rest for night! Or, they need shrewd, crook and selfish mafia who can support Communist Party of Soviet Union. They support only those who become spy of own work areas and family!" Ghost turned around Yogi to say more, "What you will speak to them?"

Yogi raised his hands to silence ghosts. Fun time was over! Yogi said, "Lord Sun is coming…" They began to look at skies and applauded with laughter. That moment, few ghosts who were wiser and had higher spiritual quotient, rushed in front to silence the crowd. One of them, bowed Yogi and said, "Pardon me on their behalf. Actually, we have laughed after so many months. We have talked with living person like you…what a fortune! (Pause) I understand, you have come a long way so it means you will not go without your functions are over. I welcome you, Yogi...I understand your concern for our world. You at Himalaya are so much serious about our planet and mankind...I am proud of you as you are keeping an eye on us." He paused and again continued, "You look probably like our Jesus as narrated in Holy Bible and we are useless and condemned species of Soviet Union! Tell us, how can we help you in your mission, what a contrasting event!" (And all ghosts bowed systematically! They have turned suddenly wise!) Old ghost said, "If you can throw some light about your visit...now!" Yogi smiled at their wisdom and blessed them. Soon, he began his visionary speech to a large group of Ghosts. Here, Yogi started:

"A Human takes birth with Emotional Quotient higher than animals. You are supposed to grow to still higher levels of vibes...so much that a human can become an Angel. And, you, the humans are the bridge between Earth and Heavens, between Angels and Animals. Either divine souls may come to our planet or you can rise high.

This was a possibility unfulfilled. Since ages, the Brahma, the God or Krishna had tried so as man can evolve spiritually not by dead matters. I have come to pave pathway so as when you will take birth, you will breath in Sun Land.

See, 'someone' has designed an invisible prison, in which human race is trapped. Most of people spend life after earning for their livelihoods. They suffer from fear, survival issues and defense preparation. A common man lives for security of life, which is not that required if you are the humans. If you are the animals, then yes, you need to have strong teeth and nails and killing instinct. That way, you remain half-humans- born like animals and failed to get wings to fly. A human is the one who can fly, sore to higher consciousness.

Those invisible forces have succeeded to captivate humankind in such a way that you work only for them and they sanction 'ration' enough for your survival. The profits from all human activities go to where? To whom? You are happy that life is fast-forwards in pace, (enjoying fast life) but then, you are reaching to last terminal earlier. The Human race shows scientific discoveries and mechanical growth. They excavate earth, make bridges and tall buildings but the size of 'human' is receding. Man has become dispensable and replaceable and exile-able, traffic-able, sellable (as slaves), organ-harvestable (taking organs from prototypes for rich people)! You are the pawns of some invisible conspirators who have made you work for them- starting from farmers to salaried people to common man and woman. They have exploited the Mother Nature too.

"Who is it?" Asked one ghost.

"Animal that sits within you!" Yogi answered, "A man is born like animal but soon, we give them Sanskara[33] of Humanity, of love and kindness and higher moral values since childhood first by mothers, then by teachers. Today, women's mind is polluted they live by body consciousness. What they will teach to their children? Sanskara are given by stories and own experiences, not by 'don't do it' orders. We have had a strong set of Purana, Ramayana, Bhagavat stories that give beautiful messages to empty childhood. I don't know what you have but true evolution shall begin with improving women's mindset and emotional quotient. They should leave body-consciousness level early once married and have own family." Ghosts were listening something new. "To fight with darkness, women always take a lead role in directing the human race. I have come to teach your people what is higher level consciousness and how first the mothers and daughters should rise. Their choices for life should be changed, the first." All ghosts were so happy that they applauded. Yestlin saw the First Ray of Hope- improving vibrations of women.

You will be released from here, soon when you see Golden glow of Sun Land in Siberia. You will come to Sun

---

[33] Character-building that raises not only IQ or EQ but Spiritual Quotient also.

Land. Then, you will not repent in coming at wrong place." Few of ghosts, chuckled.

Yestlin whispered, "What if, they don't understand what you want to say and don't evolve as you wish?"

Yogi said, "They will be purged!"(pause) "Yes! Seriously...Nature has programmed it, and we have to save the lives." He stopped and asked to guide where some nomad and medical center were. It was about 3 AM and that way, first day of Yogi on Siberia would be over at 4 AM. Yogi entered in meditation as it was his routine time to enter in within at 3.15 AM. Yestlin was imitating. Ghosts also tried to sit quiet and many entered in their soils. [34]

The Leader of Ghosts sat in front of Yogi. He saw beautiful monk with whitish blue aura going from vortex of head to heart level and then it ascended. Again, it started to return. The Leader Ghost prayed to his Jesus, "See, that you are not crucified twice."

Yestlin could not focus in meditation and came out. He saw the sky as the playground of clouds; with the background of stars. "From those stars, one has come to Earth for me, for my people, for the country. Bears came to see him, ghosts bowed down to him! This wild Siberia is also, cozy for him!" he murmured. Yogi opened his eyes, and asked Yestlin, "Yest! What do you suggest to stop violence?" Ghost leader was listening their conversation happily.

Question for Non-Violence:

Yestlin wondered and took time to answer, "Hmm...this Exile, Gulag Camps and forced labors have taken toll of more than 20 millions of people since 18th and 19th Century. As if, women were producing children for those camps! I will advocate forgiveness, compassion and practice 'non-violence'. Keep the heart considerate and merciful if there is a mistake."

[34]It was difficult to cross a territory of Permafrost at night hours, in fogs! Soil would be wet and soft; it will make cracking sounds while walking.- Yestlin explained why they spent time with ghosts.

Yogi smiled and said, "No! You are so lovely! But, you are talking to please me. You understand that virtues are very much personal. Non-violence is a personal virtue, it springs when you reach to certain level of Pure Consciousness. Violence is an essential virtue in Nature. Creation and Destruction goes in Sine-wave. I won't talk of non-violence for Russian Government. History of Indian Sub-Continent teaches a good lesson. Lord Buddha came in about 600 BCE (563-483 BCE, by some scholars). Emperor of Maurya Dynasty, Ashok the Great (lived from 304-232 BCE) unified various states and tribes by wars and created an Ancient Asia. Then, he adopted Non-Violence of Buddhism. It was a good decision for him but not for nation. Slowly, invasions from Middle East started and infiltrated Hindustan and nation disintegrated. Today's India is the smallest part of original kingdom. Non-violence is not good when you take responsibility to protect the nation."Then, both became silent- Yogi entered in meditation and Yestlin in sleep!

Yogi left the physical body and reached out to Moscow. It was about 4 PM of Saturday while it was 2 AM Sunday, at Magadan. He saw Kremlin Officers in hustles. There were few meetings in various conference rooms at Kremlin and officers were preparing for emergency meeting of Politburo next day, at central hall with opposition party leaders. Next day, it was () The President's Secretary was drafting documents.

[Now, what happened on that day all around Russia will be narrated on day 1 of Yogi. It means, it was the time period of 1974 to 1985 to 1990 as I explained before that one day of Yogi's stay was equal to 10-15 years of history of Soviet Union.- Yestlin]

Section:

3

C: Moscow

(Year: 1973-1988)

Summary of what happened in Soviet Union, on Day 1 of Yogi's stay. (The time period of 1974 to 85-90)

13. Russian Orthodox Church (ROC)

(Eastern Orthodox Church, Moscow, 1.30 P.M.)

Patriarch or Kirill (Russian name cognates with English Cyril.) of Moscow, aged 74 years, was sitting on his royal seat with leaning posture in his prayer room facing his beloved Jesus on statue of Holy Cross, at chancel[35]. His head was lowered to hide his tears. He had all bad news today, from North Caucasus region, Ukraine and even from Moscow. As an old pious Patriarch, he couldn't handle all demanding situations, in a single day.

It was difficult to digest and understand why two communities living together yesterday were at daggers drawn! Their hatred for each other was irreconcilable. Muslims were at daggers drawn with Christians and Slavics or natives.Why Christians from Armenia were at unrest[36] and why Chechens[37]

---

[35]***Chancel****: The space around the altar- where religious rites are performed in a church, it is often enclosed for use by the clergy and choir.*

[36]**Armenia**: Armenia is in South Caucasus region of Eurasia- with Turkey on West, Georgia on North, Azerbaijan on East and Iran towards South. Main religion is Armenian independent Apostolic (Orthodox) Church, in communion with Rome. It became first country to adopt Christianity in 301 AC. Armenian Church changed from Syriac alphabet to Armenian by 5th Century. Armenia is one of the oldest civilization. 900 BC, first Kingdom of Urartu was established in Armenian Plateau. Persian and Byzanthine rule came in 4th to 6th Century. 7th and 8th Century was ruled by Arabs. In 15th Century, Western Armenia came under Ottoman Empire. In 1828, area around capital Yerevan and Nahichevan were awarded to Russia by a treaty of Turkmanchay. From 1885, Kurdish and Turkish forces invaded from Constantinople and killed 200 Thousands Armenians. Then, till 1915,systematic Ethnic Cleansing was done by Ottoman

123

attacked local Slavic, Christians and army men, ruthlessly. 'Killing too, should be at least humane! Descent!!' he whispered.

His heart was agitated when he recalled a video released by Chechen rebel group showing tortures over captivated soldiers, enucleating eyeball and decapitation. Slavic and Christians were fleeing from Chechen areas into deep forests and up-hills of Azerbaijan, Kazakhstan and Turkmenistan. He was brewing for growing religious intolerance between Muslims, Slovaks and Christian community. How Soviet Union would remain intact, he asked to himself. Air was divisive, doubts had shaken the foundation of society and rumors were spreading like wild fires in dried our forest of Mankind. People were uncertain how the Church would help them. He recalled that both religions were derived from Abraham Religions, or Judaism[38]. He whispered,

---

Empire and 2 millions of Armenians were killed. On 28[th]May 1918, independence was proclaimed. Eastern part of Armenia was Sovietized in 1921. Then, according to Trans-Caucasian treaty in 1922, Armenia, Azerbaijan and Georgia were combined and made a single unit. Ethnic tension mounted when the area of Nagorno-Karabakh was given to Azerbaijan while majority of population were Armenian. They voted to join Armenia. There, Ethnic war precipitated between two former Republics of Soviet Union.(information derived from internet)

[37] **Chechen Conflicts**: Russian Empire had little interest in North Caucasus other than communication route to its ally, the Kingdom of Kartli-Kakheti (Eastern Georgia) against their enemies- Persian and Ottoman Empires. Russian Activities triggered an uprising of Chechen in 1785 and clashes resulted in 1817 –Caucasian War. Russia defeated Chechen forces in 1877. After regime of Communism, in 1921, Caucasian nations became Sovietized! Confrontations began against collectivization. In 1930, Chechen leaders were arrested and killed or sentenced to Exile. Chechen Uprising broke out in 1932. In 1944, with dubious allegations of widespread collaboration with advancing German forces, Chechens were transferred forcibly to Central Asia in an act of ethnic cleansing. This triggered very cruel phase where both sides suffered heavy casualties. In 1991, Chechens declared independence when Soviet Union was disintegrated. 1994, first Chechen war broke out. In 1999, it restarted when large numbers of Casualties resulted in that Battle of Grozny. By 2017, centuries old conflicts ended. (information derived from internet)

"We both are brothers that way!" He sighed as Kremlin won't help Churches and Christians expediently because Cyril or Kirill or Patriarch had less control over Kremlin. After establishment of Communism, Communist Party had become party of Atheists. Stalin era was a worst hit to Churches. Many churches were demolished and Believers of God were not favored in Government posts. Therefore, he was helpless!

Though sermons or discourses are given by clergy to the gathering of the faithful (Commune) to teach 'words of God' and to encourage faith, Patriarch came that morning on pulpit. He walked waveringly and all of segregation stood up. Soon, he began. His words were soft and whispering...so segregation found it difficult to listen at him. There was a pin drop silence.

"Prepare! Prepare for uncertainty. Ocean will rise, darkness will fall. Animals will enter in humans and they will run amok. You will be clueless; and may run helpless. You may not find anyone trustworthy- not even military personal. Violence may escalate and harmony will shatter in many parts of Ukraine, Armenia and Caucasian Territory. Government may not support you, the innocents. Prepare for a night fall. Don't sleep. Keep reserves of foodstuffs. Neither Government nor the guardians (police and Judiciary system) may be of help. Remember, your true Savior is Jesus Christ. Faith! Have faith on Jesus! Endure the present moment, that is the fruits of your own pasts; Sacrifices will make you pure. Sacrifice what you have to help your fellow citizens, especially neighbors. Lord Jesus will guide you in dark. Run away to safer place if required. Amen!"

He recalled such of his oration in that afternoon, sighed for his helplessness, looking at his beloved Jesus who was standing in front of bright Eye of Horus or Fish Eye (representing the Third Eye or pineal gland) and he asked, "Why...why this cataclysm! Why not peace- if we were humans? I saw glimpses of future in my dreams. 'The world is coming to a standstill. Clock will stop for a

---

[38]**Abraham Religions**: Both religions (Christian and Islamic) take name of Abraham as the first person, to whom God revealed Himself.

while! I have seen haunted cities, no life on roads, fear gripped people hiding in their homes or underground shelters. Soon, they ran towards Siberia looking to East with Hope. In smaller towns and villages, I saw people running amok, law and order gone. In Ukraine, thousands of people taking shelter in mountain, government will shun from its duties instead it will send army to cities. Children will cry for food; shops and stores will remain closed for weeks. People will spend time, standing in queue like ghosts, for hours. Children of Abraham will fight with each other, street will be drenched with human blood and communities will clash." He, then sobbed and whispered, "And, unlucky as I am, I will have to see the massacre! And, I can't prevent! Won't be able to hear those cries and their moans, O Jesus! If I can't do anything, then take me. I don't want to live, Jesus! Or, please, show me the path." On back flash, he visualized the past of Christianity. And, he had more pain to recall. Glories are always watered with blood drenched past. Kirill understood this principle of Nature, either pay first then get the fruits or get first and then pay with interest!!Kirill understood as a time for payment with interest! "This is the time to accept the Judgment by Christ." Bishop (Kirill) understood.

14. Brief History of Christianity:

Semitic religions are 'Abrahamic' religion that includes Judaism (of ancient Israelites and worship the God of Abraham), Christianity and Islam. Ancient Semitic religion was monotheistic. Tanakh and Quran describe Abraham, the Patriarch as a major figure and all Jews, Christians and Muslims recognize him with serenity. Abraham (535 BCE) is hailed as the first Hebrew and the father of the Jewish People. One of his great-grandsons was Judah from which Judaism started. Israelities were intially living in tribes in Kingdom

of Judah.Abraham had two sons- Jews and Christians recognize his second son- ISSAC and Muslims recognize the first son, ISHMAEL. Abrahamic religions were adopted by Roman Empire in 4th Century after Christ, while Islam was adopted from 7th Century. Both religions spread globally. There are few religions from Abrahamic Faith, namely- Samaritans (Israel) Druze Faith (Ismaili Islam- in Syria, Lebanon, Jordon), Bahai Faith (Iran) and Rastafari (Jamaica). Some say that main was Judaism that birthed Christianity and Islam. Abrahamic religions accept that God himself revealed to Patriarch Abraham.

God is a transcendental Creator and source of moral laws. Believers that way are positive about similarity amongst various groups. To them, God, Universe and individuals are separate, so one seeks Salvation by pleasing God by obedience and surrender to divine laws. Christians believe in Trinity form of God, Islam and Judaism believe in One God. Judaism puts more emphasis on laws and follows them completely. That way, Christianity talks more of Love for all. Both of Abrahamic Religions spread widely and globally. After all, the fall of Roman Empire in 4th century gave birth of Christianity making Pope as the (History of Christianity continues.) State Head! That way, probably, ruling over the world was perfectly designed again! Christians are monotheistic -believe that there is only 'One' God who created and sustains the Heavens and Earth. Doctrine of believing in Divine Godhead having 3 parts:

God, Son (Jesus Christ) and Holy Spirit is called as Trinity. People who follow Trinity were called as Trinitarians and who defer in their faith are Non-Trinitarians.) Christianity revolves around the life and preaching of Jesus. Christian believes that Jesus is the 'only messiah' to save the world. Jesus was crucified to forgive the sins of others and was resurrected 3 days after death. An insignificant man, John saw him enthroned in heavens and is returning as ruler of world.

After the crucifixion of Jesus, in 64 A.D. Emperor Nero blamed Christians for a fire that broke out in Rome. They were tortured and killed. Domitian made Christianity illegal and he ordered execution. In 303 A.D. Christians faced the most severe persecution under the co-emperors Diocletian and Galerius. Roman Emperor Constantine then, was converted to Christianity and that way, religious tolerance entered in Roman Empire. Emperor lifted ban from Christianity and he tried to unify Christianity and resolve divisions. In 380 A.D. Emperor Theodosius I declared Catholicism[39] (Western Christian Church as compared to Eastern Orthodox Church (EOC)). As the state Religion of Roman Emperor, the head of Roman Church was the Pope. Catholics have deep devotion for Virgin Mary, seven sacraments (A sacred act or ceremony as an outward sign instituted by Christ to give grace.) and honor relics (That which remains- like part of body of a saint or ancient religious objects

---

[39]**Catholicism**: Christianity is the world's largest monotheistic religion. It is based on the life and principles taught by Jesus Christ. Catholicism is relating to or being a Christian church having a hierarchy of priests and bishops under the pope, a liturgy centered in the Mass, veneration of the Virgin Mary and saints, clerical celibacy and a body of dogma including transubstantiation and papal infallibility. Catholics worship the One and Only God, who is **the Trinity (Father, Son, and Holy Spirit.)** He is ONE God, in three divine Persons, and his name is YHWH or **Yahweh**. The second Person of this Trinity (the Son) came to earth and took on humanity. Catholics follow teachings of Jesus Christ but do so through the church, whom they consider as the path to Jesus. They believe in the special authority of the Pope, which other Christians may not believe in, whereas Christians are free to accept or reject individual teachings and interpretations of the bible.

kept for veneration- (religious zeal or profound respect.) and sacred sites.

In 476 A.D. Roman Emperor collapsed, two major divisions, Eastern and Western Christian churches emerged. In 1054 A.D. Roman Catholic Church (ROC) and Eastern Orthodox Church (EOC) came in existence. In 1095 A.D. to 1230 A.D. a series of holy wars (Crusades) took place between Christians and Islamic Rulers to reclaim holy land in city of Jerusalem. At the end, Christians were defeated.

Apostle Andrewfounded Russian Orthodox Church. He visited Scythia and Greek colonies along the Northern coast of the Black Sea. Andrew reached the future location of Kiev and the spot where he reportedly, erected a cross, is now marked by St. Andrew's Cathedral.

By the end of the first millennium AD, Eastern Slavic lands started to come under the cultural influence of the Eastern Roman Empire. In 863-869, Saint Cyril and Saint Methodius translated parts of the Bible into Old Church Slavonic language for the first time, paving the way for the Christianization of the Slavs. By the mid-10th century, there was a Christian community among Kievan nobility, under the leadership of Greek and Byzantine[40] priests, Princess Olga of Kiev was the first ruler of Kievan Rus to convert to Christianity, either in 945 or 957. Her grandson, Vladimir the Great, made Kievan Rus' a Christian state.

As a result of the Christianization of Kievan Rus' in 988, Prince Vladimir I of Kiev officially adopted Byzantine Rite Christianity — the religion of the Eastern Roman Empire — as the state religion of Kievan Rus'. This date is often considered the official birthday of the Russian Orthodox Church. Kievan church was originally a Metropolitanate of the Patriarchate of Constantinople and the Byzantine patriarch appointed the metropolitan who governed the

---

[40]**Byzantine Priests**: Byzantine is from Byzantium an ancient Greek Colony founded by a man named Byzas, in 330 AD. Roman Emperor Constantine I chose to Byzantium as capital, now it is Constantinople. Byzantine Empire turned into Eastern Orthodox Church.

Church of Rus'. The Metropolitan's residence was originally located in Kiev. As Kiev was losing its political, cultural, and economical significance due to the Mongol invasion, Metropolitan Maximus moved to Vladimir in 1299; his successor, Metropolitan Peter moved the residence to Moscow in 1325. Following the tribulations of the Mongol invasion, the Russian Church was pivotal in the survival and life of the Russian state. Such holy figures as Sergius of Radonezh and Metropolitan Alexis helped the country to withstand years of Tatar oppression, and to expand both economically and spiritually.

St. Sergius founded monastery known as Trinity-St. Sergius Lavra near Moscow, was one of the defining events of medieval Russian history. Then, followers founded four hundred monasteries, thus greatly extending the geographical extent of his influence and authority. The spiritual resurgence of the late 14th century, associated with the names of St. Sergius, the missionary Stephen of Perm and the writer Epiphanius the Wise, contributed to the consolidation of the Russian nation. The Suzdalians, Vladimirians, Rostovians, Pskovians received the blessing of St. Sergius to make a stand against the Tatars, went as representatives of their principalities but returned after the victory as Russians, although living in different towns, a dictum which has been endorsed by modern church functionaries. That was how Russian Unification came in existence.

At the Council of Florence (1439), a group of Roman Catholic and Eastern Orthodox Church leaders agreed upon terms of reunification of the two branches of Christianity. The Russian Prince Basil II of Moscow, however, rejected the concessions to the Catholic Church and forbade the proclamation of the acts of the Council in Russia in 1452, after a short-lived East-West reunion. Metropolitan Isidore was in the same year expelled from his position as an apostate. In 1448, the Russian Church became independent from the Patriarchate of Constantinople. Metropolitan Jonas, installed by the Council of Russian bishops in 1448, was given the title of Metropolitan of Moscow and All Russia. This was just five years before the fall of Constantinople in

1453. From this point onwards, the Russian Orthodox Church saw Moscow as the Third Rome, legitimate successor to Constantinople, and the Primate of Moscow as head of the Russian Orthodox Church.

Monastic life flourished in Russia, focusing on prayer and spiritual growth. The disciples of St. Sergius left the Trinity-St. Sergius Lavra to found hundreds of monasteries across Russia. Some of the most famous monasteries were located in the Russian North, even as far north as Pechenga, in order to demonstrate how faith could flourish in the most inhospitable lands. In the 1540s, Metropolitan Macarius codified Russian hagiography (study of life of saints and documentations) and convened a number of church synods, which culminated in the Hundred Chapter Synod of 1551. This assembly unified Church ceremonies and duties in the whole territory of Russia. At the demand of the Church hierarchy, the government canceled the tsar's jurisdiction over ecclesiastics (French word: pertaining about Church). Reinforced by these reforms, the Church felt strong enough to challenge the policies of the Tsar. Philip of Moscow, in particular, decried (Condemned) many abuses of Ivan the Terrible, who eventually engineered his defrocking (removal of rights/authority of of a member of clergy) and murder.

In 1517 A.D. Martin Luther, a German Monk, began to protest some of practices and priorities of ROC by publishing a text of 95 Theses. He said that Bible didn't give the Pope the sole right to read and interpret Scriptures. Here Reformation started and Protestants were separated from Catholic Church. That way, 3 main branches of Christianity came to exist: Catholic governed by Pope and Bishops. Eastern Orthodox is governed by Holy Synod. There is no central governing body akin to the Pope. Protestants have many denominations- Evangelist, Methodist, Presbyterian, Lutheran, Anglican, and Evangelical and so on.

[All these data are derived from Wikipedia and such references from Goggle. The validation is not cross-checked. The purpose of writing history is to illuminate the Pathway to Unification of Religions. See Later.]

*

Kirill in afternoon, sitting in his room sighed and murmured, "Everyone on Earth tries to centralize the Powers, and Churches were not exceptional. Churches were stranded in between own Mind and own heart! Actually true devotion is a matter of Heart; we taught prayers from heart while use mind to get donation, favor and authority. We had preached Love but we have created hierarchy as a wall in defense! This speaks of Politics!' He paused and whispered, "I have got answers, O Lord, for my question, 'why Christians are passing through resistance and pressures, all over world? We are probably not doing well in Your Eye'!" He became blank observing Jesus, with sobbing mind and melting heart! 'A candle was burning in isolation.'

15. Conversation with Jesus:

When his Mind became thoughtless, subconscious became emotionless, Patriarch was dissolved who was crying for worldly favors and Earthen goals. Then, his crystal clear inner eyes and inner Peace received the glimpses of Sun shining behind his eyes, in center of his skull! When the waters of Lake become still, without vibrations and waves, full moon can be seen in its waters. There, he saw Jesus coming out of the Glory of Sun. He opened his eyes and gazed at Jesus on Cross. Hall was suddenly tranquil, no air currents and no sounds from other rooms of church. Stillness was right medium to receive the God. In such a glorious moment, a whitish glow emerged from the heart of Jesus, slowly descended and entered in heart of Patriarch (Kirill). Jesus was full of joy and happiness, was walking like a king, with sparkles in eyes, a sweet smile, had a great aura and he was as if, walking few inches above the floor. He lost his consciousness and his head dropped over the dining table top. He remained unconscious for a long time. Inside, he was with his Messenger, Jesus. Voice of Lord Jesus came inside his Sub-Consciousness! It was in Slavonic language[41] that amazed Kirill later when he gained consciousness.

Jesus: Don't ask 'why' to the Mother! (Jesus as if scolded him.) You are just the Kid! Your question from mind has words while the Mother Nature runs her program with Vibes that too, run in parabolic course! It makes impossible to understand the next move of Mother Nature. We don't ask, 'what', 'why', 'when' and 'how' or 'where' to Nature. We just, worship her. Mother Nature not only brings seasons or has control over Five Elements; 'She' is an Ocean of non-particulate energies from which Five Elements are derived. As her energies are non-particulate, the Mother Nature is invisible, is the mother of whole Universe. Now, you can understand; Ocean maintains Equilibrium. It tries to settle everything to Zero Level. A rise will meet a fall and life meets its end, death! Light dissolves in

---

[41] ROC speaks in an archaic liturgical Slavic language.

Darkness. That is Equilibrium. Make a plus sign and you will be minus somewhere! You get something and you need to pay or lose something somewhere. You laugh and you will be crying somewhere. You make a day and night will follow. Existence is oceanic and creations are waves! This Universe is like a wave of an invisible ocean and a wave should return back to its origin, Ocean of Existence.

Kirill: That means we are going 'down'! Doom's Day?

Jesus:Afraid? Who is feared of? Rise and release yourself from mortal emotions. (Pause) 'Your' Christianity is a Wave, it was 'created' once upon a time, understand and leave it to Mother! Whole Existence is on a swing, on swaying! Muslims are not reasons, they are the means for Nature for Destruction! When their functions will be over, they will suddenly realize that they were 'used' by Nature. Like Volcanoes eliminated Dinosaurs. Volcanoes were not the reasons, but means to Nature. You can't ask Mother Nature 'why'; She reserves all her rights! (Kirill nodded and looked down.)

Kirill: Rise had a reason and fall has its reasons. We are tiny atom in the Realm of Mother Nature. Without her wish, we can't move our finger next morning.

Jesus: That statement is unfair, it means you have pains and are egoistic. Reason to die is the birth itself. Mother never holds a specific reason for specific person. She has programmed so as the sea will never overflow, its surface will remain constant. Waves may come and go. For rise or fall, Mother finds resources and engineering. Mother is ingenious and the niftiest! So, when you will be humble when you know this and become wise. Your tears say you don't like decisions of Nature, you don't trust the process of Existence. Seek, who worries? It's your ego and for your attachments to your people." (Kirill nodded and looked down again.)

Kirill: Muslims are threat to Christians. We have treated with human values, tolerated them and allowed them to settle among us but now, they want whole land.

Jesus: Mother Nature won't penalize 'Her' children. Remember the God loves! He can only love! No penalty norms exist in Divine Realm. When you will see Love of Father and Mother in whatever you get as the destiny, then you will be wise and intelligent. Someday, Mother washes her kids, gives a good bath, isn't it? She helps you to decelerate Christianity, cleanses your wrong deeds and will give you comfort. Actually, penalty is not a penalty...it's her process of Equilibrium! She will cleanse the deeds of Mankind! Tell me are you happy with deeds and decisions of mankind? Animals cry, trees cry and Earth, also shudders from Sins of Mankind! So, don't disturb the Nature, allow her to take her ingenious course so as to correct our mistakes. You don't cry. Mother Nature has to run whole life over this planet. She runs her own program; you don't complain but be recessive in such situation. Receive her judgment with grace, the way I walked with cross on my shoulder! I could have escaped. (Kirill became weepy...he looked at Jesus with tearful eyes. He said, "I am so sorry on behalf of our society! Please pardon us."

Jesus said, "I am not that Jesus, he is gone...by 2000 years. I am not body. Your love compelled me to come to you in a shape you have in imagination. I am ethereal. What you see is not the truth! What you hear is also not true, only vibes that create waves in your heart is my message."

Jesus said, "Judgments are pending since long. (Kirill was looking at Jesus with blank eyes, then he recovered himself.) I said, 'Judgments are pending. Good person has many dark spots. A wealthy person donates you at Church; he might be the most corrupt and a criminal. Donation and prayers are mixed with his bad deeds. So, Nature has difficulty to punish him. That way, a poor has his sins yet, he is more honest and pure heart. Again, mixed attributes, he has. Almost every human has been living in Mosaic shade; you at the Church are also, neither in white or black.

Kirill: What wrong, we have done?

Jesus: How did you spread message of Bible in Far East, in Western areas of mountain? How you destroyed religions of local Nature Lovers- Shamanic?![42] None receives his/her destiny in time. That is slowly, Whole system has come to standstill so, you find agitations all over, hatred and violence will erupt like volcanoes. And, you will be sitting, unhappy.

Kirill: Yes! Now, what to do?

Jesus: You can't do anything; instead you do less to the world. You do more for your Salvation instead of thinking about others. Grace of Father descends to someone Chosen. You come upon in Being state, rather that doing state. Doing represents ego. The mankind has overdone and damaged the Planet Earth. (pause) The ONE from Himalaya, the Chosen One has arrived in Siberia for this divine purpose. He will come to you in 1-2 days. He will release everyone from deadlock situation; will help Mother Nature to Justice to all, that way he will bring Equilibrium and Peace.

Kirill tremulously whispered, "Churches will definitely survive, we have done good! We deserve good fruits as we have made great sacrifices on your name. We spread your words, taught Holy Bible; instilled principles of Love and brother-hood. We brought all people from diversified Ethnic groups under one umbrella, under your holy cross! We unified them, made them free from their old prisons of misconception, beliefs, sinful traditions and idol worshiping which was a fraud. We taught them science, brought modernization, comfort in life. We have done great work on your name. Our missionaries had sacrificed to reach to the darkest corners of world. We truly, loved the people so we will be safe!

---

[42]Russia's main religion is **Orthodox Christianity**; however, other religions, such as Catholicism, Protestantism, Islam, Judaism, Buddhism, and even Shamanism are professed as well. The second Russian religion by the percentage of the population is Islam, followed by Roman Catholicism and Judaism.

Jesus stared amusingly at Kirill and began to discuss at length; but here are few points Kirill remembered and jotted down in his diary, later on. Jesus said so.

- "I did not ask you to bring whole world under my 'Cross'! This is all, my realm. I was very shy...spoke short sentences and you created whole treasure of literatures! Love is expressed in few words. Why so thick are holy literatures?

- I did not use my mind; that is why I was arrested and punished. I could have corrected my stance, could have escaped before arrest. And, you use mind to spread your religion.

- You should revise history and review how and why you started new Religion upon my name. It's interesting for me that you crucified and later after 300 years, I became useful to take charge of innocent people. From Roman Empire, you established Christian Catholic Empire! You must research! Actually, I did not start 'this' religion. I talked of love for all!" Kirill was now tearful, he bowed at Jesus.

- What is wrong in ideology of other people and what is wrong with their idols? Cross is an idol, isn't it? (His voice was so sweet (!) that Kirill nodded and he sobbed, as he used to spent hours focusing on Cross!) Anything that helps you to focus, concentrate and help to be unified is the Idol. May it be Sun, Star, Moon, Ocean, Mountain, river, Ocean , trees or an Idol. Who are you to judge what is good and what is bad for a race! Never envy or distrust the pathway of other people. All the rivers are going towards the Ocean. Eastern Spirituality yielded Enlightenments- Father or God have come there as Humans! They had golden age in their civilization before I was born, before your Christianity began. You are a younger brother to world's religions. Show respect. Don't dismiss their logics, concepts and ideology! A mountain peak can be reached from any direction, isn't it? Why you have a grudge? Dismissing other's faith is dismissing me and it's Ego and Ego means no spiritual growth! Different flowers and various fruits are in our Garden, how generous is our God!" Kirill smiled at Jesus and asked, "But, now what to do? I foresee a class war, civil war between two Communities. Would you show me a pathway?"

- Jesus: Two religions fight? Property issue!! Two brothers of one family... are fighting this world; they don't know that they are going to get buried in same soil! This soil is mysterious. It has engulfed flowers, stars and mountains; it has got civilizations buried. Don't make this land as your goal! This is not your permanent address, you came here to express the great divine virtues and experience your royalty. Then you return to us. Staying here and fighting for a piece of land is sheer stupidity? About your concern let me tell, we, the holy Saints or Rishis don't do anything in world's business. (Jesus smiled at him.) Better if 'you' drop your ego, become zero... and dissolve. You dissolve and disappear and your bondages or chains will drop by itself. Let the Nature takes her course. Drop imperialistic goals and raise your spiritual level before Doom.

- Kirill, "Why Doom? Why?" Jesus remained silent and took time to answer, "Creations will meet demolitions. Follow the Pathway of Eastern Civilizations, follow the Hindus...they have Sanatan Dharma (Eternal Dharma)- I live with their Rishis or Yogis of the highest clan. We don't have a one religion nor one God! Our God is 'Everywhere' and in 'Everyone'! They perceive Divinity in everyone and worship Him by all the ways! I also came across holiest Buddhist Yogis and we have to tell that the God can project Himself in any way and He has presented in all the ways. It's your responsibility to recognize him, be open to receive Him from any direction! May be, Muslim with sword might be in form of your God's wish. Death is little painful but relieving. Accept the death and walk over. Such are the principles of Rishis and Yogis accepting air from every direction and loving all events as the Gift of God. They call 'Raza' or 'Wish' of the God. In this oceanic existence anything can happen to you at anytime, instead of fearing like a dewdrop on a leaf, forget what can happen to you and start your spiritual Journey. Himalayan Religion is as high as Himalaya. We respect atheism, too. Don't go on comparing and fighting with them to show you are great. You have one Bible...they have endless holy Granth (Holy Books).

- A yogi from Himalaya will visit you, just find the way to sublime! You are emotionally labile, have tears, fear of losses and you hate one class (Muslims), then you can't love the God. Hatred is logical and love is illogical. Both are on extremes of spectrum. You need to choose whether you will love everyone or not.

  Kirill interrupted, "Muslims don't love anyone!"

  Jesus interrupted, "It means you too, don't love anyone! World is your mirror, that's the beauty of this Matrix!" Kirill fumbled for words.

  Kirill: How can I meet that Yogi?

  Jesus: Send off vibes of pure love from your heart towards Siberia! Yogi will follow your heart. He will reach to you in time, if you emit your vibes of love constantly. In East...Sun is rising, it's dawn, there. Wipe of tears, my Son, wise you are and should welcome tomorrow. I know you won't adhere to your past.

- You said that you served the Humankind but for your cause! You ran parallel government. You established your Kingdom, your followers, have your rules and own court, your judgments, your voice, run own hierarchy of Ministers and Priests, have commandedeven, the Kings, you have your army and now, you have your enemy!" Kirill argued, "It's required for smooth religious administration. Is it wrong?

  Jesus: You must have sentenced many innocent Jesus so far. (Kirill was shocked with that unbearable accusation from Lord.)

- Jesus continued, "A wave that comes up shall perish! Everything is mortal, Russell, everything! (Russell was his pet name of Childhood.) The whole existence tends to zero. See, I was also a wave!" Jesus waited his words. Kirill argued, "No! You are still immortal. You were not a wave, you and your teaching were immortal."

- Jesus looked at his inner conflicts...and smiled. Jesus said, "I am gone...but you keep me alive in memory. You transfer memories from one gen to another generation. When I was there, you were also there but you did not recognize me. Now it is 2000 years and still you are calling me. Your religion is rancid." Again, Kirill was as if, stabbed by such a sentence.

- Kirill: (in broken sentence) All religions on Earth worship their Gods from the Past. There is no Fresh God of Today. Whom should we follow? We behold your Holy Preaching. What more we can do?"

- Jesus: Forget me, don't adhere to the past. When you send vibration to me, you will feel intense love, a desire to unify for me. Then, you should fly. When there is a fire, you become a spaceship and leave the Planet Earth, go beyond the Gravity Pull and enter in another dimension. Function of all religions is to set every human heart afire with Love. Then they will enter in vertical axis and that is Spirituality. There, we will see all birds liberated from this planet and fly high towards the God. Followers of all religions of Earth will stand on one stratum, one platform in skies. Like different birds, flying at one level together in air; how sweet it will appear?

- Kirill: How is it possible? Who will give up possession of all churches and temples, the properties of billions dollars? Priests will object.

- Jesus: No, those who want to cling with temples and churches can adhere there. People will understand me one day, my message and will be to give up this platform of Planet Earth, being ready to sublime. Your churches and properties will be yours, your hearts and love will be ours! (Jesus first time, laughed and Kirill also, chuckled.)

- Kirill: Is it possible? It means we are reaching to confluence of all religions. (He was extremely happy then, became serious and asked.) "But...how will it be possible? Who is he from Siberia, you are talking about?"

- Jesus: He's the Himalayan Yogi who have landed in Siberia. He will reach out to you, so be prepared. He will take you first to my height. You will find that 'you are the Son of God.' Every spark within an atom belongs to 'Him' and every life is 'His' revelation. There is 'no Son and Father' relation. We say to God, "I am as You are! And, 'You' are as I am! Aham Brahma Asmi! (Sanskrit) I am the God!' is the final revelation. Come, Russell, come to higher levels and drop the worry of life on this planet. This soil is all messy, why do you shade tears? Pains come to awaken people, to teach them about higher authority."

Kirill bowed down and Jesus slowly disappeared. Kirill fainted on dining table until late in evening.

16. Kremlin Boils

(Moscow Time: 7.15 pm, Day 1: Siberian Time: 3 am Day 2)

An 'eye' of an observer entered in Golden Gate of Kremlin passing through long aisle. Viewer could see eyes without security personals, people with utter soft words or silence, air was cold and 'heavy' and no smiles on sincere faces! Visitors were coming with eye-to- eye gossiping! There were rooms and all the walls had 'eyes', even flowers in bookies had 'eyes' and 'ears'! Every room, every table and every person was systematized! Rooms were active, around which many more rooms were scrutinizing them. Ocean displayed small waves of joy and happiness, but it was too serious and deep inside! Rooms behind thick walls where panels of computers; security officers were watching each activity, listening all conversations of every room. All sounds and conversations were recorded and stored for future reference. Few experts of psychology were looking at the behaviors of staffs, body language of visitors and ministers. Still, there was a second tier of security offices around the Kremlin, with computers with great speed (Super-Computers- seen in 1974) and analysis. Security officers of various departments of KGB were busy with inputs from secret services from the Russian, Trans-Caucasian, Ukrainian and Belorussian Soviet Socialist Republics (SSR) since 1922. KGB[43]

---

[43] **KGB** (Komitet Gosudarstvennoy Bezopasnosti) means Committee for State Security, foreign Intelligence and domestic security agency) was the primary security agency to Soviet Union from 1954 to 1991. It started as Cheka from 1917, then GPU, OGPU, NKVD USSR in 1934, MGB 1941, GBUB NKVD, NKGB 1943, MGB in 1946, MVD in 1953 and last KGB was redefined for its work. It had multi-faceted role inside Russia as well outside too! It was under Department of Homeland Security devoted to safeguard country, means Communist Party ruling. KGB apex agency resided in Office of Mr. President of USSR. Its reputation was not as notorious as imagined as far as its external affairs; but it was infamous for its activities at home. Primary roll was to quell dissents who promote anti-communist political or religious ideas and silence them. For that agents used extreme violence. Instead of national security, KGB became prey and began to protect Party leaders and maintained party orders.

(Committee for State Security) was the primary security agency to Soviet Union from 1954 to 1991. The observer's eye was running from one room to another, innocently gazing at heat and hassle inside Kremlin but, he did not locate Mr. Presidential Suite so easily.

Kremlin word came from fortress inside a city, built in 13th century on left bank of Moskva River by Prince of Suzdal. Later, when radical and circular plan of center of Moscow were redesigned; Italian Architects renovated it, from 13thto 17th century that included fortification of Europe and churches on Cathedral Square (Cathedral of Dormition, Church of Archangel, Church of Annunciation and Bell tower of Ivan Veliki. Five domed Assumption Cathedral was also built in 1475. The cathedral became major Russian Orthodox Church and a wedding and coronation place for great princes, Tsars and emperors as well the shrine for metropolitans and patriarchs. Italian Architect constructed in 15th Century 'The Palace of Facets'. It was a great hall for state ceremonies, celebrations and receiving foreign ambassadors. The Senate was built in 18th century and it's today residence of Russian President. In 1849, Great Kremlin palace was built. Red Square lies East to Palace that is a political, historical and religious center of Russia. Once it was the palace for Great Prince. Today, it's world heritage site from UNESCO. At the foot of its ramparts on Red Square, St. Basil's Basilica is the most beautiful Russian Orthodox monuments.

Mr. President had 3 Presidential Conference rooms and had consultations with different visitors that evening and he was in his personal Presidential Cabinet at Senate building, Kremlin. His Home resident was at Novo-Ogaryovo in Kremlin. Windows of his rooms opened in an aisle that was secured totally. (There was a fear that America could attack Kremlin through Hawks. Windows did not open outside.) Filtered and conditioned Air was blowing through aisle, into windows of his offices. The outer walls of his suite were reinforced by heavy metals. The carpet was about 1.5" thick so walking was difficult for many visitors as well staffs.

That day, internal staff was under pressure, as usual! Almost all Ministers of Politburo were engaged in respective regional rooms. The noise of printers, typing, rings of telephone, flashing screens of Computers and running fingers of operators were speaking of burden the Government was walking with! A giant ship may look picturesque from distance but its basement is always too noisy. (Turbines, propeller shafts and other machineries make a great noise.) Mr. President was seen poised and at equilibrium but internally he was standing on warzones and walking through mines. He was not traceable easily, constantly changing his offices dealing with visitors in various suites. This time, eye of observer was searching him, "Where is he?"

Mr. President had a lunch-break. (3.30 PM.)

He was sitting with his daughter in his private room; she had brought lunch at 3.30 PM. Daughter was 20 years old, very passionate for her father. She was in fighting mood for not coming home for lunch. She silently observed him, who was taking rapid bites, chewing fast, busy thinking. She whispered, "Always in accelerated mode! Even if, a mountaineer climbs fast the peak of mountain, he has to return earlier. Runners are losers on long run, daddy! A rolling mouse gathers no moss." She got up, went behind the seat of father, bent on to hug him from behind saying, "Last night also, you came late to bed at 12.30 am." She rubbed her cheek with dad's cheek who was chewing; he smiled, tapped her left cheek by left hand and whispered, "I Love You, Nomi (Short form of Naomie)!" Daughter rubbed cheek with left cheek of father and whispered, "Hum, Me too!"

She whispered, "Do you love working for rest of world at cost of your lunch and sleep?" She pressed her cheek against father's cheek and said, "Slow, daddy, slow! Time really runs slow... and it's elastic. You can put many things in time frame...no need to hurry! (Father looked at his daughter and smiled.) And, Time should not make you run...you should make Time to wait for you. You are our President! World will roll over like bicycle, even if you don't peddle, most of traffic clears by itself and traffic police has just, to see! Many presidents in world have done nothing in their tenures...and were called 'Great!"

She went back to her seat saying, "I was reading a novel, its author writes, 'You can hold whole world on your head like Atlas but, can't put it on heart! I see you have been growing serious, not fair dad! Even, you do not smile with me! (Dad laughed out.) Heart should sing, your cheek should smile and eyes be relaxed." She was childlike. Mr. President observed and became proud of his daughter. Mr. President went to washroom.

Naomie asked, "Dad, when you meet 'no one' and relax? May I suggest, dad, add one name in schedule of visitors, name him, 'Mr. Peace' and observe silence for 5 to 7 minutes every hour. Improve your oxygen levels then, return to your work."

Father chuckled and said, "Enough, dear. I know you have grown up and have become wiser. Great, I am proud of you. My minute is greater than your day! See, when a man runs his family, he has certain times to relax. When he drives a car, he should be cautious as his family waits at home. When he is a pilot, his little mistake may cost lives of passengers. When I am a Captain of a huge cruise, then still more serious I will become." He raised his glass of water high and said, "Cheers, Naomie!" She smiled and answered, "You are not alone, dad...a sea captain, ship's captain, captain, master, or shipmaster are all there, doing their works.

Naomie asked, "Just tell me one most irritating problem for you!" Father began to narrate the situation, "Violence at Northern Caucasian territory where areas have Muslim Majorities (Chechen Republic, Azerbaijan and Kazakh) and they ask for freedom!" Naomie jumped from her seat and began as an expert advisor, "Do they use guns of own?"

Mr. President, "They use even mines and missiles to attack military convoy. They kill innocent people ruthlessly."

Naomie, "Who is the source of their powers? Who support their rebel? Who supply them guns and missiles?"

Mr.President, "Afghanistan and Iran!"

Naomie, "Why don't we focus on Afghanistan?" Father became alert; his daughter was on right track. (His Intelligentsia (KGB) was insistent to focus on Afghanistan. Soviet Union had never been aggressive upon its neighbors. But, time had compelled Soviet Union to enter in Afghanistan.)

Father nodded and whispered, "Everyone insists but we don't invade in countries as our basic policies. We have enough troubles of our own land."

Naomie: Then, give them internal trouble; so they get weakened by themselves and forget our states. Create their internal enemy.

Mr. President, "US is working on that line."

Naomie continued, "Good, so now, second issue is about their freedom. Hmm...(She thought, nodded here head, looked in eyes of her father and said.) Be a fatherly figure and give them what they ask; their Freedom if they are right, of course. I would ask them to pay for freedom and remember our old relations of past." Mr. President commented briskly, "*Land is the costlier than lives. Land makes a nation where people come to live. We give importance to borders and integrity.*" Naomie became softer and said, "Daddy, you can't stop flood; you can lead them or allow the waters to pass away. Let the Nature work, for sometimes! Bend with dignity and allow waters to pass over'. Give but, conditionally; with proper costing!"

Father was looking at his 'highly mature' daughter. He felt proud of herself. 'You will be a good trader.' He remarked. Daughter hugged her father and whispered at his shoulder, "I am! I started thinking in your ways. It's all your intelligence; just, I wanted you to laugh at me. Now, should I go? Our five minutes are over. Take care." She left presidential suite leaving behind her father astonished, he murmured, 'She was right by all means!'

*

Meeting at conference hall, Kremlin (8 PM)

Few members of State Dumas[44] ('Gosduma' in Russian) who constitute lower house of Federal Assembly of Russia while Upper house is Council of Federation arrived in emergency at Conference Hall D at Kremlin. They were involved as it was a case of Human Right Violation case filed by Muslim Representatives of three states:

(1) Chechen (North Caucasian territory whose conflict with Russia was since 17th century) Popular Front members,

(2) Azerbaijan (South Caucasian Oil-rich territory and East to Armenia)

(3) Kazakhstan[45] (Southern State of Soviet Union former member of Soviet SSR)

Politburo asked representatives for Eastern Orthodox Church too to present their views. Mr. President presided with his Minister of Internal Affairs (Home Minister) as well few more of Ministers. Proceedings started with reading following letter written by Muslim Representatives.

Rebel groups from above states (Chechen, Azerbaijan, Kazakhstan and many groups of Christian churches from Ukraine) have filed a long complaint at Human Right Commission, accusing Government of Soviet Union in many ways. Government invites debate in which Dumas, all party ministers and rep of all concerned party representatives are present." (pause) "Here is the

---

[44]**Dumas:** The first representative body of legislative power was created in the Russian Empire in 1905 as result of the revolution when the government was desperate to divide the opposition during an uprising. On 6 August 1905, Emperor Nicholas II issued a Manifesto on Establishment and Organizational Rules of one of the parliament chambers. The **State Dumas,** commonly abbreviated in Russian as **Gosduma** (Russian: Госду́ма), is the lower house of the Federal Assembly of Russia, while the upper house is the Federation Council. Its members are referred to as **deputies**. The State Duma replaced the Supreme Soviet as a result of the new constitution introduced by Boris Yeltsin in the aftermath of the Russian constitutional crisis of 1993, and approved in a nationwide referendum.

[45]Kazakhstan became independent in 1991 with dissolution of USSR.

complaint, it is distributed to everyone." (Papers were distributed on round table conference.) It read as under:

"Religion is one of the forms of spiritual oppression, lying everywhere. The helplessness of the exploited classes in their struggle with the exploiters just as inevitably generates faith in a better life beyond the grave as the helplessness of the savage in his struggle with nature produces faith in gods, devils, miracles, etc. To him who works and is poor all his life religion teaches passivity and patience in earthly life, consoling him with the hope of a heavenly reward. To those who live on the labor of others religion teaches benevolence in earthly life, offering them a very cheap justification for all their exploiting existence and selling tickets to heavenly happiness at a reduced price. Religion is opium for the people. (Vladimir Lenin in Thoughts of Lenin about Religion)

The draft was read as under:

"The government of the Soviet Union follows an unofficial policy of state atheism, aiming to gradually eliminate religious belief within our borders since 1930 onwards. While it never officially made religion illegal; the state nevertheless made great efforts to reduce the prevalence of religious belief within society in government agencies. To this end, at various times in its history it engaged in anti-religious persecutions of varying intensity and methodology. Believers were never officially, attacked for being believers, but they were officially attacked for real or perceived political opposition to the state and to its policies. These attacks, however, in the broader ideological context are meant to serve the ultimate goal of eliminating religion. The perceived political opposition acted as a legal pretext to carry this out. Thus, although the Soviet Union was officially a secular state and guaranteed freedom of religion in its constitutions, in practice, believers suffered discrimination and were widely attacked for promoting religion."

"As part of its anti-religious campaigns, the Soviet state enacted a significant body of legislation that regulated and curtailed religious practices. This, along with many secret instructions that were not published, formed the legal basis for the Soviet state's anti-religious stance. Laws were designed in order to hurt and hamper religious activities, and the state often vigilantly watched religious believers for their breaking of these laws to justify arresting them. In some places, volunteer neighbor-hood committees, called "public commissions for control over observance on the laws about religious cults", watched their religious neighbors and reported violations of the law to the appropriate authorities. The state sought to control religious bodies through such laws with the intention of making those bodies disappear. Often such laws incorporated many ambiguities that allowed the state to abuse them in order to persecute believers.

"With this as our primary concern, we have approached to Human Right Commission for justice. We need freedom as living with our faith in Soviet Union is stressful. Government is too much made of laws and words...operated with mind and controls rather than feelings and heart as our religions and the God explain."

All three parties as well few Christian groups from Armenia and Ukrainian Rebel groups had signed that draft.

One of members from SSR of Chechen Republic began:

"We have been an integral component of Soviet Union. We love our land, mountains and do not want to be separate from Soviet Union for few trivial issues that have amicable solutions. (He viewed Mr. President through upper border of frame of his spectacle.) Our Muslim community has not yet, entered in regular stream of Russian Society, devoid of Education, Health facilities and representations in governance. Muslim community does not get posts into Judiciary system, Police department and Administrative stream as well in militaries. Hardly 3% of youth enter into collage. Their voice is unheard and crushed under the shoes of soviet Army. Government agencies hate us. Muslims live poor; did not get priority in rations. Our ladies stand for long hours in queues, ration does not reach to us in time, We are not in priority even though we are in majority in our region by now. As Muslims are feeling insecure and agitated, young blood rebelled and government punished them harsh and sent them to Siberia. We would request to bring them back, release all prisoners of Chechen leaders to fortify our mutual trust. Rebel is named when own citizen try to cry out, to draw attention of government! Actually, they need not, reprisal but sympathy and more caring. (He looked at Dumas.) Otherwise, we love our neighbors. Muslims also favor integrity of social fabrics but they would love to live with their 'own' norms!" (Home Minister whispered to his secretary.)

In response, representative of ROC (Russian Orthodox Church) and some Members of Politburo argued:

Muslims, Christians, Serbians and Slovak people have dwelled in peace since centuries and have family ties. We make a matrix, that we can't shred or grate! Wounds always bleed unless the body has died. None did advocate their religious norms to be instituted till now. Government is secular and we accepted their vision as the foundation of our social integrity. We pay to enjoy fruits from those trees we had not grown! Co-existence is a sign of maturity of Society where giving is more valued than getting! Today, Muslims have been poisoned...they ask more than the most the Government can give. Soviet Union is the biggest nation in world and transport is also a problem. I suggest that 'our Rights shall be titrated with responsibilities we share.' As you have the right to flourish, rest of communities have also the same right and, you can't insist for your laws! 'Sharia' Law!

An officer from Ministry of Internal Affair submitted papers on desk and said: "Here are statistical data; that 'Sia' Muslims community has been already favored in jobs, government employments, in health care and in Maternity care, though Russian Orthodoxy is major denominator in Soviet Union. Presence of Muslims in Army and police is increasing." He paused and ROC member added, "Actually, Christians and Slovaks are deprived of their rights in Ukraine and Armenia."

One member from team of Azerian SSR, made an egoistic remark, "Natural resources of Oil and natural Gas are with 'us'; we produce wheat, maize, barley, potatoes, cotton, grapes, vegetables, fruits and tea and tobacco. As such, we are self-sufficient and still we are with Soviet Union since 1921. Muslim community is in majority at Azerbaijan and we get disproportionate opportunity. We have the first right to use our resources but we deliver oil and gas to Confederation." Community party CPSU members were annoyed.

---

[46] **Secretary of CPSU party:** (He was Gorbochov but author did not know his name in 1974. This is mere coincidence.) He had law degree in 1955 and moved to Stavropol, First, he worked for the Komsomol youth organization and after Stalin's death, became a keen proponent of the de-Stalinization reforms of Soviet leader Nikita Khrushchev. He was appointed the First Party Secretary of the Stavropol Regional Committee in 1970, in which position he oversaw construction of the Great Stavropol Canal. In 1978, he returned to Moscow to become a Secretary of the party's Central Committee, and in 1979 joined its governing Politburo. Within three years of the death of Soviet leader Leonid Brezhnev, following the brief regimes of Yuri Andropov and Konstantin Chernenko, the Politburo elected Gorbachev as General Secretary, the de facto head of government, in 1985.

Although committed to preserving the Soviet state and to its socialist ideals, Gorbachev believed significant reform was necessary, particularly after the 1986 Chernobyl disaster. He withdrew from the Soviet–Afghan War and embarked on summits with United States president Ronald Reagan to limit nuclear weapons and end the Cold War. Domestically, his policy of glasnost ("openness") allowed for enhanced freedom of speech and press, while his perestroika ("restructuring") sought to decentralize economic decision-making to improve efficiency. His democratization measures and formation of the elected Congress of People's Deputies undermined the one-party state. Gorbachev declined to intervene militarily when various Eastern Bloc countries abandoned Marxist–Leninist governance in 1989–1990. Internally, growing nationalist sentiment threatened to break up the Soviet Union, leading Marxist–Leninist hardliners to launch the unsuccessful August Coup against Gorbachev in 1991. In the wake of this, the Soviet Union dissolved against Gorbachev's wishes and he resigned. After leaving office, he launched his Gorbachev Foundation.

One Secretary[46]from CPSU Party's Central Committee raised his hand and light-hearted, open-minded gem of Politburo upon whom everybody had full trust. He got up. He was square-faced, smart and self-made man from Stavropol Regional Committee. He said, "As I feel, what you said so far is that you are not satisfied with what government has paid to you at Azerbaijan, Chechen land and Kazakhstan. But, let me tell you that when you come to Kremlin, talk any word, remember that we talk with only balanced people in conference. Unsatisfied people just put their demands, one after another. Unwise and unintelligent people remain unsatisfied. Values are different and things we extract values from, are different. When matters are converted into values, they become the same, the one. We are Government are wiser than what you understand. If you have paid as you listed, government paid in infra-structure, road and modernization of cities, mining and developments, exploration of Oil in Basins are costlier affairs. We provide protection-the priceless service, medics help and operate various systems so as Dushbara and Plov[47], bread (lavash) or cracked wheat (bulgur) to maize and rice reach to plates in every house. What is the price, do you tag? Being Human means being considerate, first. Thinking of others, first!" (Dumas applauded and they tapped their desk and rebel groups shouted and got furious.)There, we have to safeguard minorities. too. (He was pointing at Armenians living at Karabakh range of Lesser Caucasus and extending up to margin of Kura River law land at its foot.)"

Azerbaijan's representative: Our motherland was independent before 1813, acquired by Russia and incorporated in Soviet Government in 1923 as 'Armenian' majority Autonomous Oblast of Azerbaijan. West to Karabakh range, Nagorno area comes, that is our land. Now, they demand to transfer this oblast (Nagorno-Karabakh Oblast) to Armenian jurisdiction; you can't purchase our land by any means. We will oppose, you can't play. This oblast is

---

[47] **Dushbara and Plov**: Azerbaijan food, former traditional food with meat and herbs; Plov is Rice with meat cuisine.

like an island within Azerbaijan and Armenians were prompted to colonize by Soviet Union. You stop pampering Armenians."

Government officer: It can't terrorize by populating another community just by populating at faster! Incidences of violence, kidnapping and rapes are increasing! People are running away from homes, town and villages. I have a suggestion. Muslims have populated in many nomads. They are happy there and let Armenians be happy at Karabakh. We should remain ONE, as Soviet Union! That is our strength."

The Leader of Chechen Revolutionary group revolted, "If we were the One, then why our leaders are exiled to Siberia? Why you break our unity? Judiciary system is deaf to us. It doesn't take any complaint. You don't recruit us in Military and Judiciary system. We do not represent in higher posts in Police department. It means you don't trust us and you don't incorporate us in Russia."

Azerbaijan representative argued, "See, the world is ruled by Majority, not by loyalty of a few!"

The Minister of Internal Affairs sternly spoke out, "Majority? We stand for our Commune. We will not indulge in majority-minority issue, it's bloody democratic game! We stand for those who respect the nation, stand with us with loyalty and solidarity. And, if I may tell you, you too respect minority. They have their right to exist. **The world without contrast will be boring**, take it from me. (pause) Those who respect our Communist Manifesto are in our concern.

Azerian rep asked, "Why so much hatred for majority?"

Minister of Internal affairs answered, "We don't trust in number games. The crowd may have 'backseat drivers', tell me whom do you represent? Your voice is not yours. (Rebel groups became agitated...) You should be loyal to our treaty of 1922, (Declaration and Treaty on Creation of USSR in 1922). We will strengthen our Socialistic philosophy."

A Cabinet Member from Politburo said, "Many Muslims are misled and instigated for violence. We have come to know that they go to Afghan and Iran, get training and return with arms from terrorist groups. They make bands of mercenaries in various cities or rest of them stay in mountains! You were asking us to sanction higher posts in administration...hmm! Live in peace and let's adhere honestly. When Ukraine will need, we will stand up to defend. When Azerbaijan will have problem, they will look for help from parents. Soviet Union is great nation, like a continent; we have enough for all. Give your cooperation."

Azerbaijan SSR representative interrupted, "We signed 1922 Treaty and made a Union of Soviet Socialistic of Russia so as borders are eased, for crossing of Red Army. Slowly, all our local autonomies were systemically, erased! Azerbaijan used to have own force, now it's gone! We are losing our identity in Soviet Union. Now, you are inviting others- say Slovak and Russian to settle, you recruit them on government jobs and they make permanent residence. We are sacrificing so much for Soviet Union. Now, we have decided to maintain our own cultural and geo-political identity."

The hall became stunned. Experts sitting sighed at in despair. The Azerbaijan representative added, "Fault is not that people are trained, become rebellious; fault lies with your possessiveness about the land and to establish your authority, you don't peace at heart. You are hyperactive and create unrest wherever you have inserted your nose in! Slowly, you want to eradicate the past, history and local folk on long run. You have discrimination so our attitude is a defensive measure. You said of mirrors...yes, we are your mirrors!" Minister of Internal Affairs had no answer, but they breathed heavy. Their arguments were not bad, not far from truth!

After a long silence in that Hall of Conference at Kremlin, the Gen. Secretary from CPSU Party's Central Committee broke the ice, "You know, what trouble we have. Other Governments have 'one eye' to look at its people, but we have 'hundred eyes'! (All laughed out. Secretary was so much, loved by Mr. President and Home Minister that they laughed loud and tapped the conference table.) Naturally, we have problem in brain...current passing here and there...bit of chaos...inside our head! That is why we use our heart, not our brain! (All were silent became serious.) See, we listen with hundreds of ears and speak with just one mouth. That is the smartness of Communist Party. What you have talked, we have reviewed before coming to this hall. You are not talking 'something new'. We don't give you a piece of our brain...no logics, paper works...arguments, legality...can deviate us. We offer you our heart or we reject you. A mother may punish a mischievous child, even though he is right. We look at the rights of weaker sections too. We look at your background, loyalty, intelligence and wisdom before you enter in governance! Government posts are not like ponds...that it can be filled with dirty waters. It's rightly said, that when we get rough roads...we must revise our plans...probably, you have chosen wrong path. Your stubborn attitude might have inhibited government in giving you desired posts in administration. I understand that there are genuine loyal people all over and we will respect them. If their applications are neglected then, I will look in that matters and they will be selected for administrative posts in Judiciary, police and government offices."

A secretary, PMO said, "Here I have something to show." Everyone became attentive. "We spent about 18% of budget from Home Ministry to uplift Muslims of Ukraine, Azerbaijan, Kazakhstan and Chechen republic. It's a huge amount. Then, we increased the funding up to 21 % in 1986- for schools and collage, for Primary health centers at grass root level and built hospitals with free medical services to 'your' pregnant women and most of benefits go to your community!" Someone shouted, "What do you mean 'your' pregnant women? Hmm...?" Secretary answered with poise, "It's number game, my brother! Maximum benefit will reach to whom, you tell me? You are flourishing; you should thank us! (Many Dumas chuckled.) Now, in just 3 years, you ask more sanctions worth 25% of total budget."

One voice came, "Crude Oil! We provide crude oil in return." A Muslim representative of Ukraine raised his hand to draw attention. His long 'thin' face with dark thick spectacles and thin white beard depicted him ugly. He reiterated, "You are not obliging. Take an account of oil from our seashore; as well metals and minerals from Kazakhstan and grains from Ukraine that feeds almost whole of Russia. What you do for us in repayment is not enough." Most of Ministers of Politburo had one single thought, 'to shoot that guy!' The leader of Chechen Republic added shamelessly, "Our people are starving... leaders are dying...being exiled. Their judicial cases are kept, pending... women and families are crying...look at our tears, not words, Mr. President!"

Mr. President was now furious, he whispered, "Shame!" He got up and last statement was, "See, what others do not have, what they don't get! Don't keep crying, making noise, we have many matters to address. If somewhere we have missed something, take it as unintentional. Remember. CPSU never wants to trouble any community, unless it's behaving like traitors. Take it from me." He left the hall. Azerbaijan leader raised voice so Mr. President could listen at, "Our demands are just pea-nuts against the oil you extracted so far! If something happens to our oil pipes, tomorrow then only, you will heed at our problems."

Secretary from Home Minister office fumed and said, "For sure, we can sanction troops to deliver what you asked so far." Suddenly, the Chechen and Azerian group stood up saying, "We will receive them with 'open arms'." Hall became shocked again. The meeting was adjourned for a second date.

*

Eye of Yogi also, returned fast from Golden Gate of Kremlin, here, Yogi returned and opened his eyes at Siberia. It was 4.00 am and First day of Yogi was over. He too, sighed and sent his first day remark to his Masters at Gyan-Ganj, as under:

"I had never ever experienced such puzzle of human ambitions at crosswords, since last 700 years! I have returned after a long gap, and it's difficult for me to reconcile human issues. I have no past memories of this world, this society. To me, everything is painful. (Yestlin noted tears pouring out.) Their pains are unbearable to me, tales of ghosts were sickening, to wedge myself in your State is

156

a serious issue, I understand. Often I feel like to withdraw from Human Society but the purpose with what my Great Masters have sent me compel me to live forwards. Otherwise, you have built a very painful society. People 'breed' to populate the nations like fungi, bacteria or virus and pigs! Lol!! They want to consume whole world and they call it ruling! It shall be called devouring. Another type of human race wants to rule the world with power and intelligence. They have weapons. Both of them will die of discontent because the Mother Nature and this planet had been faithful to none! Ultimately, all of them will be buried under the ruins of cities."

Yestlin noticed real pain of a divine saint what he had to tolerate when he had arrived after 700 years with no retrograde memories or convictions to navigate in this human society. He stared at Yogi, noticed very slow breathing of his Master; as if he was dying! Yestlin was also, frozen white, blank and too silent and chilling! He had a bad dream. He saw a chaos coming up to their land. Long long queues at stores for bread, grains, goods and kerosene. He saw people on streets, guards chasing and even firing at them. He saw fragmentation of Soviet Union after military operations at various terrines of Soviet Union. He saw whole of Soviet Union was submerged in darkness!

Yogi said, "Don't dream; don't presume. Emotions and presumptions blind your inner eye, here!" He placed a finger on center of forehead. Yogi was serious and he explained, "I saw, Yestlin what is going on in Kremlin. The days are not going smooth, military will march in many states...and it will erode faith in Soviet Union." Yestlin looked at him intently; he admitted that he had seen such a dream.

Yogi said, "I am worried from where I am going to start. They have enough of their own problems...and I am going to add one more. I am not related to you or the authority anyway;why should I meddle? Should I stir an ocean?" Yestlin smiled at Yogi and asked childishly, "How are you going to bring Golden Era, then? Are you going to create autonomous group of Siberia to rebel?

Yogi chuckled, "You are wiser now." Both laughed.....the laughter echoed in Siberian plains. Yogi uttered:

"Their local problems are not 'real' problems. Let them finish unbalanced internal accounts, meanwhile we will awaken the society. We want people to be eligible for Grace of God and then, they will enter in New World Order. As far as I am concerned, I must pay first then I can begin a new game."Yestlin did not understand a word so far.

[THIS IS THE END OF FIRST DAY OF YOGI AT SIBERIA. 4 AM TO 4 AM NEXT DAY.]

4

D: Welcome to Our Hell

Day 2:

[From 4 AM to 12 midnight]

17. Earth is not our permanent Address!

Yestlin notes:

"We started for medical center at about 4 AM and crossed Taiga Forest[48]. I was stunned at beautiful Light and Shadows game played by branches and leaves of trees with sunrise. The Light showered through leaves. Clouds were sleeping, yet and they slowly got awakened, began to rise. Yogi whispered in my ear, 'You are blessed, Yestlin! You have got Siberia, the Heaven of Soviet Union!! Who would like to chop trees, kill bears?" He looked at Yestlin who answered, "Only the fools!'

Yogi explained, "Divine life is reflected from everything that surrounds. Man should learn to find God from very existence. Look at the shadows; they exhibit presence of Light and its significance. The God prefers to present Himself in indirect manners. Do not complain for shadows; focus on showers of Light. Shadows beautify the scene. That way, you will be grateful to all troubles in your life, as they exhibit the Spray of Light beams. Even Lord Sun needs dark amber around to shine. Contrasts are must in life; Thunderstorms may bring rain. Nights bring dawn! Don't keep focus at mud, but find the lotus! Find the good, from every condition! Bad and good co-exist to make zero! Ultimate experience of life is 'Zero'- nothing is taken from here so far,

---

[48] Taiga means pure or untouched in Russian language. Retreating glaciers from the last ice age smoothed much of the taiga land mass. High plains cover most of the area with some mountain ranges dotted throughout. The soil underneath the taiga is often contains permafrost , in other areas layers of bedrock lies underneath the soil ,but they both prevent water from draining from the top layer of soil. The Taiga (Boreal) Forest has several characteristics; first is their evergreen trees or coniferous trees (spruce, pine, and fir). Coniferous trees have needles instead of broad leaves and their seeds grow inside protective, woody cones. Needles have less water so, in cold, they don't go frozen otherwise, leaves would drop out. Mammals living in the taiga include foxes, lynxes, bears, minks, squirrels, while larger ones include grey wolves and their prey such as caribou, reindeers and moose. Taiga forest stretches from Ural Mountains in West in sub-arctic region in North to westwards, at Tundra Forests.

except the experiences! Sum total of your pains and gains in life make Zero! Life is zeroed with death!" Master ended.

Yestlin had noted later, "Actually, what I search in life will hide behind the leaves and branches. If I surrender to Mother Nature, my Light will seek me, will follow me and reach to me at end. It's in Process of Nature.

If we have complaints, then our focus is over the mud, darkness and so we will enter in darkness. Life is the Game of Shadows. Flip the shadow and find your Light. Leave all the mess and soar high to come to me! I am waiting. This planet is not yours!! This Planet is not your permanent Address. Don't spend time kidding with the Time, dark shadows scattered all around. – Yestlin.

*

'It was dawn and my heart beats were raised. 'It was my day!' He thought. Till then, time was as if, frozen, but Yestlin was getting nervous and treulous! What will happen next, was his puzzle. It was a full moon in West and East was fired up on horizon. The clouds that had rested on Taiga Forest trees, whole night began to move like sleeping kids turn and twist in bed. Slowly, cold breeze began from East and clouds began to drift to West. Yogi stood with

help of a creeper on a tree and became a part of picturesque scene! Yestlin looked down in valley and found the realm of Snow. 'The Siberia is as dead as a Graveyard.' he noted. There, Yogi was happy at frozen trees of forest.

Soon, they crossed dense forest of Taiga and Yestlin saw algae and fungi brewing on still waters in ponds- Siberian bog[49]. Yogi was exalted with first

---

[49]Probably, Siberian Bog is the first evidence of beginning of Life on our planet.

161

darshana or glance at Sun from hilltop; He whispered at Yestlin, "Sun is your Heavenly Abode. We all arrived from there. Yestlin, always wake up early, observe for sunrise, recall me what I said, 'It's your true home. and Sun is your Father!' And, you belong to Him, not to Earth! Then, you will never play in soil and desire of worldly gain. You will always rise in every moment, a step higher than where you are! We came here to express His divine attributes, we hold in Genes our parents have given as endowment. Then after, you should aim to return back to Sun. Earth is not our permanent residence; you can't take anything from here."

Yestlin argued, "But, Earth is so beautiful and all elements here, are in full exposition, that man is tempted to wonder here, love every flower. Even carbon takes form of diamonds here and vapors role over as clouds, rain and become rivers and oceans. Air is fragrant and soil is the final destination of every life, we embrace the soil of Mother Earth. What to say for Gold and Silver, whole mankind is running after them? Oceans also, yield pearls, see and...they hold so beautiful sea life!"

Yogi added, "Sea gave nectar, also to us but, still I say, that all are the raw matters! They help to understand who you are! Everest peak invites the all; all climb and reach there. But, do they make their residence there? They return to their home soon. Everest gave them a chance to express their endurance, strength and valor.

Every beauty here is its own innocent expression; stars in space express themselves! They all say that, 'you too, are beautiful, so shiny, a star in yourself.' And a man usually, seek his identity from reflections! He asks to all, "Who am I?" and hopes for smile and appreciations from others. If I smile at you, you will feel 'good'! Look around and feel that you too are a flower; you too, are a star, a diamond or a pearl! These soil, stones and sand provide you raw matters so as you can make your nest, you livelihood and your reflection. Nature gives you chances to show your intelligence, prudence, virtues and powers. At the end of day, you're your play is over; there, the Sun invites you! He says, "Come

On!" He belongs to you. One day, you will have to reach there as Ethereal form, on Heavenly Abode! Otherwise, you will take birth and die, repeatedly here."

Yestlin did not understand a word, stood blank for a moment and then he found Yogi was moving downhill now. They were reaching to a village (Nomad).

"My Master taught me following principles:

Actually, what I search in life will seek me, will follow me and reach to me at end, in 'its' time. I need to have Perseverance on my activities and path as well Patience if I have Faith in Process of Nature. Till then, I should stay 'alert' with hope.

In this game of shadows, whatever comes as shadow or light, accept gracefully. Stay focus over root source of Light, the Lord Sun! And, meanwhile, let me flow over like a river. Life is itself, a flow, a current (Detachment initiates a flow. It gives you Ananda!)- Life that way, is without a gain or loss!

Nature plays with shadows and root source is Sun; while life is a game of detachment and flow. Go on rolling that gives Ananda and you will reach to higher conscience. Reach to Everest peak and get ananda and return to base camp. Adhere not to earthen clay; it will make you dirty, and add worry as everything created is dying!"–Yestlin.

*

A small nomad was sleeping down there in a valley and now, Yestlin became nervous. His worry surfaced up, 'what will happen to him.' He intelligently began to talk to Yogi, "I heard a small incidence. A farmer's dog used to chase every car that passed on highway. A man watching him, thought, "Even if that dog catches a car, what will it do?" The saint stopped, turned back to see him with piercing eyes and smiled and continued walking.

163

Yestlin continued," Let me frankly ask. Do you truly, mean to give me anti-rabies vaccine or you have your agenda, there? (Pause) Even if, you make the authority sit in front of you; you can request them to release rest of prisoners. Words are just words...feather like! What magic your words will create? Even if you catch the govern, what are going to do?"

The saint didn't look behind, continued walking and gave answer in whisper. "It's the call of Mother Nature. I am posted as the Catalyst. Justice must reach to person in time. It's high time for justice to prevail. Pending files will be closed soon."

Yestlin asked, "So...you won't initiate a rebel group?"

Yogi looked in the eyes of Yestlin, stern faces and continued to walk and whispered, "No. Violence and Hatred change the heads. Swords just, change the hands! That is not the way to eliminate violence from the mankind. It's like cleansing a street to dump up rubbish at seashore!!"

Yestlin was curious then and asked again,"I don't see any of my role...then why I am walking with you?" Master shrugged shoulder and said, "Come and lead me on!" He smiled at Yestlin and later was confused. The bark of street dogs drew his attention. That was followed by a neigh from a free horse that had bulging flanks and muscular hindquarter muscles. He walked straight to Yogi, was looking beautiful and Yogi greeted the horse. As it came closer; it moved its neck up and down and snorted. Yogi pulled its reins, brought closer, placed his right hand on forehead to bless it. Then, he palpated its throatlatch then neck, played with his thick mane and withers. Horse was puffing vapors and tried to take hand of Yogi in its mouth! They were about to enter in a village street and dogs were there to welcome them! Yogi smiled at Yestlin, "Be ready, Yestlin! Your Exam time has come!"

*

18. The Medical Center:

It was half past five of morning and two strangers were slowly

moving in search of Health Centre. The people in their houses were sleeping. Dogs were silently walking behind, as if escorting them. Few windows were shut down as a few civilians must have seen them coming. The way to Medical Center was uphill. On left, there was a steep valley covered with snow, deep down was the running river making soothing, relaxing and blissful sounds. Somewhere, river made lapping sound with gurgling. It was frozen at many places. The Saint pointed at river and said, "Waterways are good way to travel, Yestlin!" Yestlin smiled at him but became more confused. There, at the end of road, was a primary health centre. The frozen village was

ghostly in early hours in Siberia. They knocked the door of Health Center, waited and then entered in the medical centre, as there was no activity. It was early morning.

A female nurse walked out from the next room, half sleepy and with red eyes. She was amazingly 'feminine'! She saw wrist cuffs of Yestlin; then raised her gaze to study Yestlin, was surprised to see him in normalcy. She came to her full consciousness, then. She whispered inside, "So, he have come!"

Yogi said," Sister, he has dog bites..., needs vaccine."

She questioned Yestlin with harsh commanding voice, "Who is he? (She pointed at Yogi.) Then, she examined Yestlin for bites and they had healed. She asked, "Why did you escape?" Yestlin became emotional, "They killed my mother, wrongly, sent me to Siberia, sister. I am innocent sister!" (Those words were as if for begging mercy, that Yogi did not like.) She turned at Yogi and asked, "Who is 'he'?" She stared at Yogi with stone face. Yogi again, reminded to question later on and said, "He needs Vaccine, first. Question answer session, we may take later on!" She was annoyed and asked stern voice to Yogi, "Who are you?"Yogi smiled a little, while she walked in her next room, whispering, 'Wait, coming!' Yestlin could listen at breaking of ampoules, then there was a silence and then, she asked Yestlin to lay down on table with Macintosh cover. Meanwhile, she came out rushing, thrust a large syringe in his buttock through his pant and injected about 4 cc of drugs speedily. (A rabies vaccine is just one cc. per dose, only.) Yogi was alarmed, looked intently in her eyes (He could see, she had informed police on phone.) Yogi sharply, asked, "4 cc. Morphine[50] you injected!" She whispered, "I relieved him from all pains!" She smiled at Yogi. "I know everything, he jumped from running train." Yogi heard a police wagon slowly, humming uphill to medical center! A band of security guards was marching taking position around the medical center. She laughed at Yogi saying, "Now, your turn!" pointing at upcoming police and became proud of herself. Yogi turned to her, made an attempt to slap on her left cheek violently; she turned her face to left to withdraw, to escape from that sharp slap. She felt dead![51] Yestlin could see this

---

[50]<u>Faults when a nurse injected 4 amps. Morphine as bolus</u>: Yestlin had no pain, then, why morphine? Intentional?(First crime) Four ampoules! 40 mg Morphine, a lethal dose!As a bolus injection? She wanted to kill.(a second crime) Being a Nurse, she discriminated a good man and bad man! Against humanity? (Third crime) You became judgmental, though there was an order, as she said. (Fourth crime) And, she was a woman; sympathy and caring were expected, whensecond person had brought the wanted person! She was expected wisdom, a good cultured woman always show! (Forth crime.)

[51]Yogi's right hand did not touch her face but her violent and abrupt twisting of neck broke her cervical spine and she immediately fell dead! She had broken her cervical spine!

event but, hazily. He was 'sinking' because of high dose of Morphine, respiration became slow, eyes gloomy and he felt suffocation. Yogi saw him getting cyanosed. His eyes got wide opened! He was unable to speak, by then. Luckily, nurse had injected lethal dose intramuscularly!

Yogi had time; he quickly, rolled Macintosh (A rubber sheet cover placed over examination dressing table over Yestlin, packed him up tightly, thrust the table top from below to detach from its legs, took few bandages and tied Yestlin, wrapped in rubber sheet with table top. Yogi was giving instructions rapidly, to 'sinking' Yestlin, "You will reach to Wombick, Remember. Tell him, it's the time to leave caves and come with all, at Prison." Yestlin observed his Master blankly who continued his orders, "You will sleep now, your respirations will stop...better you enter in Samadhi!" He, gracefully placed his right thumb on his forehead; Yestlin got a divine current that blanked his consciousness, his body jerked and became as silent as dead. Yogi immediately, lifted table top, with that Yestlin wrapped in Macintosh (the Human Parcel), opened the window on backside of medical centre and glided the red colored (Macintosh color was red.) 'human' parcel through the window over slope of hill. It glided immediately and Yestlin reached to bottom of valley, where a river was flowing. The Human parcel entered in that snow covered river. Red parcel was carried away swiftly in torrential current, dangling. It twisted and then disappeared. Yogi saw the red mackintosh submerged in river and then entered deep inside the glaciers. Yestlin began his horrifying journey through sub-glacial and en-glacial water channels. There were lot of ramifications, tree like channels, many waterfalls inside glaciers; many rocks in under surface tumbled his board.

He was moving fast, wobbling, tumbling and hitting sharp edges of snow (Board took care of.) His body was relaxed by morphine, his muscles and joints were almost flaccid so body was twisting frantically. The wood sheet was making a way through thick ice, but it would last for a while only! Then, Macintosh would wither and then Yestlin as a dead body would continue his journey through rough underground- Sub-glacial passage[52].

Here, the medical center was secured by police; Yogi, viewing the river with tears in eyes, was easily arrested. Police rushed down in valley in search of Yestlin! They looked at wild horizon and found vast field of glaciers. Dead body of the nurse was secured, was not to be subjected to post-mortem examination because of various dubious reasons. Yogi was accessed, ill-treated, inquired why he killed the nurse and Yogi remained silent. There

were no injury marks on that nurse! Next moment, van proceeded towards Prison of Gulag.

---

[52]**Passage through Glaciers:** Stretch your imagination now. (1) After ice age, most of glaciers melted leaving behind valley in between two rows of mountains. Actually, glaciers were formed by thawing of waters or snow that filled valleys. They erode, make sediments and carry them down from mountains. That is how we find unusually large stones (rocks) in valleys. (2) Temperate glacial ice is Deformable due to frequent thawing and cooling, in response to changes in pressures, melting of passage walls by heat generated by viscous dissipation and expansion and contraction of passage by pressure of ice slabs. Passage of waters under glacier is determined by topography of glacial bed. Network of passages tends to become arborescent (tree-like), with (1) **a super-glacial part** like an ordinary river, (2) **an en-glacial part** – tree like system penetrating the ice from bed to surface and (3) **sub-glacial part-** consisting of tunnels carrying water and sediments. Waters may thaw, sediments settle to create eskers (long, narrow, sinuous ridges). There is a sheet-like smooth basal water layer under glacier allowed Yestlin to glide swiftly through spiral networks of water channels. Yestlin was near dead and so he passed through such a horrible terrain.

[This way, Yogi replaced himself in place of Yestlin; though he didn't wanted to enter in human society. A man with higher vibrations reached to a level of complex human mind, logics and arguments.]

*

19. 'Welcome to our Hell!'

A police wagon was running 27 miles North-east of the nomad. It began to cross a thin strip of land across a frozen lake on either side. As it was summer, waters were less so, strip of land was usable as passage. It stopped at a huge building with gate made of thick iron bars. The Prison was surrounded by lake that remains frozen throughout the year. Security guards at the iron-gate were surprised to see anew arrival, a holy saint, coming out of wagon, wrist-locked! He smiled at guards, who bowed a little! Yogi looked up over the height of the prison, thought a little, sighed and entered in. He looked around the security and turned around to notice so isolated prison was. A security guard commented to next fellow, "Is he a prisoner? Not a criminal, I am sure! Not, even Russian citizen!"

Second guard whispered, "Police sometimes, catches a wrong prey! Stupid!! Rats have made a hole in basket of a snake!" They chuckled.

Third guard whispered, "This person is not an ordinary person, a holy monk."

First guard said, "We have seen battered prisoners, crying, hesitant; guards used to pull them like a pig. While this gentle man smiled and looked around before entering. They should understand his intention.

Forth guard whispered, "I think, this monk must be stupid, why to come to this slaughter house? Actually, everyone who is admitted here ascended vertically!"

There, they saw dark clouds looming in Far East. (It was unusual to see such dark clouds in morning hours in Siberia.) The prison inside was relatively dark, damp, stinging and unhygienic. Light had gone off since last 36 hours and there were few fire torches[53], mounted in walls of prison lobby. In the office, there

---

[53] A wooden stick with ragged clothes wrapped at the top. Then it was dipped

were few candles, also. Jailor opened a ragged register[54],flipped pages. Yogi saw many names that were stricken through red lines. ('They must have been dead.'). On last few pages, many names were scribbled at corners of page. New separate pages were added loose. Here, registration of Yogi began.

"Name?"

"Yogi." (Jailor looked at Yogi in anticipation for full name.)

"No father, no surname, now." (Jailor was not able to understand.)

"Yogi" (Yogi repeated with very composed gesture & stable voice.

"Address?"

"Himalaya!" Pen stopped. He looked at him intently, took time and said, "O Man, you are at wrong place at wrong time!"

Yogi: Sun does not come up, unless it's dawn.

Another assistant was observing smiling face of Yogi...He asked, "Why you came here?" Yogi smiled innocently at them and said, "Just for you!" A shock wave spread in corners of whole prison! Prisoners were able to listen at conversation. "Who sent you- Human Rightists?"

"What is that?" (He nodded.) "I hear these words for first time. You mean, human rightists are those who ask rights for humans from humans; is it so? Either they are silly or you, as human admins are." (He chuckled.) Jailor dropped his pen, spread his hand on his bald scalp and nodded, "Good! Humorous you are! (pause) Why you came here, tell us in detail. Speak out whatever you want to speak."

---

in animal fat oil and was alit and kept on walls.

[54] Register was ragged: It was old, unorganized register. None has taken care about entry and exits, higher officers did not checking about valid entries. It was not maintained year wise.

"I have come from Himalaya, we reside in caves in ethereal bodies sometimes. My Himalayan Masters heard the cries from Siberia; I have come to inquire out of empathy. Second reason is major. Something great is going to occur from Siberia. (All guards leaned forwards to hear the Himalayan Yogi.) Stars are going to be born, Lord Sun will bless here, and Era of Pious Land will begin. We are passing through a bottle neck area. We feel compression. Many will be eliminated. Mankind will be purified soon. So, I have come with message of love and a request to release all prisoners, they had paid you enough by now- through sweats, through their tears and through flesh and blood!" – Yogi.

Prisoners rose in their cubicles of prisons, tears began to shower from stony faces and dried eyes; a ray of Hope had warmed up their frozen slow hearts! Someone whispered, "If he is wrong, then he is a mouse talking with a lion!"Others believed and prayed to Lord, 'His words shall come true.' The security officers across table were frozen, missed breaths for about a full minute! Pin-drop silence prevailed. Then, officer wrote down whole statement from Yogi. They were blank for a long time; later they tried to find out who is behind Yogi. They had not found any papers from Yogi. Jailor asked, "How did you come here?"

"Via sea-route, from India! Came by boat and, it's there near that village at seashore (Magadan)!" Jailor and many could not digest that information, 'Can a man travel thousands of miles across sea, over a tiny boat?' The writer made a remark in his note. He was writing everything prisoner was saying.

The Jailor closed down his register and sternly said, at Yogi, "If your information is wrong, see what I will do. Many crimes, you have committed in just one day and you talk of innocence. You are an enemy of states, to our land. You protected an escaped exiled prisoner; killed 'our' dear, nurse! (Few guards smiled at extra love of Jailor!) Her ghost will kill you."

Yogi said," I had a few, you have millions of crimes by now, how will you escape, how will you repay, if Mother Nature starts giving you judgment?" Fear of Unknown loomed in hearts of interviewers. Two wardens were annoyed and punched Yogi from behind, at head and shoulder blades. Treatment was started.

The noise of sliding iron grills, snapping of gates, walking with thick shoes alerted whole prison. All prisoners came to their grills to watch a man from Himalaya, who travelled across sea to reach for them, into Siberia! They saw three men entering in corridor. A rose fragrance suddenly spread all over that delighted all prisoners. Wardens walking with Yogi spread away and walked with distance. The scene was spectacular. Guards were

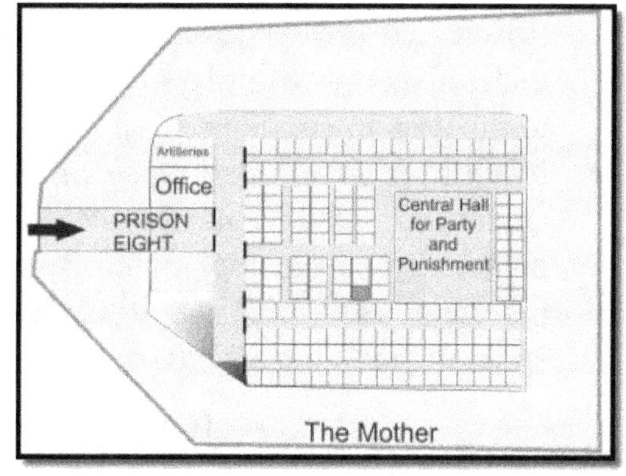

in dark figures and surprisingly, the Yogi was having extreme glare! They saw glory of Lord walking, blessings of their prayers flowing in corridor! As the saint walked slowly, silently, with dignity, he was just like a lion. The sounds of his chains were though rhythmic like a bell from church; the corridor of prison resonated the sound his chains, though it was disheartening.

Most of prisoners knew that none had escaped from here; none was released so far in a single piece! Only the dead had exited from their prison! They closed their eyes to pray mercy for this divine bird that has flown from the heaven!

Meanwhile, a mad prisoner came into him as if, driving his bike in corridor, making humming sound of vehicle and putting tongue out, spraying saliva from mouth. He crossed Yogi and wardens then he turned back, imaginarily parked his bike and began to observe Yogi from all around. (The guards chuckled at his madness.) began to study Yogi from head to toe, from front to behind. Soon, he came over the face, eyes met with his eyes and looked at the hand-cuffs of Yogi and cried loudly saying, "So... 'you' arrived at last! Bloody people will never understood divinity, innocence, the beauty of life and the piousness." He laughed out mad and whispered in ear of Yogi, "Why came here, hmm? You can't do anything here. Anyway, it's nice to see you, here." He greeted Yogi with laughter, embraced Yogi (So, fortunate!) and began to cry on his shoulder!! Then, in broken words he uttered,

"An eagle has landed from heavens to inspect our Prison." He bowed down and picked up the calves of Yogi and whispered with tears, "You have taken so much pain to meet us in condemnation here! Thank you, Sire! *Well taken* (our cries), *well received* (their complaints, sighs, curses to Communism), *well answered* (you came personally!), *welcome*, my Lord to our Hell!" He clung to his legs and cried a little. He began to sing his spontaneous song as under:

Welcome to our Hell!

Sun shone in darkest cells
Blinding us and wardens mad,
World will see what will be the next!
Welcome, Yogi! Welcome to our Hell!!

Our cried, you well heard
And, Prayers Answered well!
Blood and tears well registered in Heavens today.
Welcome, Yogi! Welcome to our Hell!!

Shine Lord Sun, Shine furiously in Hell,
Late you are and have miles to go, mind you well."

Then, Albee whispered in right ear of Yogi, "None came to see us where we are dying." He kissed Yogi's locked hands; a guard slammed the butt of gun on left side of forehead of Albee[55], the Mad Prisoner, who fell unconscious in hands of Yogi. Yogi gracefully placed his right hand over his vortex and left of forehead to heal his scars of frontal lobe of brain. Albee was extremely an emaciated prisoner on the verge of death, 'fully' starved. He was an entertainer to wardens and jailor, by his exceptional wit and he was given food, just so as he would survive. He was allowed to wonder in Prison, to remind other prisoners of their potential fate if they didn't work as per schedules.

Every morning, prisoners were taken to work in vast fields of Siberia- may it be to build bridges, to construct roads in forests or villages or Nomads. Many were sent to mines and Trans-Siberian Railway line was built by such prisoners, against their will! Their breakfast was given there, at working place. That way, those who were ready to work would get breakfast. Rest of prisoners who failed to come to field was starved in prison. Food was proportionate to their work output. If they failed to finish daily work, they would work with a single hot drink cup till late in night in snow storms or in thunders; even though, they might develop frostbites or die. Many a times, they would return to prison late in midnight, hungry and they would fall asleep like dead to get up

---

[55]**Albee**: He was a 52 years of age, post-graduate in Commerce, consultant to Planning Commission of State at Kiev, Ukraine. In Stalin Era, he was framed by seniors, for his visionary statement-
'The Economy follows the Rules of Waters! Waters percolate to lowest levels. Waters flow in sinus rhythm; makes waves and waves may collide with eachother; water level of an ocean remains constant for each country and civilization. Government should see that economy should not be concentric; it will create whorls and may sink the nation. Forces of Nature and waters can't be controlled, can be channelized to our advantage and passed over to next generation.'
That advice was sufficient for Communist party to label him pro-America and 'anti-national'. To approve patriotism was the burden of the accused. Biased Communist Party sent him to Exile. Here, he was regularly tortured until he became mad. He was getting regular hits on left of his forehead as a part of experimental study by a crooked medical doctor. His madness was recreational for wardens. "Welcome to our Hell!"

again at 6 morning! Those weak prisoners, starved for a day would be ready to go to work next morning. Nights were deadlier. The stonewalls would freeze in sub-zero temperature, a crust of snow would appear, urine pool in corner of cell would also freeze and prisoners would sleep embracing each other, adhere to each other for warmth, for survival. Those wardens would hit them hard and keep separate to freezing level. Those who show disrespect to wardens, would be tortured in presence of all prisoners and might be killed! That was to intimidate and depress other prisoners. That was a hell, and Albee was singing!

*

Yogi was left in the dark cubicle. The vision from behind bars was different, it was like a bird viewing from the cage! It was 'spectacular'! He smelt urine, excreta, blood and meat spread around! It was dark and atmosphere was just like a freeze, 4-7 degrees Centigrade! It took time to see the things around and found many curious faces of prisoners from next cubicles, eager to talk to him. In very dim light, it was easy to listen than to see others. Yogi closed his eyes and his divine vision reached to Albee, who was still lying unattended, on chilled frozen floor! It was great that he always recovered to charming personality as before.

One prisoner began conversation, "shh...Are you from India?" Someone said, "I don't think you are a conspirator, anti-national, invader and so on...!" Third voice came, "Why have you come here? You could have gone anywhere, but not to Russia, not in Siberia and worst, not to Prison Eight. Now, you will not be able return." Yogi remained silent and he was making a tour inside the prison. He was stretching his inner vision across the prison....he could enter all cubicles, went across iron frames...went upstairs, saw all prisoners. There was an operation theatre with blood stained instruments in trays. There, he noted a trained doctor doing frontal Lobectomy to punish a violent prisoner. He reached to a corridor where only women were kept; they were malnourished and terrified like guinea pigs in a laboratory. Dead silence prevailed all over. He opened his tearful eyes.There were hundreds of prisoners all around.

A voice came from a dark corner, "What have you achieved in coming here?" Yogi has returned to his consciousness. Another old prisoner intervened, "Don't joke." Then, he came closer to his grill and asked with politeness, "I have heard you. It's great to see you here, you have dived from Himalayan heights to Siberian Cell. There has to be strong reason, I am asking you; but you should have some backup to protect you. They will ascertain what you said, then frame many crimes against you, you may not have imagined and then they will order your fate. How will you defend you?"

Yogi gave a smile in response. Meanwhile, Albee had recovered a bit, did not stand up, crawled to Yogi and saint asked him sympathetically," You said this prison as Hell...so they got annoyed and gave a hit!" Albee nodded. He got closer by crawling, to the iron grill and whispered, "Why you have come here?" He again whispered, "Devils dare not enter, they would rush out from here and you as a fool, have entered! How can I say you are a wise person? You call yourself as a Himalyan Yogi! This is the most defamed prison of Gulag Camp[56] in Siberia. What are you going to achieve from Communism? Here, gardeners shaved off trees to level of shrubs...everyone should be equal here!This is the rule of Commune according to Marx Theory. Ideology was distorted by Lenin."

---

[56]**GULAG Camp 1:** Russian acronym for Main Administration of Camps, a branch of the <u>NKVD</u> (Previous name of KGB) dedicated to the running of Soviet slave labour camps. By extension, the term is also used to describe the network of camps over which the Gulag presided. The Gulag was conceived in order to transform human matter into a docile, exhausted, ill-smelling mass of individuals living only for themselves and thinking of nothing else but how to appease the constant torture of hunger, living in the instant, concerned with nothing apart from evading kicks, cold and ill treatment.All human emotions—love, friendship, envy, concern for one's fellow man, compassion, longing for fame, honesty—had left them with the flesh that had melted from their bodies...

Yogi asked innocently, "What is Communism, according to Marx and why it was distorted, what is Leninism?" An old man, namely 'Zorcov', torn out by starvation and extreme labor, with thick beard and rough skin of face and shrunken eyes, began to narrate from a cell exactly across the corridor, The Communist Manifesto, section II. It all started by inequalities between classes of society. Richer were the most powerful and didn't care for poor. So, this Mutation came in place, that eliminated Czars and rich class. Here, if I go, if you want to understand:

2.2.1: Communist Manifesto II and gulag camps:

1. Abolition of property in land and application of all rents of land to public purposes: (That way, people lost charm of properties and personal development.) (Completely implemented in the USSR)

2. A heavy progressive or graduated income tax: (USSR went way further by implementing government pay scale for all, removing any income from private activity.)

3. Abolition of all rights of inheritance: (This one was almost implemented, since there was no private ownership of means of production left. Inheritance was retained only in a sense that the government would still allow children to live in the apartment where parents used to live.)

4. Confiscation of the property of all emigrants and rebels: (That one was complete by mid 1920-s)

5. Centralization of credit in the banks of the state, by means of a national bank with state capital and an exclusive monopoly: (Nationalization of banks was complete in the early 1920s.)

6. Centralization of the means of communication and transport in the hands of the state: (No private communication or transportation means except for an occasional private car owner illegally acting as black market taxi.)

7. Extension of factories and instruments of production owned by the state; the bringing into cultivation of waste land and the improvement of the soil generally in accordance with a common

plan. (Fully implemented in the USSR (Example: Virgin Lands program in Kazakhstan, 1955-1965)

8. Equal obligation of all to work: Establishment of industrial armies, especially for agriculture/ Failure to work (to have a government job) was a crime in the USSR. Joseph Brodsky was imprisoned for exactly that, since he claimed he was a poet, but the judge said 'you did not have a job.' so he was guilty.

9. Combination of agriculture with manufacturing industries

    (a) Gradual abolition of all the distinction between town and country by a more equable distribution of the populace over the country,

    (b) The most difficult of them all, but finally implemented in the USSR by the 1970-s with full scale transition from collective farms (kolkhoz) where at least some relation between productivity and pay was retained, to soviet farms (sovkhoz) where agricultural workers received salaries just like their industrial counterparts

10. Free education for all children in public schools: Abolition of children's factory labor in its present form. Combination of education with industrial production etc. (The last sentence is the key here. Industrial production was an integral part of education in the USSR. Starting at 15, most of the students were moved from regular schools to "technical" schools where curriculum was heavily slanted towards machining, lathing, etc. Pupils would spend significant portion of their time at work, rather then, in a classroom.)Those were Marx's ideas, but distorted by Lenin.

Lenin reviewed: History marched on an "inevitable" path from hunter-gatherer to slavery to feudalism to capitalism to imperialism to socialism and finally to communism. He stated that each of these stages morphed into the next stage when they were fully mature and through a process, he called 'class struggle'. Lenin believed that, although Russia had only just shaken off feudalism and was barely, capitalist (although it was imperialist) this stage could be "telescoped" - shortened - allowing for a socialist revolution. His other major revision was that although Marx claimed that the peasantry was always conservative and would support the existing regime; the workers would be the motor of the socialist revolution. Lenin realized that because in Russia the working class was so small then the peasants also had to be part of the socialist revolution. Marxism-Leninism is, therefore an alliance of workers and peasants.

*

Albee continued, "You won't survive their inhumane treatment, tortures and art of breaking an egoistic prisoner. Now you will know what they feed us and how we live and sleep! If you complain, you are tortured. If you speak more, more you will be made silent. If you speak less, more and more you get work load

till you cry. They love silent obedient prisoner who can work like a horse. If someone talks loud or leadership, conspire, speak bad words against Wardens, or prison authority; his tongue might be chopped off. If you ask for food, they will starve for 5 days! If you work less at Enforced Labor camps, we will be forced to work for day and night in subzero temperatures. Someone made mischief repeatedly; he was exposed to snow storms till I will be dead frozen! He was made to stand in storm, with thin wet clothes. Some prisoners were buried in snow and head subjected to special

dogs. Here we are guinea pigs; what else? Therefore, I said it as a perfect hell!" He waited for Yogi and resumed, "Do you think, you will fly out from here?" He nodded his face crying, "Wrong! Die first if you want get freedom. Dead bodies have gone out...! Death is certain and we urge for; that is in our daily prayers. We envy and feel happy when someone dies! We advise him as last time come; 'don't return' to this land! This is the land of merciless aliens! T don't like us and they have to live for us. They have many slaves, so you too, are an unwanted guest! You should have asked me before coming here!" Albee had last words, staggering and he felt unconscious. Saint began to sooth their souls:

"We don't wish to see, even a single bird in cage; here are hundreds of humans in prison- humiliated, battered, terrorized and engaged in forced labor! Government is has lost the gems of your society, they are selling gems so cheap! You are the real power of States; you are the intelligence, wisdom and future of Soviet society. When you will be freed, nation will soar high." Yogi continued, "There are different stratifications of Human Powers: from body, mind, Sub-Consciousness and Universal Consciousness. You have high emotional as well Spiritual Powers of your Sub-Consciousness, therefore, your ideas and words were different from their anticipation. I see, treasure of your nation, here in Prison Eight! Communism, is like a snake, eating its own tail! It's a waste of Humanity!" All prisoners became silent; felt as if someone had wiped their tears from cheeks. Yogi continued, "I have truly, come for you; my Grand Masters have sent me from Himalaya. I am begun the game, dices are in their hands. Next step, I will be waiting."

A prisoner, in next cell, 6.5' tall, Massie squeezed his grills and asked, "Anyway, what are you going to do?" His voice was thick. He added, "We know what they will do to you- either will kill you tomorrow or will take you to forced labor in remote area and you will not come back. (pause) We don't need your words... If you are going to break prison for us; then okay...if no, then please, shut up!" Everyone was stunned at his statement. Yogi smiled at him. He whispered, "I have come to take you all, with me." Prisoner continued, "We have a priest coming, regularly on Sunday. He says, 'Your heaven is there behind clouds. Bullshit! Why Heavens don't descend on this ground? Why is the mankind so weird? Why 120 kg able-bodied man is behind bars? So I said, don't try to please us; if possible, protect the self first." He turned away from the grill.

All became silent, went to rest for a while. Soon, a sunbeam entered from a top window; fell over Yogi like a spotlight. He was illuminated like Buddha. Here, a wakeup call was given. It was a time to go for work. Prisoners were brought out from cell, one after one, with hands cuffed from behind and guard would raise arm cuffs above shoulder level so a prisoner would have to bend down, then they walked out to a wagon. That way, they were transported to work. [When they were sent to next building, they were blindfolded (so they won't get idea about the map of the prison.]

*

Yogi went back to his Great Masters in meditation. Second Master smiled at him at welcome and said, "Landed? And, landed in a prison?" He smiled at Yogi, "Great! Who can dare to dive into such prison?" Another Master added, "That young disciple was right...you used him as a bait." Another Master said, "You have challenged them by entering in their prison...so be ready to pay price. In addition, you pay more so as you can take few more steps in this play!" Yogi smiled at him as he understood the Law of Karma, "Pay and get the fruits. (Do Karma, action or reaction then you will get the crops.) Or take the fruits first then, pay with interests to Nature. (Taking fruits first is cheating...is steeling. So, you will pay more.) On Earth, not any of your actions goes in vain." He stared at icy wall of cave and looked at his bloody future.

Grand Master said with love, "Yogi! Did you see the pains and sufferings of prisoners, isn't it? I was right in sending you, isn't it? Now, you will eradicate the system in which people sigh, weep and curse. You will be a sufferer and a Catalyst. When people will come out repressions, they will need guidance, a direction and a future. You need to pave the pathway, prepare a Neo-world Order." Yogi bowed down to take blessings.

2nd Master: Don't be shy! Don't punish less.

3rd Master: You are the Sun, why you should hide? You can't hide as such. Don't think then, that because of you, darkness will be disturbed. Sun arrives in darkest hours of nights. Promise you will not forgive wrong people, won't do less in justice when time comes. You are there, to expel animals from human flesh."

Yogi answered, "Breaking the shell of egg is not our work. It's the life that is inside, should break its limitation by itself. Still, I am convinced that 'it's better to wipe off rabid civilization. Gardens will spring from Graveyards, tomorrow.' But, people should be wise to choose their course of life by themselves. People were betrayed by their rulers, followed them and landed in Siberia! They won't trust me. I will have to wait so as they develop their own choices. I will give them a single ruling. (pause) I heard of a story when a king went on fighting...and advanced too far in warzone. Then, he looked behind to find none was following! He was alone. (He was pointing at Jesus.) I don't want to repeat that mistake." All nodded and blessed Yogi. Grand Master said softly, "Jesus must not be crucified twice."

Yogi said, "If people are not worthy of me, immature, can't make their choices of life, then I will return soon." [57] (Yogi decided to live the life and return to Himalaya soon.)

---

[57]Yogi wanted inner engineering first, before outer changes. First should be spiritual revolution or vibration changes in society, (That is a slow process.) then the emotional sublimation, then mental uprising making right decisions and then people should march into Sun Land. Otherwise, people will be, frequently cheated by those, who sell dreams.

20. The First Trial:

When all prisoners were out of their cells, taken to work, Yogi was called in Jailor Office at about 1 PM. to face the first trial. Three officers were sitting across table. One of them began, "You are a dangerous person, threat to nation! Killed so many people in one day?"He puffed smoke towards Yogi.

Another officer remarked, "Any way, you are right. Your boat is seized, we sank it. You won't need it anymore. (You are not going to return.) We found the nozzle and barrel jutting out from glacier at shore and discovered our lost team of patrol troop buried under glacier. How that happened? If you are honest, if you tell truth, we will release you faster. (A pause) You then came to health center carrying our exiled young boy...Yestlin. You killed a beautiful nurse for no reason and saved him. You made Yestlin disappear in glacier waterways, splendid idea! I gave her, order to inject 4 amps. of Morphine and kill escapee." All waited for Yogi to say few words to defend himself but he sat smiling. Another officer added, "Tell us, who sent you. Intrusion in Soviet Union, without passport and visa is a dangerous crime; know it from me! You have no papers. Tell us why should we not subject you, to our Laws of Land?"

Third officer added, "Before you utter a single word, be serious in answer. Your words will write your destiny. Tell us, who has sent you? Who is behind you? A single man can never dare to enter in Siberia." Yogi took a time and then began:

"I have been here of my own, came via sea route, have protected Yestlin as I saw he was innocent; your officer has killed his innocent mother too! I have been a witness of death of those costal guards who came on sledge and died because of fissures in glacier. I witnessed them go. Same way, I witnessed the death of a nurse when she turned her head abruptly. You won't find any external mark of injuries. She died of her fate." That was recorded at register.

Yogi emphatically said, "I am a tourist without visa and have come with love for people of Soviet Union. I am a different person.(He paused.) I have come to request release of these prisoners of all Gulag Camps. They paid enough for their petty faults, as I understand. Go through their papers and see, you are indebted by their labors. Now, I have come from Himalaya to request you to sympathize. In reaching to you, a few obstacles were cleared, it's not my fault. That Sister had many crimes on her name. You know who she was at that Nomad. (Jailor and other officers were shocked.) Have mercy on your own fellow citizen. Actually, you should ask forgiveness and award compensation for unduly prolonged detention, humiliation, physical abuses, starving and bad conditions of habitats for prisoners. They are skin to bones, have dissolved themselves. I would ask you to review their files and see their penalties were over, since long. They have paid by their blood and life. I request you to release them at the earliest." Officers were stunned and speechless for a long time, then took a deep breath and remained silent.

One officer said, "Instead, you will soon, ask mercy for your survival. Listen, we won't review their files; do what you want to do!"

Yogi smiled and joyously said, "Surely, I can do anything as I stand on fulcrum of pendulum. A person standing in equilibrium can go in any direction. (pause) You are serving a system, so you should forward my message to seniors." Voice of Yogi was commanding, "Do that..." A wave of current passed through all officers. An officer dared to smile and he counter-questioned Yogi, "If they won't respond then?"

Yogi looked at officers for a long time and answered leaning forwards, "Not, every human may be a man! He may be divine! When I have come to request you, then I can go beyond your understanding. Be feared of Mother Nature. I am her Son. (pause) My request is just in words, otherwise it's an order." (pause) "Our Interviews are bidirectional. I also, look for your wisdom. I will also, give you the Judgment. These prisoners are your brothers, politically victimized. Today, common people of Russia struggle for survival, tomorrow, your government will struggle for its own survival. Justice will be delivered aptly."

The wardens standing behind Yogi were annoyed and attacked Yogi from behind…saying, "Hell with your wisdom! And you too go to hell!" They attacked with fists, files and sticks from behind…one warden ran and grab the rifle, used the butt and hit on back of skull of Yogi, that made Yogi unconscious.

Soon, he was dragged through corridor to his cell where he was literally thrown in. Three officers were sitting silent…they felt something wrong brewing in this matter so, they referred the case, file and audio conversation to higher post at Borskiy that was situated at 2000- 3000 meters high in Kodar Mountains[58] East to Baikal Lake.

*

Yogi returns to Himalayan Masters

Yogi again reached to his Masters in his sub-consciousness. 2nd Master asked, "Does it hurt?" He was pointing to blood spot from right ear. Yogi answered, "A little, but worth to experience! People have had similar experiences since centuries. And, I should accept their scorch; a Nurse died and border security guards were killed. I should accept their punishment."

2nd Master: They have killed millions; while fighting against feudalism, imperialism; when Communism was enforced in Russia and in Stalin Era they enacted Purge! You shouldn't be soft in taking penalty on head. Don't be proud of being a Yogi! I doubt, why every saint, Yogi and devotees accept the attack of other

---

[58] Kodar Mountains: It's one of Siberia's most spectacular and remote mountain range, in most uninhabited region between Lake Baikal and Yakutia. Here, reindeer herders live in extreme weathers. (-60 degree C. in winters)The terrain includes glaciers, passes, river crossings, sandy deserts and more. Here were Gulag Camps in which thousands of 'Enemies of State' were exiled! There was a head office of KGB, with all scientific gadgets and research labs.

people. Forgiveness is not for those who live on surface of Planet Earth. Not reacting means inviting death."

3rdMaster added, "Words won't work on Earth. Preaching will be foolish in humankind. Nature is an another name of a play of powers. Use your powers against theirs, not for selfish purpose but for others. If you will fail to treat them well, Mother Nature punish you more. A Sun is refusing to shine!" Yogi looked at Grand Master who whispered, "You are walking of dreams for Human Race, isn't it? Then, you must safeguard your dreams. You are going to take those innocents to Salvation point. So, eliminate all who resist you. Make your way then, pave the way, for people. Then, you will outline the future of Mankind. Sometimes, we need to stir the whole ocean, to get pearls!" All Masters appreciated the vision of their Grand Master.

Yogi argued, "My people are still, not prepared. Time is running faster. Prisoners will be more terrified, intimidated and made clueless. I am here, early in their timeline! Let's postpone the idea of 'Sun Land'! Really, human lives for bread, survival issue!

Masters blessed him saying, "You know you are wrong...this time! They are 'made' helpless, 'made' dependent for bread, 'made' poor by injustice and humiliation. They are driven by fear; life is at Muladhar Chakra. Water the plants, roses will begin smiling tomorrow. That is too simple. Important is your survival! Jesus must not die twice!" And, Yogi opened eyes in his cubicle, with tears.

*

21. The Second Trial:

Yogi Puts Demands For Prisoners:

It was about 4.30 PM when guards came to take Yogi to face a trial. Meanwhile, four wardens dragged two wounded prisoners to their cells; they were unable to speak a word. They had broken their legs. They saw Yogi going for a trial. A wild cry of a woman came from upstairs. Wheels of military wagon stopped outside at gate of prison. When Yogi entered in jailor office; few investigating officers also entered from outside. They were amazed at a glance of fearless monk of Himalaya. It was a panel of 3 Chief Officers (One from KGB[59] office, one was Siberian Prison Superintendent from Magadan and last was from Military Court, Servobaikalsk (near Baikal Lake) and a translator. The jailor, other officers, wardens, unit managers were observers. It was truly a serious atmosphere; a crowd of 11 officers, were eager to interrogate Yogi. He as usual, gave a smile at those three chief officers. After a long silence, KGB officer picked up the notes of morning record and read loud so everyone could listen:

"Name, Yogi! From Himalaya, an Indian, via sea route and on a small boat! It's surprising! Gentleman, is this a tourist place,hmm? Enters at Magadan shore and immediately, kills border security squad with dogs. There he met a prisoner, who had escaped from exile. He is Yestlin, okay. They travelled 266 kilometers inside Siberia to meet us! Unbelievable! Impossible!! He brings the convict to medical center so as we come to know that Yestlin is alive...by pretending to give him a dog-bite vaccine. It was a great plot! When he is given a vaccine...he threw Yestlin

---

[59] **KGB:**(Komitet Gosundarstvennoy Bezopasnosti or Committee for State Security), Intelligence and secret functions service for Communist Party of Soviet Union: It served from 13th March 1954 to 3rd December 1991. Its past preceeding agencies were Cheka, OGPU,NKGB, NKVD, MGB. It was attached to Council of Ministers. It was a chief government agency of Union-Republican Jurisdiction carrying internal security, Intelligence and secret police functions. Similar agencies operated in each of republics of the Soviet Union in Russian SFSR, state committees and state commissions.

into glacial rivers. Convict escaped in Glaciers. He is going to die inside glaciers, understand? (Officer looked in eyes of Yogi.) Now, you killed a beautiful nurse...(looking at Yogi) you committed an another crime! (Pause) You should have respected the law of foreign land, do you know or not? You are without any visa papers or documents of visa or identity! You should be afraid of us, and you walked to us fearlessly. That is your third crime! Who are you; tell us?"

Jailor added, "He has come to advocate for freedom of these prisoners. He requested us to release prisoners, saying they have overpaid, more than their crimes. Actually, he asked for compensation to all prisoners. He is a Devil's Advocate!!" All laughed loud. (Those prisoners in far distant cells could listen at their conversation with echoes.)

Another officer asked, "It's a matter of concern for us, how you came to know that here is the Prison? Who called you here? Who was he from this prison? Who guided you to reach here? It's a serious matter to investigate. (pause) Tell me Yogi, what shall I do for you?" KGB officer asked.

Yogi smiled at him and whispered, "What can you do for me? You said so! (Yogi chuckled.) You are talking as if you are capable of doing everything I will propose. Even if you will agree with me, you cannot do anything. You must not talk high!" Then yogi answered as follow:

- None called me, but cries of innocents reached to us at Himalaya near Kanchenjunga glacier. Strong vibes can travel. Even vibes travel in cosmos. Someone is always watching you from heights, as you emit vibrations every moment. Now, what I want from you...

- I asked to reopen files of all prisoners and objectively reassess by neutral authority, whether their crimes were serious enough for exile.

- Stop exile to Siberia. Siberia is not a place of human habitat. It also, speaks of your mala fide intention when you send someone away from his cities or towns- not good for a government of the people and for the people! What Dumas were doing?"

- Siberia is a gift to USSR, don't exploit, stop mining, don't kill bears for their fur, don't increase human habitation in Siberia. This hostile terrain is made for a special purpose. Bears protect your land.

- Stop Forced Labor and start volunteering! Is your nation so poor that it can't pay for labor? Nation should not achieve growth with exploitation of human resources and virtues of humanity! A ruler has its own dignity, maintain your crown on your head.(pause) See, I tell you without my ego and consider you as representative of your governance. No personal accusation, so we have no enmity as such, YET! (Yogi's eyes sparked in last word, that made all officers serious.)

- Release prisoners as they have paid much more by their sweats, tears, cries, blood and life. You should thank those who died in serving your impossible tasks.

- Now, pay them compensation if they have labored in excess more than their crimes. See! Not all prisoners committed the same crimes, so all should have different tenures in labor camps. You have detained them uniformly, until they die! Is there anyone wiser and humane person in your team? (It was a great shock to them.)

- And, re-establish them in social life, their families are shredded. Rehabilitate them respectfully.

- Give the sky to all. Trees have their rights to grow. Their genes are different than those of shrubs. Every theory works at mind level and we live by heart. So, Communism might be great but see we don't give injustice to intelligent, wise great people. They might tall personality! Land belongs to none and sky is for all, people are your strength, more than that, are their ideas, thoughts, intelligence, wisdom and power to send or receive intuitions. Why you waste them in making roads and train tracks in Siberia? (pause) See, I may be... or say, I am coming after few centuries...therefore if I have poor connection with our flow of human life. I may be wrong a little.

- I have come unintentionally, have nothing to take or to get from your land. I will not take a sip of your waters! (Albee heard him.) I am here just to give and therefore, I have entered in your prison of my own!

All officers in office were spellbound...little feared of the knowledge and guts to speak against policies of Communist Party! There was deep silence and all looked embarrassed at each other. One officer asked, "I ask you in reverse, do you love your life or not? You said to a lion, 'Your mouth is stinging!' (pause) What will happen in next moment?" (All chuckled and tapped the table.)

Yogi also, smiled and said, "I did not say communism has done wrong, but every system has never been fool-proof and foul-proof because Mother Nature is ingenious and nifty. A birth is stamped for death so, we need our systems to review and rectify. (pause) When someone has come from a height (of Himalaya), and from distance, enters of his own will, just to request you for release of prisoners. You must stop joking and start thinking. Be serious as I am. (Yogi looked all around and all were as if devitalized, became frozen.) You are the representatives of Communist Party of USSR and your government will abide by your decisions." Many officers became numb.

The Judge from Servobaikalsk took the control and said, "You asked as if you have come for a basketful shopping! We can't do anything about what you asked. You need to go to Kremlin. By the way, what will you pay if you want all prisoners free."

Yogi chuckled, "My clients have already paid by blood and sweats. Your plump 'fatty cheery red cheeks' and smiles are the proof that they have watered their blood enough. Cities like Magadan, this prison, those roads, mines are all their creation. 'My' clients have transferred all their properties and fortunes on name of Communism. What more you want? Or I will label you power-thirsty people. Please, release them. Sky is for all, not only for Communist Party."

Judge, suddenly shouted, he thumbed the table, leaned forwards, appeared like a beast sitting opposite to Yogi, "Bloody, as such you are a criminal. We have ascertained your crimes. You accepted all accusations. Notary, write down and take his thumb print!" (Writer scribbled fast and took right hand, inked the thumb and took a print!) Jailor Rudley whispered, "Have you anyone to protect you?"

Yogi argued, "I am talking to humans, I suppose; then why shall I need an advocate for defense?"

Meanwhile, postmortem report of Nurse came to be negative. No mark of external injuries and a fracture of Atlas of 2nd Cervical Spine, leading to crush of Spinal Cord, cardio-respiratory arrest in a moment! Now, officers sighed, as death of nurse was not easily explained. Those injuries are just possible by hanging!

Next officer suddenly burst out, "Bloody fool!" He turned to his officers and shouted, "'Shoot' him!"

Yogi leaned towards the table and said, "Do you know numbers of Gulag Camps and prisons? Do you know numbers of prisoners or Goners? Siberia is your waste-paper basket. Do you have any record of people dying every year, here? Your register here, on

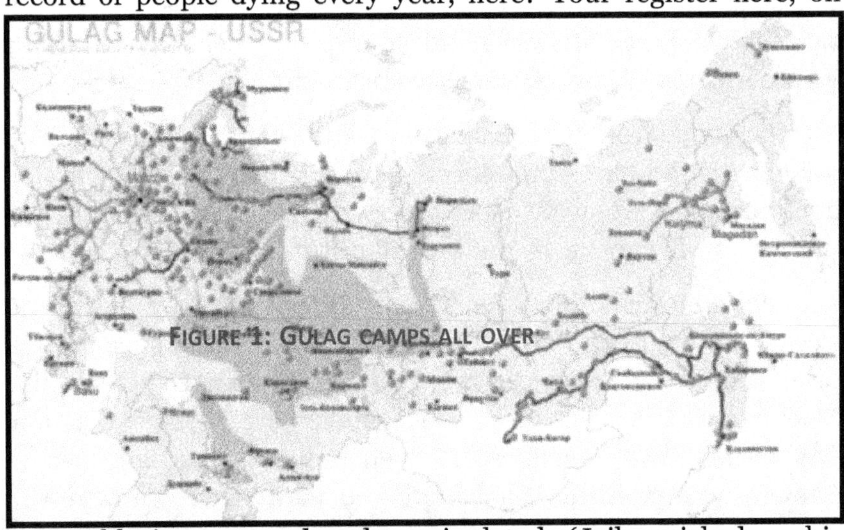

your table is so ragged and manipulated. (Jailor picked up his register and hide in drawer.) Saint became tearful. "Your people could have made sacrifice by themselves for growth of your nation if they were asked to help the Nation. It would be an act of patriotism. Your people are loyal to nation. They were humiliated by distrust from emperors and now by Communism. (pause) World is a mirror, what else is it? You don't love them, they won't love and trust you."

*

22. The Judgment:

Officers had to listen whatever a stranger said in their prison. They asked wardens to take Yogi to his cell for a short time. Officers discussed in their room, their comments were like these: 'Yogi has no backup.'; 'He is a dangerous man; we can't release him and he can't stay with prisoners either or he may start a rebel within prison.' They typed the judgment and all five people signed the papers. Then, Yogi was called back to listen the verdict from Judge. He began to read the destiny of Yogi:

"Yogi, from Himalaya has made a sudden entry from seashore at Magadan at Sea of Okhotsk without any identity and visa permission. You are charged for serious crimes:

1. Entry without Visa and Passport: Have nothing to support your identity with ambiguous intentions.
2. Helping and hiding a convict, an escaped prisoner of State is attracts a criminal penalty to you.
3. Death of our security personals and our civilian after your entry in Siberia in mysterious manners is your next crime.
4. More to add are following articles:

4.1: **Article 277.** Encroachment on the Life of a Statesman or a Public Figure

Encroachment on the life of a statesman or a public figure, committed for the purpose of terminating his government or any other political activity, or out of revenge for such activity (a terrorist act), shall be punishable by deprivation of liberty for a term of 12 to 20 years, or by capital punishment, or by imprisonment for life. (Yogi had 'killed' border security force troop as well a nurse.)

4.2: **Article 317.** Encroachment on the Life of an Officer of a Law-enforcement Agency

Encroachment on the life of an officer of a law-enforcement body, or of a serviceman, and also of their relatives, for the purpose of obstructing the lawful activity of said persons to protect the public order and security, or out of vengeance for such activity shall be punishable by deprivation of liberty for a term of twelve to twenty years, or by capital punishment or life imprisonment. (Slapping a Nurse at Health Center.)

4.3: **Article 318**. Use of Violence Against a Representative of the Authority

- Use of violence that does not endanger human life or health, or threats to use violence against a representative of the authority, or his relatives, in connection with the discharge by his official duties, shall be punishable by a fine in the amount of 200 to 500 minimum wages, or in the amount of the wage or salary, or any other income of the convicted person for a period of two to five months, or by arrest for a term of three to six months, or by deprivation of liberty for a term of up to five years.
- The use of violence endangering the lives or health of the persons referred to in the first part of this Article shall be punishable by deprivation of liberty for a term of five to ten years.
- Note: A public officer of a law-enforcement or controlling body, and also other public officials vested in the statutory order with regulatory powers in respect of persons who are not dependent on them by virtue of employment, shall be deemed to be a representative of the authority in this and other Articles of the present code.

4.4: **Article 319**. Insult of a Representative of the Authority: you have tried to teach us wisdom that is the insult.

- Public insult of a representative of the authority during the discharge by him of his official duties, or in connection with their discharge, shall be punishable by a fine in the amount of 50 to 100 minimum wages, or in the amount of the wage or salary, or any other income of the convicted person for a period of up to one month, or by compulsory works for a term of 120 to 180 hours, or by corrective labor for a term of six to twelve months.

- Accessing vital information of our government offices, our prisons, security services of Siberia, Gulag camps activities are all major crimes. You are dangerous to our Communist Party by now.

4.5: **Article 275**. High Treason

- High treason that is espionage, disclosure of state secrets or any other assistance rendered to a foreign State, a foreign organization, or their representatives in hostile activities to the detriment of the external security of the Russian Federation, committed by a citizen of the Russian Federation, shall be punishable by deprivation of liberty for a term of 12 to 20 years with confiscation of property or without such confiscation. (Yogi, you know more than what is needed by common man. You are dangerous for government. It may carry out spy activities, hostile activities.)

- Note: A person who has committed crimes stipulated in this Article, or by Articles 276 and 278 of this Code, shall be relieved from criminal responsibility if he has facilitated the prevention of further damage to the interests of the Russian Federation by informing the governmental authorities of his own free will and in due time, or in any other way, if his actions contain no other corpus delicti. Proclaiming the innocence for all prisoners and convicts without any knowledge of our laws and system and asking to release all prisoners from territory of Soviet Union is a serious threat to working Communist Party of Soviet Union. You have capacity to split the society and wedge a class-war in Soviet Union again after 1917.

4.6: **Article 278**. Forcible Seizure of Power or Forcible Retention of Power:

Actions aimed at the forcible seizure of power or forcible retention of power in contravention of the Constitution of the Russian Federation, or aimed at the forcible change of the constitutional system of the Russian Federation, shall be punishable by deprivation of liberty for a term of 12 to 20 years.

4.7: **Article 279**. Armed Rebellion

Organization of an armed rebellion or active participation in it for the purpose of overthrowing or forcibly changing the constitutional system of the Russian Federation, or of breaching the territorial integrity of the Russian Federation, shall be punishable by deprivation of liberty for a term of 12 to 20 years.

4.8: Article 280. Public Appeals for a Forcible Change of the Constitutional System of the Russian Federation

Your next step is to appeal people to pressurize government and/or for a forcible seizure of state power or its forcible retention, or for a forcible change of the constitutional system of the Russian Federation. It shall be punishable by a fine in the amount of 500 to 700 minimum wages, or in the amount of the wage or salary, or any other income of the convicted person for a period of five to seven months, or by arrest for a term of four to six months, or by deprivation of liberty for a term of up to three years

"My Yogi, we don't entertain Third Party advocacy on behalf of those prisoners. That belittles our ego and wisdom. Tell me, why shall we not treat you as Enemy of States? Such acts, committed with the use of the mass media, shall be punishable by deprivation of liberty for a term from three up to five years entailing the deprivation of the right to hold certain jobs or engage in certain occupations for a term up to three years.

4.9: **Article 282**. Incitement of National, Racial, or Religious Enmity

Actions aimed at the incitement of national, racial, or religious enmity, abasement of human dignity, and also propaganda of the exceptionality, superiority, or inferiority of individuals by reason of their attitude to religion, national, or racial affiliation. If these acts have been committed in public or with the use of mass media, it shall be punishable by a fine in the amount of 500 to 800 minimum wages, or in the amount of the wage or salaryor any other income of the convicted person for a period of five to eight months or by restraint of liberty for a term of up to three years, or by deprivation of liberty for a term of two to four years.

The same acts committed:

   a) with the use of violence or with the threat of its use;
   b) by a person through his official position;
   c) by an organized group,

shall be punishable by deprivation of liberty for a term of three to five years.

4.10: **Article 283**. Disclosure of a State Secret

Disclosure of information comprising a state secret, by a person to whom it has been entrusted or to whom it has become known through his office or work, if this information has become the property of other persons, in the absence of the characteristic features of high treason, shall be punishable by arrest for a term of four to six months, or by deprivation of liberty for up to four years, with disqualification to hold specified offices or to engage in specified activities for a term of up to three years, or without such disqualification.

Mr. Yogi, we can't allow you to go out of this prison. You will disclose what you have seen. Your case is different but I will apply clauses as for ordinary people in a favor. 'The same deed, which involved through negligence grave consequences, shall be punishable by deprivation of liberty for a term of three to seven years, with disqualification to hold specified offices or to engage in specified activities for a term of up to three years.

4.11: **Article 353**. Planning, Preparing, Unleashing, or Waging on Aggressive War -(chapter 34: Crimes against Peace and Mankind's Security)

Planning, preparing, or unleashing an aggressive war,(Class war civic against government) shall be punishable by deprivation of liberty for a term of seven to fifteen years.

Waging an aggressive war shall be punishable by deprivation of liberty for a term of 10 to 20 years.

4.12: Article 354. Public Appeals to Unleash an Aggressive War

Public appeals to unleash an aggressive war shall be punishable by a fine in the amount of 500 to 700 minimum wages, or in the amount of the wage or salary, or any other income of the convicted person for a period of a five to seven months, or by deprivation of liberty for a term of up to three years.

The same deeds, committed with the use of the mass media or by a person who holds a state post of the Russian Federation or a state post of a subject of the Russian Federation, shall be punishable by a fine in the amount of 700 to 1,000 minimum wages, or in the amount of the wage or salary, or any other income of the convicted person for a period of seven to twelve months, or by deprivation of liberty for a term of two to five years, with disqualification to hold specified offices or to engage in specified activities for a term of up to three years. Mr. Yogi, all together, we are deciding capital punishment for you."

*

The Judge was reading constantly and looking at the face of Yogi and he found him smiling...so, he concentrated reading...till end. Then, he looked at Yogi again. There was a pin-drop silence. All were waiting for reaction of Yogi who looked at Judge for a time, then other officers, jailor and turned back at wardens standing behind....and then returned at Judge.

Yogi: You have taken lot of pains to frame me. When intentions drive you, why need words to support? Most of clauses are wrongly applied and there is no counter-checking system in your judiciary. I have no right to get advocates either. Therefore, you are the one and only one judge to decide my fate as well yours. Mind well, the way I am sitting alone, you are lone responsible person for what you decide. Your government does not know yet. So, inform them beforehand. I will accept you as sole representatives of your government and submit your case to my Krishna, my God. I asked for mercy for your citizen behind bars; was it inhumane? You have placed an elephant's foot over an ant!

(pause) What you have at heart; that only you can deliver! Once, you lost Jesus in same way, then you began to worship him in repentance! (pause) We are closing dialogues. Now, it's my time." (Outside, guards observed dark clouds looming at corners of skies with thunders and lightening.)

Jailor retorted, "You have a big mouth! Go on talking. What a fool you are! You don't see your end! The wisdom does not work in life Yogi, it only, guides! It's the 'Might' that rules. And, we don't believe in fortune, God or Nature."

Yogi thundered, "Might? Your Powers? You have not faced such a Yogi, yet. Your powers are limited. Divine people can play with Five Elements[60] for selfless cause. Think, I have penetrated in Siberia for so many miles to reach to this prison and have summoned you to discuss here! I have made you worry since morning. Now, your decision, I heard. Now, my turn has come. (Thunderous storm was heard, from outside.) Human Race has become mad after material powers and knowledge. Don't be machines who execute you laws otherwise you should not exist as humans. Be humble and liberate those prisoners."

Judge frantically, threw papers on table, wardens standing behind Yogi grabbed the hands of Yogi, took fingers impressions on every page and then they pounced upon the 'newly convicted prisoner' in darkness. (Thunderous lightening fell over the prison and all lights were gone. Utter darkness was established.) None saw Yogi was severely bitten from all sides and then, Judge stood up, (Someone took up a torch.) he was pointing at Yogi to say, "Capital..., to night! **Dinner with his death**!" Officers sarcastically remarked, "I love flesh." His big teeth were shining in torch light. Soon, all officers left the prison in their cars. Car Driver asked, "Why this storm? This is the wrong season for it!" Here, Yogi was over-beaten and became unconscious and pulled down to his cell, wounded! Meanwhile, almost all prisoners had returned from

---

[60] Space, Fire, Air, Water and Earth

labor. Wardens shouted at them, "Look at your savior! Look! Your advocate asked for your release! Who invited him, tell me or I will I will punish everyone. I will starve you for whole week. Few old prisoners cried and urged, "Have mercy! He is an outsider, a monk, did not know your powers!" Many began to sob...as that type of capital punishment was routinely, given to very strong person in prison. Few fire sticks were brought in corridors for lights!

23. Grand Masters from Himalaya:

Yogi was semi-conscious in his cell; prisoners were moaning around, Albee was standing in corridor, crying like a small child. Prisoners had avoided their day's only dinner. They all, fasted. Yogi from within was gripped in an emotional storm. He thought:

- 'Judgment was right as I have intruded in their territory, asked for release of prisoners, started disturbances and instigated a false hope among prisoners. Prisoners confirmed that they are innocent and would be free.' Penalty might be anything...according to their customs but, they were probably right!'

- Yogi recalled a dictum of wisdom, 'When the people don't understand or they are fools, better remain silent!' He changed, "When people don't understand you, you are probably too early or too late to visit the Mankind therefore, you better, make an exit!"

- 'Now, I pay out and exit,' he whispered, "and finish this story!" They don't have their own inner voice. It's all mind, programmed mind and mechanized mind! Man is a dead machine living by body and mind.' Slowly Yogi accepted his death penalty, decided to quit.

Grand Masters at Himalaya saw Yogi sinking in his own whirlpool of thoughts. One of them echoed his voice, "Once, Arjun refused to fight in Mahabharat[61]; Jesus too, decided to give up his

---

[61]**Mahabharata** (Sanskrit: "Great Epic of the Bharata Dynasty"): One of the two Sanskrit epic poems of ancient India (the other being the *Ramayana*). The *Mahabharata* is an important source of information on the Hinduism. It's regarded by Hindus; as both a text about dharma (Hindu moral law) and a history (*itihasa*, literally "that's what happened"). The *Mahabharata* consists of a mass of mythological and didactic material arranged around a central heroic narrative that tells of the struggle for sovereignty between two groups of cousins, the Kauravas (sons of Dhritarashtra, the descendant of Kuru) and the Pandavas (sons of Pandu, Arjun was one of them.). The poem is made up of almost 100,000 couplets—about seven times the length of the *Iliad* and the *Odyssey* combined—divided into 18 *parvans*, or

life...otherwise he could have done wonders.' All good people forgive evils; then who will punish them?" They soon, appeared in the prison cell where Yogi had just recovered and divine conference started. His face was blood splashed. Masters of Himalaya had surrounded Yogi who smiled at them. Few prisoners felt that Yogi was not alone this time. They experienced 'Divine Tranquility' extraordinary fragrance and some assurance that good was going to happen!

One of the Masters said with lot of love, to Yogi, "Yogi...! O Yogi! This is a rough terrain, you have not walked since last 8 to 10 centuries.[62] You know a little about this human race. Little scratches, little wounds...few diseases and just a once death...otherwise the life as a human, is good! A different experience; isn't it! (Yogi chuckled at them.)

Yogi whispered, "For whom, I shall stand for? These prisoners are half-dead! Morale gone. They survive just to live a day further. If I lit a lamp, pave a pathway of Truth, then also, they will not walk unless they calculate their profits, benefits, they will buy the Heavens but will not build own house by themselves. Hopeless species!!" Yogi began to cry. "Hopeless is the governance and hopeless are the people. Government does not give without their profits and people don't choose them without their interests! All are selfish!! I would say, give up this planet. Let's spread divine life somewhere else." All masters were hurt.

2nd Master lovingly whispered, "So, fast you want to retire? Do you remember our purpose? Great tasks, great Yogis are requested to reach to Earth. Now, don't die like a Human being! Die divine! Don't focus on validity of their reasoning. Their truth is different than our truth. Evils have indeed, a different truth. (pause) Humanity is in seed form, trust me. This land has not been barren

---

sections, plus a supplement titled *Harivamsha* ("Genealogy of the God Hari"; i.e., of Vishnu). Its authorship is traditionally ascribed to the sage Vyasa and was written by Lord Ganesha.

[62] Sublimed souls don't take birth so often, so frequent. Yogi had descended after 8-10 centuries, so he did not know about human mentality.

yet! Don't lose the hope. (His voice became emotional.) The divine person is selfless and so lonely! Slowly, you will get millions of beautiful souls soon, to support you, I know. Your love is magnetic. Identify who you are!" (pause) See, you are not alone. We are here and Fortune of all pious sanctified people is with you. Soon, you will find Mother Nature on your side. Life from various planets look at you, with hope. Everything is set ready to support, you need to walk in exile like Shri Ram walked from Ayodhyay to Panchavati Forest. So, pass through this test."

3rd Master: We know that you don't care about result- victory or loss then, why do you worry? When you are selfless then why do you worry? Just be the responsible person to help Mother Nature and execute your powers. It's routine; evil forces or demons frame rules to trap and victimize people. You should break all rules, even rules of Nature and punish them. Sun will never pity upon Darkness! He just shines! Darkness is repelled passively." Yogi nodded at their arguments.

3rd Master: To give up is a selfish way, it's easy to die and escape from responsibility. Standing against the storm for the innocents, for the human cause is admirable."

Grand Master said with love, "They can use minds. You use power of Sub-Conscious mind. Devils play with words; you will use vibrations. They use powers of Earth, Water, Air or Fire; you will use Powers of Space and Non-particulate energy of Ohm.[63] Break their rules and dissolve this prison today. Release them (prisoners)so as they can soar like free birds!" Yogi opened his ecchymosed eyes, looked in space (towards his Masters) and smiled! (Albee wondered to whom Yogi smiled!)

Yogi argued, "Will these prisoners and people of Russia be able to handle the freedom? Indians wasted their freedom, as we know. They remained slaves to a party instead of British Rules. They did not rise for the Nationalism for about 70 years post-independence."

---

[63]Ohm is the most powerful mantra on Earth and Cosmos. All five elements were condensed from non-particulate energies of Ohm!

2nd Master argued, "How can you opine about Soviet People? You have changed after coming to prison! (He chuckled.) The people of Soviet Union are gems or pure gold. They have been in furnace since last 2-3 centuries. Pure Gold, but you need to harness them. It will be their time of celebration, when you have arrived here. Pains will always give birth to a newborn. Pain of civilization will give birth of New Dawn. If you want to die, then, die for the people of Soviet Union!" Yogi became tearful.

"See, that is your next responsibility to give free world to suitable people." Grand Master interrupted, "If we want to give, then let us give them 'Full Moon' rather than 'crescent' of a moon."

3rd Master inspired, "He gave you his judgment, now you implement your judgment. Mother Nature is waiting for your signals as you are her beloved pure soul. You have come for Mother. Now, don't be emotional after coming to Earth. Remember your reason of being a human. Emotions are the first mistake in a fall." And, all Masters blessed their beloved Yogi and left. Yogi whispered, "Reason of being a human...I have recalled." And, Albee heard standing outside the cell. He ran in corridor and gave message to many prisoners, "Yogi has recalled his reason of being a Human! Something is going to happen....don't tell to anyone!"

*

24. Dinner and Death

Outside, gale of wind sprayed sleet of freezing snow and guards of prisons were chilled. Inside prison was dark due to electrical power failure. Wardens were active using torches.

A wagon was crossing a small semi-frozen lake at distance. Driver observed vapor rising from lake and dancing like ghosts on frozen lake. (When atmosphere suddenly cools down, while waters remain warm, vapors rise. It is a rare phenomenon.) He whispered to his partner, "It's Frost Smoke!" Few sergeants looked at flood icein water bodies with bluish green aquifers at the sides of road. Small hills and rocks were passing on left side, with knife edged snow ridges. Kingdom of snow and storm were in full form. Driver slowed down while the wagon began to cross a small shallow semi-frozen lake, wheels began to make cracking sounds crushing 'anchor ice' (bottom ice). There was a beautiful reflection of sky and clouds ('blink' or Otblesk (Russian)) on glossy surface of lake ahead! When wagon entered in, image was lost. Later, wagon began to run over aggraded Permafrost making special noise. Soon the weather turned thunderous with snowfall ('Blizzard' or'Purga' (Russian)) and heavy ice began to fall. Driver whispered, 'Oh My God! Ill omen!' He turned back to officers and said, "Are you sure, we are going to return tonight?" Officers were speechless, someone grunted, 'Judge is an idiot! He has chosen wrong date.' Dark clouds lowered, came overhead and heavy snow spills started over windows of wagon, with crashing sounds. Driver switched on light and wipers. He saw Prison Eight gripped in darkness with whorls of dark clouds hanging over prison and it looked ghastly with no lights. Many more vehicles later arrived to Prison Eight with same frightening feelings.

When they reached, guards of Prison Eight received with salutation, in snow storm, saying, "Lightening has struck, Comrades! Power station, blown at Irkutsk; we don't expect light tonight. Whole Siberia and Baikal areas are in dark." Officer who opened the gate of wagon informed, "An Earthquake of 7 scales has hit Alma-Ata, Kazakh. Lights are down there....also." (Incidence occurred in 1978.)

*

Albee sat down at grill, spread hands in dark cell, to find Yogi and touch him. Soon, he whispered, "Why did you take our favor?" Yogi had a gentle smile;he palpated the head of Albee and said, "I saw what they have to give us. They are just like dried husk, we can set them afire."

Prisoner from next cell shouted, 'They will give a cruel death sentence! Don't take it lightly. Death is certain. He was Jesus who was resurrected! He was swooned (fell unconscious) and revived from Spot of Crucifixion- Golgotha[64], outside Jerusalem. What about you, hmm...?"

Yogi became serious, "I am not that innocent Jesus. If I die then, my intentions of coming here will be aborted. For a new divine future, we will have to see today must die. And, I am not religious, I am righteous." Everyone became speechless for a long time.

Albee changed topic of discussion, he asked, "I have a question, none has answered till today. Tell me...why a candle has a life, a fixed time while Darkness is infinite and for forever. I have a life; stars, civilizations, planets and galaxies have a life! Everything is mortal, I will return into the Darkness, which is immortal, timeless and universal! So... I may say, that the God is Dark."

Yogi extended his hand with love, from grill, patted on his shoulder and said, "God is neither in Divine Life nor in life of Satan. He is not in plus or in minus. He is there, in Great Zero. God or Brahma is beyond Zero. God is not recognized as the Light,

---

[64]Golgotha, (Aramaic: "Skull") also called Calvary, (from Latin calva: "bald head" or "skull"), **skull-shaped hill in ancient Jerusalem, the site of Jesus' crucifixion**. It is referred to in all four Gospels (Matthew 27:33, Mark 15:22, Luke 23:33 and John 19:17).a hill near Jerusalem where Jesus was crucified; Calvary: A place of suffering or sacrifice. a place of burial.

but the Light is due to Him! The Fire of Sun is due to Him! Both darkness and Light are derived from Him when 'Zero' was split by Him into Light and Darkness! In Zero, there is Eternal Peace. Zero was the precursor of existence and it's the end too, 'Omega'!"

Albee became serious to ask, "Are we entering in 'Omega'?" Yogi smiled at his intelligence. Albee continued, "You are taking us in 'Great Zero', Omega, isn't it?" He bowed down and shouted at other prisoners, "Omega! Omega!" Be prepared; darkness and Light will meet tonight."

Then, Albee leaned at grills to ask Yogi, "How will you survive?" Yogi answered:

> "Forget about me...I want you to answer: Are you prepared for new world order? Are you going to rise after my fall? Otherwise, no more Jesus will return to your Planet! Will you choose to live of your own? Will you bear your own powers to shape your future? A wave is coming! Are you able to ride over it? Don't panic, no cry, no shouting, no tears and no fear. Just emanate same frequencies of wish, intensely in harmony I am feeling for you. Let your waves overlap to create constructive convergence. Recall what your parents had envisaged about your land, recall what your wise people thought of Russia. Give blessing to your Unseen Unborn Divine Future and pray so as divine life will come to lie in your cradles. Together you fly in one direction and you will lift net in which you are trapped since centuries. Remember, in this Prison, you have only direction to go and that is the 'Up!' , it is the Sublimation. Then, you will draw divine forces in your alliance!"

All nodded but a few understood. They understood two lines: 'Don't cry! And, don't run!'

*

Jailor Calls him. (8.30 PM):

Meanwhile, wardens opened the gates of corridors, generators began and lights were on! Few fire sticks were placed in dark corners of corridors. The central hall was well illuminated and wardens arranged dining tables. Rattling sounds of plates and tinkles of glass utensils were audible in far corners. That made many prisoners nervous, 'Royal dinner, in prison?!'It was just to intimidate prisoners. Such a feast, death with dinner was infrequent. The sentenced prisoner was killed in piecemeal while officers and jailors would witness and rejoice delicious feast!

Guards arrived, asked Yogi, who was physically feeble, so they grabbed him from shoulders and pulled him to the office. The Jailor did not allow him to sit now. He gave a paper in Russian language, showing death order that came from Vladivostok stating:

'Mr. Yogi, you are a risk for prison as well for the people around as he may start rebel. We can't liberate you. You are given capital punishment for the crimes you have committed so far, in our land!' Yogi stared at Jailor. Who smiled at him sarcastically, "We will take you to your end. You are finished! Sign here!" He cried. Yogi seriously, asked, "Any reply for my demands?" Jailor was in scotching mood, he cried, "Sign!" Yogi said, "This is a fake order! Typed from Intelligence department, Amur Oblast, not from any judiciary! You have not waited for Court of Internal Security at Vladivostok, just NKVD officer has written and signed this fake death warrant. This is your last crime." Jailor was shocked. Yogi added, "I met all your victims who were given death warrants in your past 3.5 years of tenure in Taiga forest! They narrated your deeds. Same place, Amur Oblast, same NKVD officer has signed! This is your modus operandi." The guards became furious and began their action. Yogi suddenly turned at them and guards felt their arms frozen! Yogi walked out himself and entered in his cell. The jailor shivered, remained seated in office for a long time, till other officers came in. Guards also, stood for a long time demoralized!

*

25. Death Sentence: (9 PM)

Yogi while going to the site of death sentence, stopped at NKVD Officer and Jailor chatting in cheerful mood and said, "This judgment should be from intelligent agency, after consulting with seniors. It matters life and death for someone. This judgment should not be based upon individual conflict of thought, between us. He walked a step and turned at jailor, "Are you not missing an opportunity, again? I hold my right for self-defense." Guards pulled Yogi forcibly, ahead and brought where his feet were tied and then, hooked at a giant bolt fixed in ground.

Now, wardens were free to take revenge and they made Yogi semi-unconscious. He was flabbergasted and damned. Clouds burst out with lightening at windows of prison! Generators and Transformer of Prison blasted and lights in prison again, went off! Few guards ran for oil lamps and candle or torches and got multiple flambeaus. Few wooden fire sticks were brought for light. The hall was blazed with yellow orange lights from fires all around. Prisoners became tearful when they saw unconscious Yogi being pulled high on roller chain drive, (sprockets)[65] by guards. With little light of burning flames and flambeaus, body of Yogi was looking like an animal fixed for sacrifice!

Yogi's hands were tied and pulled up on a hook to ceiling of central hall so as he was extremely stretched- arms up and legs tied to ground. Jailor, Police, Intelligence and Judiciary department officers were satisfied and smiled, and approved. There were about 43 people in central hall who took their seats on dining table. Prisoners sighed at hanging body of Yogi in flashes of Lightening. His clothes were stripped off! Jailor read judgment: 'To be whipped till Death.' Dining tables were arranged at about 40 feet away from the execution site. Few prisoners shouted to stop, "Have mercy!", they cried. Rest were watching from their grills and shading tears! Few had seen similar penalty in past to

---

[65]*A chain and sprocket drive is a type of power transmission in which a roller chain engages with two or more toothed wheels or sprockets, used in engines as a drive from crankshaft to camshaft.*

terrorize prisoners! Albee was tremulous, crying, shouting and a warden hit his head hard so he fell unconscious. Many remembered how a victim was wiped by razor sharp blades, that would strip meat and intestines from the body, how vessels from axillae were cut and how fountains of blood were sprayed in hall. They remembered that officers were taking their dinner with least concern of dying man! They relished the terrifying cries of victim, when sharp edges of chain cut deep in chest and abdomen. Massie closed his eyes, tears began to flow...and he prayed God for mercy. He was atheist and many more had lost their Faith in God, were there in prison. They all, raised their hands crying and worshiped the Unknown to help Yogi.

Now, Yogi had a short time! He sent messages to his Masters from Himalayas, "Two fields to work. I will send all animals that live in human flesh, back to animal kingdom!! They are returning to animal kingdom. You manage their efflux. Second area to work is to protect myself, destroy the prison, release prisoners and uplift them, from demoralized life."

2nd Master whispered, "Yes, violence is welcomed here Shiva! Shiva!! You serve Mother Nature. So many Judgments are pending."

3rd Master said, "Devils are those who don't and can't listen own inner voice[66] You are facing devils, so no mercy, remember!

Grand Master blessed and guided: "You won't get second chance, my Yogi! It's the right place, right time and right people-sitting in front of you! First, break all their rules! Be unpredictable! Ask, the Mother Nature to change her rules now. Ask Lord of Fire, Sun to help you burn the weeds. Your time has come!"

Yogi opened his eyes and focused on that chain that had hanged him high to ceiling. He whispered, "Ohm"! And, Ohm was

---

[66]They are the vibration of Love, Sympathy, Mercy, Servitude and Tolerance. They work with minds- logic and fear and use their rules at weapons to captivate own people.

echoed from every wall. The sound was so loud, deafening and thunderous lightening sound added that rattled the glasses of windows of office. Guards standing outside ran inside the prison and stood in central hall. Yogi looked at iron chain and said, "Let all elements return to their roots source....Return to Ohm."

Meanwhile, two strong athletic Executioners[67]men of 6.3' height pulled out a heavy trunk to hall. Its wheels made a great sound. Few prisoners began to shout, "Stop them...no no, don't do that! Yogi is innocent." A guard cried at them, furiously, "Do you want to replace... hmm? Come on!" And, all prisoners became quiet. The judge looked at his watch; it was exactly nine o'clock and was the show time. Outside, the thunderstorm was in its worse phase, giant snowballs began to bang upon the roof of prison like drummers. That made a great noise...and most of lights became dull and dimmed, 'shivering' when Yogi opened his eyes from mediation. He looked down, stared at all officers busy ondinner table and took away 'fire' from their hearts'! (Their life came to an end!) A sudden silence came upon! Pin drop silence was frightening. Officers presaged of wrong going to happen. They stopped their dinner, gazed at Yogi, then at those two executioners. They pulled out thick snake like Cuban curb chains as whips from trunk and splashed on floor to make terrifying metallic sounds! The rings of chains were sharpened like razors, at outer sides. They gave shining in fire lights! That chain would cut even a iron rod! Yogi looked above at his hands and then, chains; he smiled at it and sent a request:

"You were used to kill animals and innocent people so far! You are defamed as you are used in all 'Weapons of Destruction'! You have fallen in hands of Satan and wrong persons. You must be getting pain, when you take a life! I bless and relieve you from properties fixed by Mother

---

[67]In middle age, execution was bestowed to someone in past. In some cases, butchers were roped in to become executioners, or convicts were offered the job as an alternative to their own deaths. But typically, executioners came into the jobs through family ties; most in the profession were men whose fathers had been executioners before them.

Nature today. If you want to change your properties, if you are feeling pains in killing millions of lives so far, then you can change your properties, 'NOW'! I bless to all the elements to return to your root sources... into Fire! Ohm!" All flames in hall became wild! That was too, scary too. Yogi added, "O Fire, you devour all elements!" Graveyards can be converted into gardens." With a tear in his eyes, the gateway of return for elements was opened!

And, prisoners heard some indistinct soft hissing sounds from all over....as if there were great snakes around! They were horrified till they found emission of gases from grills and all stones of prison walls. There, the chain and pulley showed a sign of vaporization...with little fumes! A thin fire line appeared on cuff near hands of Yogi. It was intermittently sparkling, having different colors- golden yellow to greenish red tone! It spread away from his hands. Meanwhile, executioners charged two chains that came like flying snakes in whipping action into Yogi! First whip wrapped the trunk of Yogi and shattered away strip of skin with splash of blood! Yogi screamed, "Oh!" Second chain imprinted deep cut over the abdomen. Blood flushed in eyes of Yogi. There, hissing sound continued and fuming went up towards pulley. Chain as well pulley vaporized and vanished; that freed Yogi. That moment, chains that tied his legs vaporized with fumes. Guests were busy in their tasty meals when Yogi descended from air with wide-open arms! He had golden red divine aura, and he landed on ground, grabbing the incoming next whip from air. One executioner (slayer) had charged second round of whip; its razor sharp edges of chains came in towards eyes of Yogi, with shining blades in firelights. Like a warrior, Yogi picked up whipping blade, took control over the whip. Officers stooped in shock from dining table, with wide opened mouth when they heard 'Oh!' from executioners and saw the whips in hands of Yogi!Handles of whips came flying from Executioners and Yogi immediately, whipped those slayers. Prisoners saw whips encircling their necks and with a jerk from Yogi, executioners were beheaded, head rolled over the floor towards officers relishing dinner. All screamed! Officers and their guards were terrified and ran mad when headless corpses tried to walk towards them with fountains of blood! Prison echoed thunders from the skies; hail-storm outside was in its extreme. Soon, beheaded executioners fell on ground with pool of blood.

Yogi was dripping blood from own trunk; he said to officers, "Who you are...just 'animals' in human flesh! You are blemish on name of humanity; you don't deserve to be human. I order you to leave the human figures, right NOW!" He took life instantly. The officers, shivering meanwhile, silently fell dead...A few sitting on dining table dropped their heads on dining table. Yogi looked all over prison; saw all wardens and guards at various places in prison, dead. Albee was afraid of Yogi, now! He had never been in dead silence! He brought some dress for prisoners, from somewhere to wrap upon his nude body. Yogi's face and eyes were blood stained, he was furious and as if, he was on 'fire'! Yogi whispered, "All guards and officers from various camps and prisons around Baikal Lake should also, leave their bodies!"

Yogi closed his eyes, prisoners found a wave of divine vibration emitted from his heart, spread through all cells of prison and went outside. Only two guards who received Yogi on gate of prison on his arrival, were alive. They wondered, entered in fearfully, bowed at Yogi, and assessed the condition of central hall. Yogi softly said, "You are free. Please, release all prisoners." They hurriedly reached to Jailor office, to find keys. One of guard reached to phone to ring up authority and he fell dead! The second guard got papers, file and audio tape of what Yogi said so far; he escaped in hailstorm and got buried and died.

Here, prisoners in their respective cells were speechless, shocked and many fainted. Unbelievable had happened. A great thunderous lightening blasted the roof of prison and snow began to enter from roof. Pin-drop silence, snow sprinkling from roof and few fire stick tremulously burning in central hall! None moved and Yogi was still for what he has done in a blink of eye. He was tearful and so was so sweet! None had seen a pious Yogi, crying upon own deeds. He visualized past prisoners, their tortures and their tolerance! Red as his head was, so wet his cheeks were! A Yogi from Anahat Chakra and Vishuddha Chakra[68] had entered in Matrix of human race...and found reasons why man didn't evolve so far! Man is always, busy making prison for other people! They know, just to compete. It's like the law of Jungle. There are spider webs in society, prisons outside prisons...in which most of humankind resides trapped and people don't know. They have come for their different purpose, for the self and they spend whole life in serving others. Man is like a farmer, who cultivated in a farm whole life to discover at the end, that that farm belonged to someone else! They are deluded, made to feel, they are living in their mini-heavens! Every new born arrives in some prison!'

Yogi began to look at prisoners standing behind bars...Oh, hundreds and hundreds of prisoners were stunned and standing. They saw Yogi standing in central hall with corpses all around. Albee was shivering at gaze of Yogi. He whispered to Albee, "See, dear! Dead matters control the human life! Machines will control the man tomorrow. This is Kali-Yug![69] He held Albee from shoulders and softly said, "I wanted to quit a few minutes before. I told my Master I will quit. But, their whips had arouse me. 'What if, I quit? What will I tell to my Masters, if I quit? What is the use of my Sadhana (devotional Practice), if I don't help you? What is the use of my Salvation,if you, my fellow brothers are begging freedom in such prison? What is fun of talking about righteousness, if I can't help women from torture?" Yogi looked so pitiable that Albee embraced him and both cried. Albee whispered, "There is darkness under the Sun! O divine saint, you reside in Himalaya and we are buried underground for worms and insects to feast! How can you go, Yogi- there is still darkness in every human heart and mind? How can you leave us when my people are in various prisons? How can you sit in Himalaya in Dhyana, when a man is killing a man, competing for rights and for a loaf of

---

[68]**Anahat & Vishuddha Chakra**: They are Kundalini Chakras, later explained.

[69]**Yug** means a timeframe of hundreds of thousands years. There are four Yug, last is Kali (Dark) Yug when Satan governs human minds! Demons decide death! More about Yug will come later.

bread? How can you leave us when hearts breed violence?" Yogi was in tremendous emotional churning. His lips were tremulous; he had experienced the pains people have suffered since ages. Albee began to cry on shoulder of Yogi and Yogi also, cried out that echoed in prison. All prisoners standing on grills also joined. That day, heavens cried.

Yogi looked around in prison, bent down to palpate the floor made of stones and whispered to stones, "Let's begin, dear! Life is more precious than your existence. You as stones can't stop the flow of life therefore, liberate the prisoners."

Yogi said to Albee, "Every stone of this prison has been the witness of killings and tortures since 1728! Thousands were brought here to die!" (He had met those ghosts...in Siberia who were laughing mad.) These stones must vanish as they had captivated prisoners."

Every Cell of prison began to be foggy...again, hissing sounds started from walls and ghosts began to emerge from the floor! Whispers from walls, thunders from hailstorm, ghostly figures encircling around Yogi and Albee...created a horror scene; prisoners cried out and yelled in their cells. Ghosts swirled towards the roof and vanished in clouds. Now there was a silence again.

Yogi had come to his normalcy; walked to a cell, prisoners were afraid of Yogi, so they stepped back. Yogi came, touched the grills saying, "Respect the human race and release. A human being is the only way out for you. Better you return to root source, in Ohm! Prisons will remind us the Slavery of Human Race to Matters. It says, once, Satan used to rule this world. Please, repent and return to our root source!" Yogi ended.

Next moment, Albee noticed softening of stones under feet, hissing and fuming began; at last, stones showed little sparks, little flames and evaporation began! Hissing began from all sides, as walls of prison were making evaporation. As Yogi stepped forwards, fumes and fires spread on the floor.

Wherever Yogi touched, grills (iron bars) or stone walls, first hissing sounds as if of snakes, then little sparks that spread in either direction on iron rods and grey stones, then vaporization began and fumes began from stones and grills all around. Prisoners saw their grills vanishing with greenish blue flames[70], extreme high temperatures and fumes were nostalgic. and prisoners were released! Albee directed them to exit prison outside and wait. Now, the fire and fumes began from roof and every grill....Prisoners run out...wondering how the iron bars were getting vaporized! Every brick or stone...every iron rod was emitting hissing sound, then a line of fuming appeared and then soon, that thin line of fire advanced. Where there were grooves in between stones, they caught fire first, then stones began to fragment and fires appeared from multiple grooves, emitting a hiss and vapor. Whole stone disappeared. Prisoners had some 'bad' smell [71] of burning iron smoke! Soon, corridors of prison were foggy and became very hot! Extremely hot![72] Iron was vaporizing. As time was passing...prisoners still under evacuation were feeling suffocation. They began to shout for help.

Albee and few prisoners rushed in interiors of prisons and help evacuation, assisted weak prisoners to go out. Old man (Zorcov) saw Yogi walking with closed but tearful eyes and wherever he used to touch, every iron grill was converted into fuming pipelines. He was whispering one word, "OHM!" He stood frozen. He had been a true Yogi whom Mother Nature also, respected!

Ghosts emerged from upper floor of prison...and they ran down the stairs...Zorcov saw a chaos when prisoners were coming down staircase frantically, crying, shouting along with ghosts flying down! Hailstorm had broken the roof and that delivered

---

[70]**Flames** were yellow when part of Sulfur was burnt. Stone burning emits Hydrogen, Hydrogen sulfide (rotten egg like smell).

[71]**Smell of Iron Vapor**: Iron vapors have metallic smell. Its carbon and phosphorus when burn, give garlic smell. Sulfur also gives yellow flames and a different smell. All prisoners had no smell while passing through fumes.

[72]**Iron melts** at 1538 ^{0} C. and vaporizes at 2856 ^{0} C.

more oxygen so as burning became faster. The snowballs were showering in the prison! Roof also, soon vaporized and got lifted in air. Fumes and ghosts were going up in clouds. An orange fire was rising into sky. Yogi moved cell after cell releasing prisoners. He was becoming pale, exhausted and had dangling gait! Albee ran in, embraced him to support and then made him sit on the stair for a while. Later, he guided him upstairs, to every corner, there were about 113 cells and 260 prisoners; they were released. Yogi needed just to touch grills! Albee took him to hidden rooms where ladies were imprisoned....a touch of pure love and thick iron doors began to vaporize...shhhh...with fuming, iron sheets of door collapsed like burning plastic sheet. Crying ladies bowed to Yogi and ran out... managing their clothes. There, in a deep tunnel, Albee took Yogi to show a room, where few human bodies were mutilated! There, the authority was performing experimentation upon human brains of live prisoners! Yogi blessed those in coma and relieved them from terrible agony. Table and stones of floor began to hiss, caught fires from within.

While stepping down from first floor, on stairs, they showed havoc down in central hall. Whole prison hall was on fire, full of blazes, fumes and hissing. As if there were Fire emitting snakes encircling. The roof of central hall was blown away and fresh snowfall had just started. Every stone was in its extinction process! Prisoners were running amok, outside the prison! Passages were narrow and so was a chaos. Prisoners anyhow, tried to remain silent while going outside. Many helped disabled amputee prisoners to come out of prison. While passing through office of Jailor, Zorcov saw hoar-frosting [73] over the glass. He observed little of unusual mist over inside surface of glass.

Soon, the Prison Eight was set afire. The golden flames sore high in sky and drew attention of local Siberian tribal people living far in horizon. They soon, noticed the horizons reddish orange,

---

[73]**Hoar-frost**: Formation of dew-drops and crystals of ice on glass surface, when air is moist and outer surface is too cold. Routinely it occurs outside but Zorcov saw it from within as air inside was damp movements of prisoners, and outside was snowstorm at subzero temperature.

while skies were showering large snowballs frantically! Many prisoners died due to hits. Rest of prisoners waited for storm to settle and then, set out in sledges.

Prisoners came out...looked at their prison as a castle on fire. Walls were on glow and vaporization continued. Suddenly few of them recalled for Yogi. 'Where was he?' A prisoner asked. Albee, Zorcov and Massie were busy assisting weak feeble prisoners. They also, screamed, few more began to search but, Yogi was not there. None dared to re-enter in prison in inferno! Many prisoners began to escape thanklessly in search of surrounding nomads (villages) of Siberia. Albee had become a wise gentle man by now...he stood with tearful eyes...gazing at Prison! "How selfish we were, we are...we left behind our own Savior!" Few more prisoners stood there watching flames going to sky.

*

26. Wombick received the message:

[Yestlin was made unconscious by 4 ampoules of Injection Morphine by a Nurse at Primary Health Center in morning hours. Yogi had wrapped him in Macintosh (red/blue rubber sheet used in medical unit) and tied him with a dressing table-top. Then, he was glided over the snow out of the window. When security guards arrived at medical center, Yestlin had disappeared in bluish river running through glacier. He started his unimaginable journey through and under those glaciers. That way, Yestlin was prevented arrest and he escaped. Now, story of Yestlin needs attention.]

Cave Community was sitting dull since Yogi and Yestlin were set out for Primary Health Center. Wombick was worried about sudden aggression of Border Security Guards. If Yogi and Yestlin were arrested and they gave information about the cave, then they would have to prepare for a conflict. Wombick asked his men to be prepared for war-like situation. Ladies got ready for emergency evacuation of cave. Panic was felt on every face. Till, late afternoon, no information came in.

Guards of the cave were observing their children playing in water reservoir, in which torrent of glacial water was coming in, from outside. It was the place from where Yogi and Yestlin had made entry a day before. Sub-glacial waters had brought sands to that reservoir from erosion of basal rocks that made its floor sandy and water was crystal clear. Children were playing in that reservoir. Suddenly guards saw a red package that wobbled from underneath of guillotine and it came to surface of water reservoir. People jumped in and pulled it out. When they cut open bandages wrapped, the package delivered Yestlin! Wombick was scarred looking at, absolutely pale white young man! Many yelled, "Oh! My God!" People worried for Yogi now. Wombick cut out bandages of health center to release Yestlin who had become like a log of wood, completely frozen, chilled, pale white, but with an occasional breath! Yes! Wombick got a hope and resuscitation began. Warm water sponging, wrapping and packaging started.

Light sources were brought closer. Wombick began to massage his feet! People began to pray for his recovery. Wombick was waiting for Yestlin to open his eyes. Frequently, he would try to listen at his heart beats, by placing ear on chest. It took about 2 hours when muscles began to twitch, eyeballs started movement, breathing improved, face became pink. Everyone was sitting as if frozen meanwhile!

Yestlin later, twisted and got up, saw himself surrounded by his commune of Siberian cave. He saw Wombick sitting at his foot end. Both embraced each other with very tight hug and Yestlin shouted as his rib was perhaps injured.

Yestlin described events and became sad...as he narrated that Yogi had replaced him! "He is arrested!" whispered Yestlin. Wombick understood what worse could happen to Yogi. Then, Yestlin remembered last words of Yogi were... he could not recollect so easily but after a long pause (That delay in memory was perhaps because of Morphine overdose and freezing of blood going to brain.) he whispered, "Yes, Yogi said, 'I will reach to you, Wombick when I will open eyes. Meanwhile...he said, "you sleep, respirations will stop...and I am doing something. Then I had a current on my forehead and became unconscious."

Wombick was a wiser man...he understood why Yogi uttered his name. Yogi had sent a proof in form of Yestlin and a message that, 'Yogi wants me!' He got up on his rock of ice cave to address his commune, "Himalayan Yogi has sent us Yestlin back as he promised. It's tricky to decode but I feel he is in great trouble at Prison Eight. I recall, he said, when Yestlin will reach to us, it will be the time to evacuate this Caves permanently. I think, it's the message of our Freedom! (Commune became hilarious and cheered up. Ladies screamed with tears. Their eyes sparkled more than their teeth!) At the same time, as I understand, something bad is going to occur, and that gentle man needs me. (Rest of commune looked at each other in confusion. Someone shouted, "Why you give so much of importance to yourself? We will also, come with you." And all shouted with their weapons.

Wombick said, "Our Yogi needs us. We can't allow a Himalayan Monk to die in our prison. God will forgive Siberia. I have seen our Future in his eyes. Our Future can't get aborted. We can't afford to lose him. I am going...who else?"

Someone raised his voice, "Better to die in open, for a good cause rather than dying here."

Wombick wiped tears and said, "Who are coming with me?" Almost all cavemen got up and cheered and a young man said, "We have got a reason for our life today! Future is calling!" It was decided that disabled persons, women and children would come late, slowly. All became hyperactive!

There, an old man took Yestlin in a corner and held his shoulder, stared in his eyes and whispered, "I am geo-physicist. I know what it means entering in sub-glacial waterways. From en-glacial channels through which melted waters drip down to reach to sub-glacial waterways, you must have entered in sub-glacial

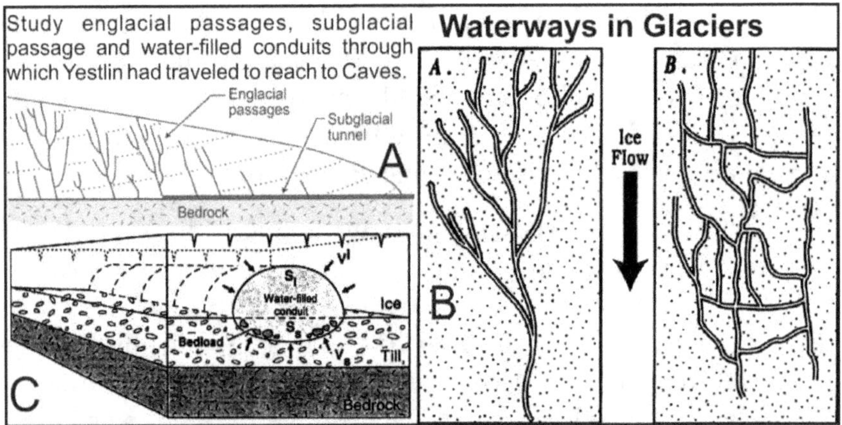

lakes, layers of Methane under glaciers may suffocate you. None survives. There are rough rocks at bottom and pits and gutters...a victim who is trapped inside glacial waters ways will be shredded and dead."

"You don't know how much you are lucky. Yogi has held your hand, forever. He took you just to enter in prison. He pushed you to sub-glacial waterways to cool your body temperature, so you can survive longer otherwise with nearly no respiration. Who can survive after 4 doses of morphine without ventilator? Who can believe that you travelled through arborescent of glacial waterways...for about 10 hours...and came alive? You must thank Yogi, he is your Guru or Master.

Yestlin sat down nervous, began to sob...tears flushed his ego and he was seriously concerned about what would have happened to his Master." Old man said to Yestlin, "Now, don't doubt him, don't insult him...don't shrug from his eyes!"

Soon, Yestlin accompanied the first batch of strong able-bodied persons from commune, who set out running with their weapons. Weather was hostile; clouds were lowered hanging over Taiga Forests and thundering. Lightening were so close from ground. Snow fall was tremendous. It was difficult to walk in soft ground. A small army led by Wombick taking fire on woods in hands was making a way through dangerous terrain at evening hours in hail storms. Wombick recalled Yogi...his holiness and he looked at sky and worshipped the God of Snow, "If we are innocent, we had not done any sin in life, then please lead us to Yogi, safely! He has called me." He took a short-cut to Prison Eight that would take just 5 hours...Hailstorm was abated and shifted towards West, over Baikal Lake. Now, team had to cross dangerous glaciers in night hours with fire sticks in hands...half buried in light snow! Their legs refused to get frostbite as their hearts were pumping 'hot' blood! Suddenly, they had been fanatic! They did not know their next step, did not think what will happen next moment. Either storm will blow off their life or glaciers might engulf them! Wombick was too serious, he doubted for survival of Yogi in Prison Eight. Meanwhile, they crossed frozen lakes and walked over glaciers. Little moonlight and more of clouds sagging over frozen lakes...their journey through darkness was terrifying. Experience of Wombick helped him to make a way in darkness. That journey of Wombick was extremely dangerous and unimaginable.

Yestlin was perplexed: Because of me, you were arrested, and I gave an example of a dog running after a car! How much you must have suffered? How, I will face Yogi? Because of me, my mom died! A Yogi came to rescue me from Himalaya and see...he also had gone in Prison instead of me.' He was feeling himself guilty, very mean! "Whoever will come in my life will suffer the most! I am a misfortune!"

He decided not to make friend. He was walking fast but weeping. He just, followed Wombick blindly, with tearful eyes. [Yogi would answer his self-degrading statements in splendid way, later!]

*

27. "Where is Yogi?"

The snow storm had halted suddenly. (Wombick had prayed to God of Snow, for help.) They were preparing for something worst. Dark clouds were low almost touching the ground! Prison Eight was about to disappear! Orange green fumes were sky-rocketing. Local tribal people were amazed about different colored fumes. They began their journey on sledges; reindeers had difficulty to run in piles of soft snow. Many prisoners began to flee for shelter in Siberian nomads in dark night and after 2-3 feet heavy snow fall! Few of them would survive. Their reason was genuine. They were afraid of action of Security guards, tomorrow. Others were waiting for the Yogi to emerge from enraged remnants of Prison Eight! Giant structure of Prison was reduced to a ruin level. Albee and few associates waited for Yogi for a long time near the main gate of Prison that was slowly disappearing with hissing and fuming. Flames were little but red fumes had made whole atmosphere spectacular! Zorcov whispered, "Who can survive in this fire?" Everyone was thoughtless.

When prison was evacuated, Yogi sat down on last step of stairs observing each stone getting vaporization! Fire began to devour everything- dead bodies of officers, the blood pool, stones of floor and walls and iron grills were 'vaporizing'! Yogi sat there watching flames all around to view that unique scene!

He looked at fumes dancing all around. He bowed down to Lord of Fire, *"You are within every atom, every element and matters. That way, you are Omni-Present. Today, matters are returningback to you, to root source. People should review this, as they want to die upon matters and materials! You are within me, within everyone, every Element and Compound. Today, you initiated process by which Fire from within has come out alive and everything is getting disintegration. People of Siberia will remember this that they are also composed of Inner Fire, Holy Fire that has taken this humanly shape! Purpose of Human Life is to seek the Root Source, through Own Fire."*

Yogi bowed to Holy Fire. (He tapped the stones of floor; movedfingers on grill and lowered his head. They had obeyed his command to return to root source. He said to all Matters that obeyed his words, 'You have dissolved own identity for selfless cause.' Yogi turned around to survey everything on fire and murmured, "If this is the beginning...then what will be the end?" A thought came, a feeling came to sacrifice the self in this whole fire. He didn't want to continue crusade for renaissance for a while. Soon, he decided to walk out...where Albee received him at gate.

*

Outside the Prison:

Albee ran at the Gate of Prison and assisted Yogi who was totally, exhausted, his clothes were blood drenched and had shaky gait. Other prisoners stood quiet at distance, slowly came to surround him. Yogi was made to sit over a ice-clad rock. Zorcov, an aged prisoner bowed taking his feet to his heart![74] All prisoners bowed with deep respect and love. Ladies were frantic, were not able to believe they were free! Many prisoners ran to embrace Yogi and cried loud. Yogi had lot of pain as he had wounds on his trunk. Albee said, "I know, you have taken our sins so as we become purified. You once, said our vibrations have summoned you, isn't it? You have come for us." Yogi looked at Albee blank and sighed, remained speechless! Eyes were crying! Yogi whispered, "It was too much of justice, Zorcov! Too much, I did to prison! (pause) Man should not give justice! It's too bad!" He pointed towards a

---

[74] Zorcov stayed in prison more than 45 years, had cried so much that he had been stone-hearted. He had taken holy feet of Yogi to his heart; as he was full of love today after 45 years! He had seen miracles in Prison, he longed so deeply in past. He used to cry when wardens used barbaric tortures to some prisoners, like breaking legs, removing eyes, beating a man until he dies! He always worshipped, "O God! You are there, watching us, then why these people don't die?" Today, same prayer came true. Prison was gone in oblivion and all wardens and officers were dead. He was released, was free today! He found that Love had emerged from his heart after 45 years like waters begin while digging a well! He had recovered Love from his heart, after a long long time. Actually, he wanted to cry while keeping foot of Yogi at heart!

cloud of fumes where there was a prison! (Now, no prison was seen!)

Zorcov argued, "Don't worry, my Lord! For new life, you requested the old to be burned. It was your request, your plea...and they were as if so ready to vaporize by themselves. (He was poignant in his voice.) I swear if there is any sin in this prison break and massacre, done by you on our behalf, let all the sins fall loose upon my head! (He held foot of Yogi tight to his heart, warm tears began to drop over foot.) We have seen, we are the witness, we declare you to be innocent; don't cry. Don't take sin on your head." People understood the feelings of Yogi. Massie, an athletic prisoner was heard in his thick voice, "It was our wish to be free and burn the prison! All sins are burnt. Now tell me, where are the sins? Where are the crimes? Why you should cry, O Yogi! We are here to answer, if anyone would question. Breaking the hell is not a crime, what do you say, my Yogi?" His voice was soft and loving.Yogi chuckled after a long time. All became hilarious.

Albee expressed to Yogi after 'being wise', "I was silly, idiotic, weak and timid person. I was insane, you have seen me, for the first time. Thank you. Will you be my Master? My Father?" He bowed down at feet of Yogi with tearful eyes. Yogi was unmoved by such emotional outburst. He bowed a little, kept his right hand on forehead and closed his own eyes chanting some Mantra. Albee got a seizure and fell unconscious. He would remain unconscious for a while.

Yogi looked around at all prisoners and whispered, "If birds can fly then, why human society can't sore up high, in open skies? That's the meaning of coming on Earth. Earth is a launching pad. You spoil your lives. Think, who holds you back? Who restricts?"

Some prisoners asked Yogi to lie down on ice so his bleeding would stop...but they saw wounds of trunk were healing fast!

There in horizon, Wombick and his small team arrived with fire torches, ran over the frozen lake. They saw a silent crowd around a fire place (where there was Prison Eight.). Prisoners were alarmed to see people with fire-torches and weapons rushing towards them. Yogi was undisturbed so they all waited for new arrivals.

Soon, Wombick and Yestlin reached to 'segregation' of prisoners and reached to Yogi getting up from his snow-bed.Both were shocked, stunned, stood frozen looking at Yogi. His trousers were blood stained. Yestlin stood with low head, speechless and Yogi smiled at him, he opened his arms calling him to embrace. Father Son scene was created and Yestlin ran like a child to put his head in his lap and he cried out, "Excuse me, Master! I betrayed you at so many places, so many times. I made great losses, for my silly attitudes. I lost my mom and today, I had lost you, my Master!! Because of me, you have suffered." He sobbed on right thigh of Yogi and slowly, became silent. Zorcov leaned over Yestlin and inquired, "Yestlin?" Yestlin nodded, looked with tearful eyes.

Zorcov introduced himself and said, "Hi buddy, you are crying at wrong place and wrong time and in front of wrong people! (Yogi chuckled after a long time.) We are free, see! It's all because of you!! We are so thankful, O Yestlin!" Massie placed his heavy hand on shoulder and ordered, "See, do we cry over our past 20 years of prison and labor? It's all past, gone in winds! Don't mourn over your spoiled milk. Just listen, thank you." (He bowed to Yestlin a little with sincerity, then all prisoners followed. Yestlin could see tears shining in fire.) Albee added, "For sending Himalyan Yogi to our Prison." Meanwhile other people from caves had arrived and were looking at Fire place with curiosity.

Yogi called Yestlin closer and said fatherly, "You don't know, who you are!" Yogi pulled his head up and stared in his eyes (Both were wet.) Yogi whispered at him, "Great!! They will remember you for long."

All became emotional, ladies began to staggering gait, Wombick was as thick muscular man as Massie was, both were ecstatic as he too, showed gratification to Yestlin. He whispered, "Without you, our life was like sleeping in graves there in caves. You brought us Himalayan Yogi." Zorcov added, "All it began with

Yestlin!" Yogi was playing with curly hairs, Yestlin was sitting at knelling posture, his head was at knees of Yogi.

Yestlin stared at Yogi and said, "You are all selfish!" You don't understand me!!" And, he began to sob looking in eyes of Yogi! He said, "Will you forgive me? I can't forgive myself." Yogi said, "You are my candle...more you burn...more I will be dissolved. When I don't have grudge for you, why you ask forgiveness?"Then something happened in his center of brain, he had a little pain and Yestlin never cried in life!

"We frequently, return to Earth, we accept the Crucifixion or take poisons again and again and bless the Earth so as you can walk happily on floral bed. You live long is my blessing!" Yogi blessed segregated crowd. You were innocent and Holy Fire liberated you, I have done nothing. You got primary justice and so you may go anywhere you want. Take control of your life, walk with your head on your shoulders and don't give heart to everyone.Stay perfect human being. Don't delegate anyone for your responsibilities. Otherwise, you will lose your authority again."

"Truly, when the Sun arrives, darkness disappears in fraction of second you need not fight with Darkness. A person should not cry at darkness, one should awaken and be enlightened, instead!-Albee

*

Local Tribes:

Prison had completely disappeared and snow began to fill the pits at the basement of previous cells and walls of prison. (Later on, it would become difficult for police squad to locate where the prison was!)

Meanwhile, herds of reindeers appeared from horizons. Their eyes shone with golden light of fire. That was so refreshing to all prisoners (ladies were much delighted at sight of reindeers. (Reindeers are auspicious in Siberia.) Many local tribal people

(Indigenous People of Siberia[75]) from surrounding nomads arrived on sledges. They were from Evanki and Yukaghir group (local tribal group). They inquired, got information about how Prison disappeared and understood the presence of a Raven spirit[76] (Kutkha), and bowed down to fire of prison site. Their leader spoke to Zorcov, "Ravens are dark black birds and we connect with

---

[75]**Indigenous Peoples of Siberia and Russian Far East**: Since 17th Century Slavic and Russians conquered Siberia and thereby opened the way of population movements. In Communist Era, (1971-1991) Russian Speaking people dominated Siberia. But, Indigenous groups still exist. (1) Uralic group: <u>Khanty and Mansi</u> live in Autonomous Okrug, previously known as Yugra. Oil and Gas companies devastated their land and communities. Samoyeds are of Northern (Nenets, Enets, Ngansan groups) and Southern (Selkup, Kamasins or Kamas, Mator (Now, extinct.)and Kobal (Now, extinct.). (2) Yukaghir group is from Kolyma and Indigirka valleys. They occupy in basin of Kolyma river, Tundra and Taiga forests, and Sakha Republic. Chuvans, Khodyn and Anaul tribes occupied once in Lena River territories. Yukaghirs are assimilated with Yakuts, Evans and Russians. (3) Tungusic group: Evenks live here, others are Ugege, Ulchs, Nania or Hezhen) (4) Eskino-Aleut group: live along the coast of Chukchi Peninsula. (5) Paleosiberian Group: Near Kamchatka and Chukchi family.

Supreme deity of Yukaghir is **PON**, meaning 'Something'. He is said to be very powerful. Nu'tenut is the chief God of Chukchi. They respect reindeer in both mortal and holy life. Tokoyoto or crabs is Chukchi God of Sea. Kutkh (also, Kutkha) is a raven spirit revered by Chukchi and other groups.

[76]**Raven Spirit**: A great number of the tragic events – deaths, drunkenness, and various disabilities – that occurred in Evenki communities in the Zabaikal region during the Soviet period and after the collapse of the Soviet Union left significant marks on the local landscape. Today, Evenki hunters and herders believe that many old and vacated reindeer herders' camps, unattended mortuary sites, and places where tragic events occurred are scattered throughout the taiga. These places have become sites where malevolent non-human beings manifest themselves. Therefore, the Evenki of the Zabaikal region link all their current difficulties to losing memory of their interaction with spirits and ritual places. People believed that various "bad places" continuously demand new victims. As a result, these bad (or tragic) places affect the wellbeing of various kin members and the community as a whole.

inner feelings. As their color suggests, the ravens are symbolic of darkness, and along with it, everything that is negative and mysterious (death, wars, despair, loneliness) are connected. As the darkness is burnt, today, we mark the death of Ravens. That is positive and it represents protection, intellect, resourcefulness, dignity, confidentiality and respect. **We have a protector in Siberia today!**' They observed Yogi from distance but with suspicion and walked away to their reindeer sledges.

Before leaving, Yakagir group leader came across Wombick and volunteered for any help, Prisoners needed. He also, warned, "Not seen such a storm in May, in last 35 years! These clouds? You won't survive till tomorrow. Siberia is known where even clouds freeze at midnight and suddenly, become transparent! Extreme cold!! Tomorrow, army troops will also come. Don't wait here, come with us." Most of prisoners took leave from Yogi and Zorcov and went away. Only 52 people remained and rest of prisoners moved along with tribal people.

28. "I should go!" Yogi

Most of crowd dispersed and about 54 prisoners and other cave commune people remained by side of Yogi. Albee whispered in mind, "Where to go? This is the realm of 'White Death'. One who freed us, will manage our survival.' He was observing Yogi from a corner when lady prisoners were sitting around Yogi to take blessings. They sat down in front of Yogi with silence compelling Yogi to speak to them. (Not all prisoners had seen Yogi in prison.) Most of them were emaciated but had sparkling eyes and hopes for future. Then rest of people also, sat down around. Yogi said:

"I have been too, harsh to prison authority and prison. (He looked at prison site.) I gave them no choice and no chance. It was weird. They decided in favor of their land. I was reacting for 'self-defense'. If this is the beginning, then what will happen ahead? (pause) He looked down at ground and whispered, "Better, I should return. Better if, I don't meddle in your matters further. Longer I will stay; more problems I will create." He looked at Wombick, Zorcov and all and asked, "Let me go. You are free and should manage your life, wisely. (pause) I was as such an unwanted guest!"Yogi became silent. A holy heart had begun to repent for what he had done to Prison and its authority.

Most of people became nervous, while a lady prisoner, Christina took permission from Albee to offer her spontaneous poetic expression to Yogi.

"From Heights, you came with Grace and Light, without delivery will you go? What the Gods will tell you? (!) U-turn is bad in our world, O great Yogi. Rivers never ascend to mountains in this world!"

Have you fulfilled the dreams of your Master by now? Give us what we deserve and give for what you wanted. Land is barren and dying... wait till spring sets in. We are primitive here; help us evolve! You have an ocean of Grace, give us a little to sublime. Wait, O Yogi, take us with you!"

Zorcov appealed: "Actually, we have 'seen' the Power of Himalayan Yogi today. And, most of young prisoners and youth of our country will decide to walk on your footsteps. Material life is inferior to even animal life. Animals do not value even diamond or gold. They value peace and their inspirations. Only the Human Being is running in wrong direction. Gold from mines to our lockers, what difference does it make? But, we think another way round! We are proud of holding as our security. We have wasted our life and you are the First Hope that inspires us to be real Human. Since centuries, mankind is busy in power play, fighting and killing each other; but today, I have seen that power, we seek from outside, resides in your heart. Your prayers can melt the stones and iron chains! Your words can take away life! (pause) We aren't satisfied by prison break, in fact! It's not enough. On contrary, you have created a trouble for us! A cage is safer than free sky, in today's world! (pause) So, don't look at fires, what damage incurred. Earthquake shakes old buildings...shatters them down so as new cities are created. Do damages, we don't mind but lead us to higher consciousness! (again, pause) As you are in human figure, you are emotional today."

Yogi gave a long oration:

This planet is like a playground for lives! Here, you quarrel, fight or kill each other; it's okay! You will return again and reenter in same game! Nature does not give penalty at all, most of times. All is "Human Play" if not in this life, then in next! That way, I need not meddle in your child's play; you play since ages. You rejoice life, drink and dance, compete and quarrel, make families and society and fight in groups. All Child's play. Enjoy! I should go!! (That was a serious allegation, Wombick thought. Probably, it was ominous presage sign of future doom. Probably, Holy Saints from Himalaya will leave the Planet before impending doom. We the human race has proved its uselessness in Nature!' He shivered at the thought.

Yogi went on, "You are the Human, came here later than rest of animals. You were better evolved, landed with divine purpose. And, after millennium, you are still, the confused species! We saw Genocide in MahaBharat and Ramayan, we know Genocide by Muslims and Christians in recent past. Nothing is changed. (Yogi became muffled. His eyes welled up.) You were supposed to be a bridge from this soil to Divine Life, for rest of lives of this planet and even aliens from all around. Actually, you are the great hope. But, you don't come out of child's play. You made a bread costlier than a life of man! Similarly, animals and birds that trust you are in your bowls on dining tables! Who can trust you? (Deep silence came.)

"You want someone to work on your behalf. That way, you are great. You can employ kings and presidents for your purpose, just by a vote. Unluckily the often become autonomous. Then, you start crying for help. You do nothing for others....such a selfish species! You are the Fire and neither you evolve nor help someone to evolve! Who will trust you? Do you trust the fellow sitting next to you, right now? No! You have lost all credits from eyes of Mother Nature. Living your life as human is a different dimension, it's not taught to you. You throb and breathe in other world of illusions and hallucinations; careless about the self and for the Nature. You don't read, listen even to your parents, great people, don't want to evolve, don't want to prove your worth in this life....just you want comfort...and, comfort is material oriented , sensual. It's an ANIMAL life. How will you show me your worth?" There were serious accusations. That pierced their hearts. Yogi said, "Animals are defined as who live by body and body consciousness.'

"That's why, I thought I should quit. End-result will be same, another religion you will establish, again you will claim your religion great and again you will begin genocide on name of your God! Then, again, you will doze. This awakening is temporary. Your life is looted my dear, and you spent life in prison. I can't see you in illusions. It needs a great effort to awaken your soul from within. Come out of illusive life and come to breathe in present tense. Then you can sore up to divine life. Better, if I return and make you free! Again, your hope creates a new prison."

29. Make us like Who You Are!

Zorcov turned towards the crowd and said, "We have no right to stop Yogi! We are too 'primal' for Him. He can't bestow blessings upon us. Prison is gone; we are free." (He dropped his head for a while, wiped tears.)

Albee took control in moment of despair and he asked Yogi, "True you are, our beloved Master! Do you think you have released us from prison? Then, you are wrong somewhere. **Is there a prison outside a prison?** And, a prison inside a prison? (pause) I know if true that there are visible prisons and invisible prisons too! Human society is like colonies nesting in Invisible Net. Who governs us, for whom we live we don't know. Life is wasted here. We don't live for ourselves. That is our darkness. (He paused for tears to run down from lips.) We are blocked at our primitive levels. And, you want to go now, hmm!"

Wombick in his thick voice, added, "If you are the Sun, then Shine! Let the rest of world burn, why worry? Prison break is first step. (Yogi smiled and respectfully looked at him.) We were like local train, stopping here and there! Now, we have got destination...if we get a chance, we will show the evolution of human race. We are like rockets on launching pad. You give us F...i...r...e, your Fire!!" (Wombick had slurred speech and became unconscious, at feet of Yogi.) None ran to help him. All were inert, detached and emotionless. They sat quiet and tearful. Death was also a good news to them!

Yestlin hesitantly added, "You promised about New world Order coming. You have seen, new dawn coming! Then, why so much of hesitation!" Mood of segregation became lighter.

Albee: We always pray when our relative or friends die that let his or her soul rest in peace! Why don't we seek that 'Peace' here, while we are alive? Please teach us the Art of Inner Peace."

A lady prisoner whispered, "We have never lived unanimously, singularly with broader sense and selfless purpose of life. We have failed as long we have been selfish. We have failed in trying Communism instead of Czar's rule. It's only a Spiritually Enlightened person who can help usrise above stupid emotional drift. Spirituality is not taught to us, so far!" She wiped her tears.

Zorcov intervened: It's true that you don't want to mess up further, your decision is respected by all. Coming in prison was your choice and going back is also your valid choice. But, you should think of us for whom you travelled so far and had suffered lot of pains. Do you see we can manage ourselves? Nations struggle today, then what its citizen would do? If you think the external conditions spring out from within, then we need inner engineering! And, who is greater than you, for us? You have everything to bestow upon us. Clouds don't think, just they shower! Sun does not retrace; just it fires the skies! Then why do you hesitate in last moment? (His voice muffled.) And, who will destroy prison, again?" (It meant that someone from Himalaya will have to return again to take care of human race.)

Wombick noted later on: 'We could not understand Yogi's resistance but late. Choice is the state in which we become choice-less then after! When all directions collapse, disappear then we come to one choice. Choice is so critical. And we were kids in his eyes. We were selfish from his eyes.'

"Beggars don't become kings even though they acquire wealth and powers! To be 'Royal' is a different energy level and different mindset. Yogi was concerned about whole nation from which such prisons were born! Society must rise to receive grace and, our Master was hesitant whether we would be able to guide whole nation tomorrow or not."

Yestlin informed later on: We promised to be selfless, will perform self-sacrifice. We will not have attachments with this world and people as they had already left us in Siberia to die. We promised we won't taste fruits of our sacrifices. We won't desire anything from them in return. Life has given us the Gem of all…Himalayan Yogi! That way, we will not stay here, longer and Master took a promise that before we leave this life, we will lit another candle the way Yogi came and lit a few. We will give everything to people of our country."

Christina explained why Yogi decided to remain with us little longer: 'We will make the society with minimal need of swords, spears and arrows; weapons will reach to smelting furnaces. Humanity will flourish with minimum machines and Artificial Intelligence. We promised to Yogi that when this will be happen, we will leave the world. We will disappear will be untraceable! I requested Yogi to accept us as his disciples and bless us with what he has! We will guard our Divine Kingdom beyond death! And he became ready to bestow upon his Grace the way, a great waterfall comes done from height. We were ready then after, to receive the Great Water Fall of Grace, so called 'The Spiritual Science' – the way to the Unknown, the God, Krishna. It's the mark of Sanatan Dharma of Ancient Bharat."

> Albee had requested, "**Make us like who you are so as we can break prisons from within and outside.** We will manage our planet for thousand of year and you need not return, so often! Great Masters of Himalaya will rest with assurance that the human kind below, will manage the cycle of Life well. We decide to be the 'Warriors of Light'! Please don't lose hope for us. We are raw diamonds, just came out of mines of charcoals!"

Albee cried out, in lap of Yogi and so did all prisoners. Yogi closed his eyes for a while and then, began to look deep in eyes of everyone, one by one.[77] He was tearful, his lips were tremulous and his fingers were unstable. He began to vibrate his head while looking at each disciple. He was reviewing the past lives of each

---

[77] *'What was our Master looking in our eyes?'* Yestlin explained. 'Master assessed energy level of disciple, his remaining Karmic bondage, fortunes and fire within! It's essential to be disengaged from mortal life and have a 'fire' within otherwise you can't soar high in meditation. (2)We are the rockets on 'His' launching pad, Master ignites! (3) Energy levels are seven as Kundalini Chakras. Blocks at various Chakras help to contain life well 'within' and live with specified behavior traits and earn his fortunes, get his family and friends and enemies at that level. Masters first recognize and break the barriers.'

one, his or her credentials, destinies, blocks in spiritual axis, the future he was going to shape...and he was opening the gates of Heavens for us!

It was a day of Divinity. It is said that a true Master hardly gets few students in life to confer upon his Grace. That night, about 52 disciples, he was adopting! A big ship he was! He was taking stranded awakened souls to Feet of Krishna, crossing the Ocean of Mortal World. We later recognized that every life here is rotating like seasons...in death and life cycles since ages. Only such a holy master can take awakened, detached souls to Spiritual Realm. Mankind is destined to rule the world...but, in immortal realm!" Zorcov added, "It's difficult to get such a Master live walking and talking with us. Siberian Exile had paid us well! Our Pranam to our visible Master!! Hari Ohm!!"

"O Yogi! Please take us from the Darkness, to Spiritual Light so as from the Matrix of Mortality, we will be released and become Immortal! From the temporary, dying and decaying planet, take us to Eternity and Realm of Truth, Love and Peace." - Zorcov.

Epilogue

How the prison was destroyed!

(Wombick shared the secret to a group of college students later.)

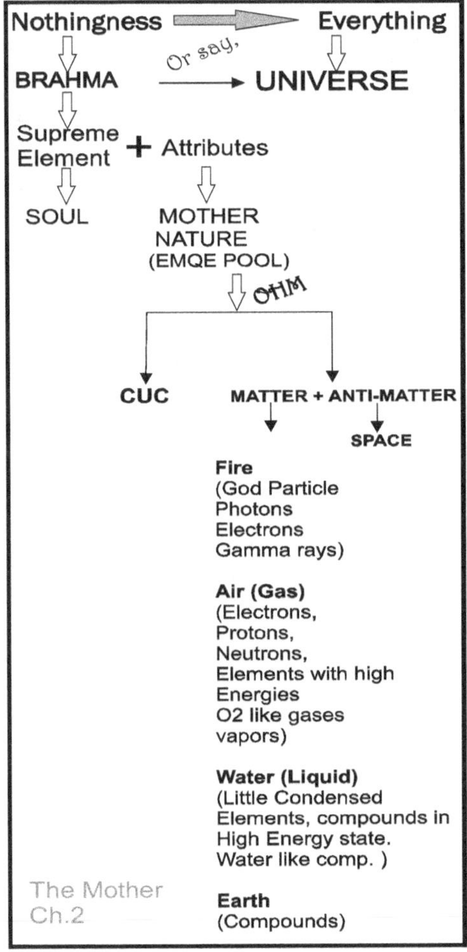

Universe flows bi-directionally, in figure of Eight. Appearance and disappearance interplay. From Nothingness, Universe was created. When Time had yet, not started, The Existence was Zero! Out of nothingness (To Whom, We call BRAHMA OR PARAMATMA in Sanskrit or GOD or ALMIGHTY. In English), everything sprang out.

It needs proactive force to create, it needs retroactive force to disintegrate. It's like precipitate of snow flakes and vaporization of waters from ocean. There are certain Regulators (regulating system or Semi-Gods of those routes. You can request them with pure heart emitting a single frequency that would reach to the God of Fire. And, that is Ohm. Himalayan yogis know and communicate with them.

The God has two moieties: The Supreme Element and His Attributes. From Element, Souls emerged the way, Rays are derived from Sun. Attributes are second moiety. They define

240

Element the way attributes (characters and powers) can define our elements for example, Oxygen.) All Attributes of God or Powers of God together are called as the Mother Nature or Prakruti in Sanskrit. Each attribute is called as Goddess and there are many more Goddesses. They define Super-Element. Collectively, they are called as 'Mahatatva'. (Over and above all attributes of Universe) Once they created Brahmand or Egg-shaped zone in which, Creator or Brahma did programming. Now was the time of manifestation. It emitted the 'First Gravitational Wave' or OHM audible sound and whole Universe came in existence. Sound came first, Light came later! The 'Sound Of OHM', the Sound of Light! Ohm is the Mother of Universe. She has Electro-Magnetic Quotient Energy Pool (EMQE). Electric Moiety runs as Kinetic Energy to make Matter. Magnetic Moiety manifests as Love, Gravity, Gravitons and 'Collective Universal Consciousness' (CUC). Our Consciousness is connected to Her Yogi contacted CUC with highest frequency vibration of Love and reversed the pathway of Kinetic Energies- Vibes to Matters to Vibes.

Kinetic Energies (The one that flows.): Attributes of Brahma (Powers of God) provide raw materials in creation of Universe. Energies are invisible and non-particulate to start, keep flowing in parabolic course. Some may say the course as cyclical or in Sine-Wave. It has Electro-Magnetic Quantum Energy (EMQE) Pool. The Kinetic Energies become quantified, condensed and would made Matters. That way, Static Form of Universe came to exist. It's just like sea and its waves. Waves go on coming! Once Matters or molecules are derived from Kinetic Energies, the return pathway (i.e. Doom's Day) is according to Program of CUC. Matters don't return of own. Same way, birth is difficult then death is also not in your wish. Pathway is one-way only. Here, comes the crux of matter: Yogi asked Iron to go reverse and return into Non-Particulate form in EMQE Pool. That way, Prison disappeared with little of flames and more of fumes and hiss of Vibrations!" Wombick added, "This theory should go further, it will disclose secrets of Universe, but I will tell you if time comes."

The Mother: Chapter: 2:

INCEPTION OF SUN LAND& AWAKENING OF ANGELS

Yogi accepted all prisoners as his disciples and it was a great task for him. He would see that everyone would be liberated. After that, each soul would be bestowed upon various attainments and will return to common life. Meanwhile, they would face the military assault at Prison Eight and it would be a matter of speculation how they defeated the armed assault.

Yogi was the right person for right people to explain them the Art of Sublimation- (The Spiritual Science) without that a human is just an animal. When the Spiritual Science unfolded, prisoners became Sages. They, then met the society. Two propositions are required: First a human though born as an animal, must recognize himself/herself as life superior to all animals. Second: He is above all religions! Religions are for his Service, not as a prison.

Welcome to next Chapter 2: INCEPTION OF SUN LAND: AWAKENING OF ANGELS- It'll be a text book of Spiritual Science.